"You have proven countless times that there are good and giving people in this world. I'll never forget your kindness in answering my first message. You don't even know me, but you took the time to explain something I didn't understand, and you did it in a way that made me feel good about myself for asking. Other people I've written to either have ignored my questions or I've felt they were talking down to me. Thank you, thank you, thank you."

—M.B.S.

This book is fabulous! I use computers and the web a lot and there are PLENTY of things in this book I find useful. And the price is right: perfect to bring instead of a stupid bottle of wine when you're invited to someone's home for dinner! The recipients of Ask Mr. Modem have been tickled at this gift! I'm here ordering my fifth copy of the book!

—Marge

I received a copy of "Ask Mr. Modem!" this past Christmas and it's the best computer book I've ever received (or purchased). I have a shelf of computer books, most of which I can't understand. This book, which is in question and answer format, is very easy to read. It's been a huge help to me and I've already given several copies of it to friends.

—Diane

I teach computer classes in Maryland and bought "Ask Mr. Modem" for my classes. I love the book! I love Mr. Modem's lighthearted approach. The questions Mr. Modem answers are questions from real people and it's true what he says, "There is no such thing as a dumb question." Thanks for a great book, Mr. Modem. I hope you're working on Volume 2.

—Franklin

Ask Mr. Modem!™

Second Edition

Richard A. Sherman

SYBEX®

San Francisco • Paris • Düsseldorf • Soest • London

Associate Publisher: Cheryl Applewood

Acquisitions and Developmental Editor: Kathy G. Yankton

Editor: Malka Geffen

Production Editor: Elizabeth Campbell

Technical Editor: Maryann Brown

Book Designer: Maureen Forys, Happenstance Type-O-Rama

Illustrator: Daniel Ziegler

Electronic Publishing Specialist: Maureen Forys, Happenstance Type-O-Rama

Proofreaders: Erika Donald, Andrea Fox, Laurie O'Connell, Nancy Riddiough, Laura Schattschneider, Suzanne Stein

Indexer: Lynnzee Elze

Cover Designer and Illustrator: Daniel Ziegler

Library of Congress Card Number: 2001093075

ISBN: 0-7821-2956-0

Manufactured in the United States of America

10 9 8 7 6 5 4 3 2 1

This book is dedicated to every person who ever sat in front of a computer and learned firsthand the true meaning of the word frustration.

Acknowledgments

Writing is usually a solitary endeavor, but that was not the case for this book. Every day, I receive several hundred e-mail messages from readers worldwide. If you are one of the thousands of individuals who have written to me with a question about your computer or the Internet, there's a very good chance you helped me write this book. In lieu of sending any royalty checks, however, let me offer my sincerest thanks for your involvement, and I hope this book inspires you to ask even more questions in the future. The community of cyberspace is full of wonderful people, and I look forward to meeting many more of you online.

Acknowledgment is also in order for several very special individuals: first and foremost, my wife Trisha, a psychiatrist by profession, who, for the last year as I've been writing this book, has provided unwavering encouragement while steadfastly refusing to bring home any pharmaceutical samples (despite my repeated requests). And it would be beyond peachy if I never hear the question "Well, so, what chapter are you on now?" during the rest of our lives together. Thank you, honey, for your love and support, and may the cappuccinos flow for years to come!

To the rest of my household: our fabulous, furry, cyber kitties, Itty and Bitty, who kept Mom company while Dad was busy answering e-mail and conducting online research, which has occasionally been described as "playing at the computer." Thank you, girls, for reminding me that, no matter how stressful life becomes at times, any stressor can be resolved by a good snooze and a big stretch.

To my parents who, though they have passed on, are with me every day and are a continual source of inspiration. And to my brother Robert who, though geographically distant, is just an e-mail away, thanks to the miracle of today's technology. To paraphrase the commercial, "I love you, man." And thank you for always being there.

A very special thank you to Mr. Paul Harvey, for his eloquent and generous support, to cyber confidante Stan Demory, and to my business manager and advisor, Win Holden.

Lastly, I acknowledge the publishing professionals at Sybex who made the process of producing this book lots of fun! Special thanks to Cheryl Applewood, Associate Publisher; Kathy Yankton, Acquisitions and Developmental Editor; Malka Geffen, Editor; Elizabeth Campbell, Production Editor; Maureen Forys, Electronic Publishing Specialist and Book Designer; Maryann Brown, Technical Editor; and Juanita Tugwell, Marketing.

Richard A. Sherman, "Mr. Modem"

Phoenix, Arizona

Contents

Introduction

Ask Mr. Modem! Not a day goes by when I don't receive oodles (technical term) of e-mail from readers of my books and columns asking questions about computers, the Internet, and life online. Many questions are prefaced with the words "This is a dumb question, but...."

Revisiting an Old Misperception

Let's set the record straight from the outset: In Mr. Modem's world, *there are no dumb questions.* Of the tens of thousands of people I've met in person and online through the years, I've never met a dummy, an idiot, or a technological moron. To the contrary, I've met lots of wonderful people who simply wanted to know how to accomplish a particular computer- or Internet-related task or who had a question about computers in general. Like we all do.

When I have a computer question, I'm not interested in long-winded, technical dissertations or in being talked down to by some technologically arrogant modem-head. I'm not even interested in long-winded introductions to computer books, for that matter—a fact that's probably not readily apparent at this juncture.

What you will discover in this book are easy-to-understand, plain-English answers to questions readers like you have asked me—FAQs, or *frequently asked questions.*

The Method to My Modemness

Each chapter in this book is chock-full of questions and answers pertaining to the overall subject of that chapter. Having conducted exhaustive, investigative research and comprehensive demographic polling, I determined (by speaking with at least two of my neighbors) that some readers will flip through the pages of this book in random fashion, reading questions of interest; other readers will use the index to find answers to questions that are tormenting them at that particular moment rather than sitting down and reading the book linearly, from cover to cover. Linear readers are most welcome, however. In fact, some of my best friends are linear readers.

Questions and answers are loosely divided into topical categories for ease of reference. You can read the book from cover to cover or pick it up and start reading anywhere. If you wish to commit the book to memory or laminate its pages so you can share this precious information with future generations, you can even do that. Most importantly, though, keep the book handy. If you don't have a question about a topic covered in the book today, chances are you will have a question tomorrow. It's an Internet truism: If you access the Internet, you will have questions.

On rare occasion, you may discover an answer or two to be closely related to another answer, and you may even find answers to specific questions appearing in more than one chapter. I embraced this approach to ensure the broadest presentation of topics possible, not to pad the final page count. That's my story and I'm sticking to it.

Whatever your level of computer or Internet expertise, you will find something of interest in this book. You may learn an alternative way to accomplish a task, or you may discover something completely new. My goal is for you to scream out at some point while reading this book, "I didn't know that! Life would hold no meaning without you, Mr. Modem." Feel free to substitute your own words, of course.

Computing Is Fun!

I want you to have fun reading this book and learning about your computer and the Internet. I also want you to know that you have a friend at the other end of the modem.

Throughout this book, you'll encounter many wonderful drawings depicting tranquil scenes of digital domesticity. The scenes generally share three common characteristics—computers, cats, and Mr. Modem—for a very good reason: Wherever I am, there invariably is a computer nearby and one or both of "my girls."

Itty and Bitty, my two cyber kitties, were introduced to readers in a previous book, *Mr. Modem's Internet Guide for Seniors* (also available from Sybex). As their fame spread worldwide and e-mail from cats, dogs, birds, fish, and assorted livestock began to arrive, I realized it was only fitting and proper to include them in this book as well. The decision to include them was an easy one because, knowing them as I do, I am well aware that I wouldn't have a meow-free moment if I didn't include them.

How to *Ask Mr. Modem*

If you have questions, comments, or your own tips and tricks to share, send an e-mail to me at MrModem@home.com or visit www.MrModem.net. I want to hear from you! Who knows, your question may even find its way into *Ask Mr. Modem!* Third Edition, making you eligible for absolutely nothing—no fabulous prizes, no valuable gifts, nothing but sincere thanks for reading, for your participation, and for your questions.

Itty and Bitty also welcome e-mail and, when they can break away from playing with a mouse or snoozing on top of a monitor, are happy to respond. You can e-mail the girls at itty-bitty@home.com.

While reading this book you'll encounter invitations to send an e-mail to a specific address in order to receive additional information that space did not permit me to include in this book. For example, you will be invited to send an e-mail addressed to cookies@MrModem.net to receive information about cookie files and how to manage them; or if you would like information about subscribing to my weekly newsletter, send an e-mail addressed to newsletter@MrModem.net. Get the idea?

When you send your e-mail, leave the Subject line and body of the e-mail blank. Itty and Bitty, my cyber kitties, will be sending you the information requested by return e-mail. Because they're so busy churning out the e-mail and foraging for crunchies—not necessarily in that order—they can't respond to personal messages included in these requests for information.

Okay, enough small talk! Let's cut to the chase, get the show on the road, and put the pedal to the metal. Perhaps more succinctly stated—coming from an author who clearly never met a cliché he didn't like—*let the questions begin!*

Richard A. Sherman, "Mr. Modem"

Phoenix, Arizona

The E-mail of the Species
Is More Efficient Than the Mail

This chapter focuses on answers to questions about sending and receiving e-mail, using file attachments and formats, avoiding viruses, and working with mailing lists, as well as helpful dos, dont's, and other tips about signature lines, spam, mailboxes, filters, and more.

Q. When I reply to an e-mail, should my reply appear before or after the quoted text of the e-mail I'm responding to?

A. For context purposes, most e-mail software programs automatically include the e-mail to which you are replying. This is called a *quote back*. Your response should appear before the quote back, not after. Responding before the quoted material is an online courtesy (called *netiquette*) and will prevent the recipient of your response from having to scroll through his or her own e-mail to get to your response.

Q. What is the best file format for sending documents as attachments?

A. All things considered, anything sent in ASCII (rhymes with *passkey*), which is a plain-text format (with the extension .TXT), can be opened by any word-processing or text-editor software. Special formatting, such as bold or italics, may be lost if you create the document with a word-processing software program, such as Word or WordPerfect. For graphics, the most frequently used format is .JPG, pronounced JAY-peg, which stands for Joint Photographic Experts Group. And, yes, it technically is JPEG, but since file extensions are traditionally three characters, it was necessary to say adios to the letter *e*. Sound files are most frequently in .WAV format, which is a Windows audio format.

For more information about file types and their associated programs, send a blank e-mail to `filetypes@MrModem.net`. By return e-mail, you'll receive a free Mr. Modem article about file formats and where to find the programs needed to open them.

Q. I received an e-mail from someone who seemed to know me, but the person didn't sign his name. How can I find out who the person is?

A. On occasion, people who would never think of sending a "snail mail" letter without signing it forget that an e-mail is really very similar. This phenomenon of forgetting to sign an e-mail is described in DSM-III-R as ENI Syndrome, or Emailus Neuronus Interruptus, and is caused by a temporary misfiring of the neural synapses. At least that's my story, and I'm sticking to it.

If you believe the e-mail received was sent by a friend or acquaintance who simply forgot to sign it, try replying with a polite "Thanks for the e-mail, but I can't identify you from your e-mail address alone. Please identify yourself." Most folks will quickly reply with an "Oops, sorry about that," and provide their name, while learning a subtle-yet-valuable netiquette lesson in the process. Works like a charm.

If the e-mail you receive is _spam_ (unsolicited commercial e-mail), never respond. Ever. Spam will generally include a sentence or two near the end that invites you to reply to be removed from the mailing list. Don't do it. Replying only confirms that your e-mail address is a valid address, and the result could be even more spam.

On a related note, receiving e-mail from friends and family members is fun, but be careful whenever you receive an attachment with an e-mail. Computer viruses can be spread through e-mail attachments. To further complicate things, certain strains of virus can attach themselves to somebody's e-mail address book and be attached to every outgoing e-mail message. An unfortunate result is that the person sending an attachment may not even be aware he or she is sending a virus with it. Eek! For that reason, if you receive a file attachment from anybody—friend, family member, and certainly if it arrives from somebody you don't know—be afraid…be very afraid. Always…_always_ e-mail the sender and ask if they intended to send the attachment, and if so, ask them to describe what it is. If you're comfortable with the explanation, be sure to check the file with a current virus-checking software program before opening it.

If you would prefer a less personal approach, try one of the reverse e-mail lookup directory services located on the Web, such as the Real White Pages (`www.realwhitepages.com/info.bls/reverse.htm`) or InfoSeek (`www.infospace.com/info/revemail.htm`).

Because the content of e-mail directories and reverse directories are gathered on a "best effort" basis, it's possible that an e-mail address or name you're looking for won't be found. There can be a number of reasons for this. For example, some people have the equivalent of an unlisted e-mail address. When they signed up with their ISP or e-mail service, they were given the option of keeping their e-mail address out of web-based directories. In those instances, you won't be able to locate their e-mail address or the name associated with an e-mail address.

Q. Sometimes e-mail I send comes back to me marked undeliverable. How can I find somebody's correct e-mail address?

A. If you know a person's name or other contact information, such as geographic location, try one of the web-based "White Pages" directories, such as `www.infospace.com`, `www.bigfoot.com`, or `www.theultimates.com`. Directory sites also provide street addresses, telephone numbers, maps, and more information than you'd probably want to make available on the Internet if you had your druthers. But this information is available through public records, so it's available on the Internet.

You might also try one of the e-mail address change registries like `www.emailchange.com` or `www.findmemail.com`.

The easiest way to find out a person's e-mail address is often frequently overlooked: Ask the person. Not exactly a high-tech solution, but it can be very effective.

Q. I received an e-mail in which the sender included the letters *LOL*. What does that mean?

A. LOL is online shorthand for Laughing Out Loud. There are hundreds of FUIAs, or Frequently Used Internet Acronyms. To obtain a copy of my personal collection of FUIAs, send a blank e-mail addressed to `acronyms@MrModem.net`. Some people collect aluminum foil; others collect acronyms. What can I say?

Q. How do you change your e-mail address? My husband picked ours, but it's so ridiculous; whenever somebody asks me for it, I tell them I can't remember it. Help!

A. I notice you didn't include your e-mail address with your question submitted by fax, so now I'm *really* curious! It's actually just your username that you would like to change. Your username appears to the left of the @ sign in your e-mail address.

You can do one of several things. First, contact your Internet Service Provider (ISP) or the organization that's providing the username you would like to replace. Tell them why you want to replace it. Depending on the provider, they may accommodate your request at no additional charge. Others may charge a fee to cancel your current e-mail account and provide a new one, so be sure to discuss this option with your husband, particularly if he's become attached to the address.

There are plenty of free e-mail services out there, such as www.hotmail.com or www.mail.yahoo.com, so the easiest solution is to let your husband keep the username he selected but establish another e-mail account for yourself. Many households are now two–e-mail address households for precisely this reason.

Q. I'm tempted to try one of the free e-mail services, but I'm afraid there's a catch to it. Are free e-mail services really free?

A. In a word, yes. Free e-mail is available through many services such as Hotmail (www.hotmail.com), Yahoo! Mail (www.mail.yahoo.com), Juno (www.juno.com), and Netscape WebMail (http://home.netscape.com/webmail/), to name just a few. Free services of this type are supported by advertising, so you can generally expect to have advertisements attached to your incoming and outgoing e-mail.

Some free e-mail programs offer an optional service to remove all the advertising. Of course, there's a fee for that service, so it's a trade-off. Other free e-mail services require that you check your e-mail periodically. If you don't, you may lose your e-mail address. Just be sure to read the terms of service that will be available for your review on each free e-mail website. Regardless of the contingencies, millions of people use free e-mail services, so if it's something of interest to you, it's well worth investigating.

Q. I know that you can send files as attachments to e-mail, but what does the recipient have to do to view an attachment?

A. The most important thing is to be sure the recipient has the same program and a compatible version that created the attachment. For example, if you send a WordPerfect 6 document as an attachment, you need to be sure the recipient has WordPerfect 6—or, at a minimum, a version of the program that will be able to open the file attachment. This holds true for spreadsheet files and many other programs. The easiest way to be certain is to send an e-mail to the intended recipient first and inquire.

Newer versions of a program usually provide the ability to save a file as an older version or even in the format of another program. Using Microsoft Word, for example, you can save a document in WordPerfect format. Most programs are what is referred to as *backward compatible*, which means that newer versions will read files created by older versions, but not vice versa.

Text files (.TXT) are universally readable, so when sending documents, if you're not sure what program(s) your intended recipient has, send your document as a .TXT file. For example, if you're using Microsoft Word and you're not sure whether the person you're sending your file to has Word, save your Word .DOC file as a .TXT file.

To do this, with your document displayed on screen, click **File ≻ Save As**, and, using the drop-down menu in the **Save As Type** field, select the .TXT format. You will also see other format options available, including .RTF, or Rich Text Format. .RTF files are also text files but include special commands to preserve formatting information, such as fonts and margins. If your file contains special formatting, such as bold or italicized text, you can save the file as .RTF.

Other common formats include .HTM; for graphics files, .GIF, .TIF, and .JPG; for sound files, .WAV, .RA, and .MP3.

If you receive a file attachment and don't recognize the three-letter extension (i.e., .TXT or .WAV), a visit to any of the following sites will shed some light on your UFO (Unidentified File Object):

- `http://extsearch.com/` is a file-extension search engine. Here you can type in the extension, click the **Search** button, and find out what it is. More than 1,700 extensions. Cool!

- `www.ace.net.nz/tech/TechFileFormat.html` contains a listing of every known file format in the world—possibly the universe—along with the program that created the file.

- `www.wotsit.org` contains file format information on hundreds of different file types.

For more information about file types, their associated programs, and where to obtain those programs so you can view virtually any file format, send a blank e-mail to `filetypes@MrModem.net`. By return e-mail, you'll receive a free Mr. Modem article about file formats and the programs that love them.

Q. Is there a way to quickly save a portion of a large e-mail message? Sometimes I don't want to save an entire e-mail if there's only a small portion of it that I'd like to save.

A. The secret here is to pretend to forward the e-mail to yourself. So start by selecting the e-mail and then click **Forward**. In the **To**: field, type in your own e-mail address as if you were going to forward it to yourself.

Inside the message area of the **Forward** window, position your mouse cursor at the beginning of the text you want to keep and click once. Next, hold down the **Ctrl** and **Shift** keys and press the **Home** key. This selects everything above the cursor's position. Then, just press **Delete**, and that part of the e-mail is vaporized.

Next, move your cursor to the end of the text you want to keep and click one time. This time, hold down the **Ctrl** and **Shift** keys, and press the **End** key. This selects everything between your cursor and the end of the message. Press the **Delete** key again to remove that text.

Now, all you have left is the text you want to keep. You can click your **Print** icon to print it or click **Send** to send the message to yourself and then save it.

Q. I tried to address an e-mail to two people, but it came back to me as undeliverable due to an improperly formatted address. What am I doing wrong?

A. When sending to more than one e-mail address, be sure to separate the e-mail addresses with a comma. For example, in the **To**: field, you might have MrModem @home.com, MrModem@lunch.com.

Failure to separate e-mail addresses with commas is among the most frequent causes of these kinds of error messages. In addition to inserting a comma between each address, however, be sure your addresses themselves are formatted properly. Double-check your addresses to make sure there are no extra characters, no commas within the address itself, and no other punctuation marks other than dots (.).

Also, be sure the address is an e-mail address and not a website address. Every now and then, a reader will tell me that they tried to send me an e-mail addressed to www.MrModem.net but that it bounced back to them as undeliverable. The reason it wasn't deliverable is because that's a website address, not an e-mail address. (My e-mail address is MrModem@home.com.)

Q. What's the difference between forwarding a message and redirecting a message?

A. If you forward a message to somebody, the original message is presented to the recipient as a quotation, and you have the ability to add a message of your own to the quoted material. A message that's redirected is sent as is, as an original message, just as you received it.

Q. I wrote a lengthy e-mail to somebody, but it kept bouncing back to me as "Undeliverable." I know the e-mail address was right. Could the length of the message have anything to do with it?

A. It sure could. Although there is theoretically no size limit for an e-mail you compose, many Internet Service Providers and networks impose a size limit on incoming e-mail messages. Before you send a large (more than 500KB, which is half a megabyte) message, including attachments, check with your intended recipient to determine whether his or her network or ISP has a size restriction for incoming messages. A size restriction could result in a message being undeliverable or an attachment being deleted.

There are a number of other reasons an e-mail might bounce back. For example, the intended recipient's mail server (computer) at their ISP could be down. Also, some Internet Service Providers don't permit multiple attachments to incoming e-mail, so if you're attempting to send several file attachments, that could cause the bounce-back as well.

Q. I have a large file I want to send to somebody as an attachment, but I was told I should compress it first. How do I do that?

A. To *compress* a file means to squeeze it in order to make it smaller—much like you can squeeze the air out of a loaf of bread. Because a compressed file is smaller in size, it's much faster to send (upload) and to receive (download) online. Before the recipient of the compressed file can view it, however, he or she has to *decompress* it to return it to its pre-compressed state.

The most common way to compress a file is to *zip* it, using a software program like WinZip (www.winzip.com). WinZip is a *shareware* program, which means you can download it and try it for 30 days. If you decide to use it beyond the 30 days, there is a $29 registration fee.

Q. I'm not sure my e-mail is working properly. How can I test it?

A. The easiest way to test your e-mail is by sending an e-mail to yourself. Unfortunately, that won't tell you whether your e-mail is routing beyond your Internet Service Provider. To see whether your e-mail is functioning beyond your ISP, send a blank e-mail to `TestHTML@wopr.com`. Check for new e-mail in a minute or two and you'll receive an HTML-formatted e-mail message, which will also let you know whether your e-mail program is capable of displaying HTML—something all self-respecting surfers simply must know.

Q. My son told me to stop sending e-mails typed in all-capital letters. He said it's offensive to people. Why would it be offensive?

A. Typing in ALL CAPS is considered shouting online and really should be avoided—unless you intend to shout. It's also more difficult to read something written in all-capital letters. "STOP SENDING SO MANY E-MAILS! DO YOU THINK E-MAIL GROWS ON TREES?" See, it's not nice to be shouted at.

Q. When I want to send an e-mail to somebody from my office, I have to type *internet:* first, then insert the recipient's e-mail address. Why is that?

A. Because you're probably on a network at your office. Messages sent from within some corporate, university, or other networks need to have the destination e-mail address preceded by *internet:*. This lets the network mail server know that the intended destination of the e-mail is outside the network so it can be routed correctly.

Q. When I send e-mail to many people, how can I prevent everybody who receives my e-mail from seeing everybody else on my mailing list?

A. Assuming you're not spamming—sending unsolicited commercial e-mail messages, which is the closest thing to a virtual felony that we have on the Internet—try this: Address the message to yourself in the **To:** field, then include everybody that you're mailing to as a *BCC* (Blind Carbon Copy or Blind Cyber Copy), and you will not reveal your entire mailing list to all recipients. From your perspective as the mailing list owner, since it's a personal list that you may have developed through the years, you understandably may not wish to share your work product or personal contacts with others.

There's another reason for using the **bcc:** field as well: It's really unfair to publish the e-mail addresses of all the people on your mailing list, many of whom probably didn't elect to be placed on your list in the first place.

By placing your intended recipient e-mail addresses in the **cc:** field and thereby making them visible to all recipients, your mailing list can easily be copied, sold, used, or abused by others, all without the permission of the recipients. The inevitable result is even more spam, or junk mail.

Q. If I receive an e-mail and there are BCC recipients that I don't know about but I hit **Reply to All** when responding, will my reply go to the people who are invisible to me as BCC recipients?

A. No, your reply will only go to the recipients shown in the **To:** and **cc:** fields. BCC recipients aren't copied even with a "Reply to All" because they're just receiving a copy of the original e-mail directly from the sender. BCC recipient addresses are not actually part of the e-mail you receive. If they were, you could "Reply to All," then go to your Outbox and quickly determine who was receiving a BCC copy, which would, of course, defeat the purpose of a BCC.

Q. How can I create a shortcut to a frequently used e-mail address? I know I can use my address book, but it would be faster if I could just click an icon on my Windows Desktop and send an e-mail to somebody.

A. Creating the shortcut you mention is easy. Just right-click on a clear area of your Desktop. Select **New ➤ Shortcut**. In the **Command Line** field, type **mailto:** followed immediately (no spaces in between) by the e-mail address of the person you're frequently e-mailing. You can include as many e-mail addresses as you wish, as long as each address is separated by a comma.

If your e-mail program permits the creation of "named" mailing lists, you can include the name of your mailing list in this shortcut instead of typing in the actual e-mail addresses. For example, if you have a mailing list titled *Family_Reunion* that includes e-mail addresses for 47 family members, in the **Command Line** field type **mailto:Family_Reunion**.

After you have inserted the e-mail address, addresses, or mailing list name of your intended recipients, click the **Next** button, and in the **Select A Name For The**

Shortcut field, type in the name you would like to use to identify your new mailing list. In this case, something like *FamilyReunion* or *Reunion* would do quite nicely, but be as creative as you wish. Note the following steps:

1. **Select A Name For The Shortcut** field.

2. Next, click **Finish**, and a new shortcut will appear on your Desktop.

3. Double-click the icon, and your default e-mail program (probably Netscape Messenger, Outlook Express, or Eudora) will open with the recipient's e-mail address in the **To:** field. How convenient!

4. All you have to do next is type in your message, click **Send**, and you're done.

Q. When I receive e-mail, I would like to automatically enter the e-mail addresses of the people I reply to in my address book. Is that possible?

A. You sure can. If you're using Outlook, select **Tools ➢ Options**, then the **Send** tab. Place a check mark beside **Automatically Put People I Reply To In My Address Book**.

If you're using Netscape Messenger, you can quickly add entries to your address book by clicking any e-mail address displayed in e-mail you receive. The **New Card** dialog box will appear, containing the selected e-mail address, and you can enter any additional information you wish.

If you're using Eudora, you can't perform this function automatically, but with an e-mail displayed, click **Special ➢ Make Address Book Entry**. You'll be prompted to give the entry a nickname or change the default nickname that appears. The e-mail address of the sender of the message to which you are replying will be added to your address book.

Q. I save all my e-mail, but are the thousands of messages on my hard drive taking up a lot of space? Should I be deleting e-mail?

A. Unless you have a particular reason to save all the "Make $10,000 per week sitting at home in your bathrobe" offers, delete junk e-mail (called spam) when it arrives. Be sure to determine whether your e-mail program actually deletes the e-mail from your computer or simply moves it to a trash bin or similar folder. If it moves it to a trash bin, don't forget to periodically empty the trash. ("Honey, don't forget to take out the trash." Now, where have I heard that before?)

For e-mail that you want to keep, it's a good idea to periodically compact or compress your e-mail folder(s) so they take up less hard drive space. Netscape Messenger 4.*x* users should click **File ➤ Compress Folders**. (Earlier versions of Netscape Messenger refer to **Compact Folders**.)

Microsoft Outlook Express users, select your **Inbox** or **Outbox**, then click **File ➤ Folder ➤ Compact All Folders**.

Eudora users, click **Special ➤ Compact Mailboxes**.

Compacting your e-mail folders will not affect your ability to access the e-mail contained within these folders; it just compresses your e-mail folders, leaving the information contained within the folders intact and accessible.

The amount of space consumed by e-mail will vary according to the size (length) of the e-mail and whether there are any attachments. Studying my own extensive collection of e-mail—and proving definitively that I have no life—I have determined that 1,000 e-mail messages consume approximately 1MB (megabyte) of disk space, which is not very much. So save the e-mail you want to retain without fear of consuming massive amounts of disk space, but I still recommend deleting the junk.

One additional point: If you wind up saving tens of thousands of e-mail messages like certain bearded authors who shall remain nameless, just be aware that your e-mail searches will be much slower due to the volume of material that needs to be scanned.

Q. I get lots of e-mail with quotations or witty sayings at the bottom. How do I add a quotation to my e-mail?

A. Those little tag lines are called *signatures,* sometimes referred to in digital shorthand as *sig lines* or *sig files*. Most e-mail programs allow you to create one or more signatures that will automatically appear at the end of your messages. Look for a signature setting under your **Tools, Preferences,** or **User Options** menu. Signature lines can be both informative and fun. A reader sent me an e-mail recently that contained the following Ross Perotesque signature line: "You can't light a porcupine on fire and expect to make gravy." And that, my friends, about says it all.

Q. What is a digital signature? Is that something I need for e-mail?

A. It's a unique, electronic imprint used to confirm and authenticate a sender's identity. It's also used to verify that the e-mail was sent and that its attachment, if any, arrived intact. Sometimes the actual e-mail is the signature itself, meaning that it's scrambled or encrypted. The e-mail recipient receives a "key" that allows him or her to unscramble the message. Unless you're sending very sensitive documents over the Internet, you probably won't need a digital signature.

Creating a digital signature is a simple process, but the specifics will vary depending on the software you're using. The good news is that the software does all the technical work.

With a document you want to "sign" displayed on screen, launch your digital signature software, select the signature you would like to use—you may have more than one digital signature—then enter your authorization code. Your authorization code lets your digital signature software know that you are entitled to affix the digital signature you have selected.

I know what you're thinking (and you're correct): If somebody swipes your authorization code and has access to the computer on which your digital signature software has been installed, they can affix your digital signature to just about anything. Hey, nobody said it was perfect!

Once you enter your authorization code, your digital signature will be affixed to the document. You don't have to do anything else.

Here's what a digital signature looks like:

```
-------BEGIN SIGNATURE------
   IQB1AwUBMVSiA5QYCuMfgNYjAQFAKgL/ZkBfbeNEsbthba4B1rcn
   jaqbcKgNv+a5kr4537y8RCd+RHm75yYh5xxAlOjELwNhhb7cltrp
   2V7L1On
   h+Rb2j5SU+rmXWru
       =QFMx
-------END  SIGNATURE------
```

For more information about digital signatures, visit the Digital Signature FAQ at http://home.earthlink.net/~hldettling/digsig.htm.

Q. How can I create a signature file using Netscape Messenger?

A. The process of creating a signature line is easy and takes a few minutes at most. Start by launching Notepad (**Start ➤ Programs ➤ Accessories ➤ Notepad**) or some other text editor.

Next, type the text of your signature. Keep it short—less than five lines tops. Nobody wants to read your life story with every e-mail received.

Save this file as a text (.TXT) file (the default format in Notepad), and remember where you save it and what you name it. I'd suggest something clever like *signature*.

In Netscape Messenger, click **Edit ➤ Preferences ➤ Mail & Newsgroups ➤ Identity**. Under **Signature File:**, click the **Choose** button to locate and select the file you just created and saved. Click **OK** when you're done.

Next, check out your handiwork by sending an e-mail to yourself. Look at your signature line from a recipient's perspective. Does it appear the way you intended it to appear? Is it formatted correctly? Is it too long? Tweak the signature file (using Notepad) as often as necessary until you get it exactly the way you want it.

Q. Can Outlook block spam? I just hate getting that stuff, and I sure would like to be able to block it so I don't have to even look at it.

A. You can't block spam completely, but the Outlook Rules Wizard located on the **Tools** menu does somewhat control the delivery of junk e-mail and messages that might contain X-rated or adult content.

The Rules Wizard allows you to create parameters for filtering your incoming e-mail so you can easily add junk e-mail senders and X-rated content to a special file. To use these e-mail features, select **Organize** from the **Tools** menu, and click **Junk E-mail**. Then highlight a junk e-mail (spam) message you received, and select **Junk E-mail** from the **Actions** menu. Choose **Add To Junk Senders List** or **Add To Adult Content Senders** list. The next time any cyber flotsam or jetsam arrives from this sender, it will be routed automatically to the appropriate file, which can then be deleted as frequently as you wish.

Several websites exist to help all of us in our never-ending quest to become a spamless Internet society. SpamCop, located at `http://spamcop.net/`, helps you punish spammers for sending you their junk mail. This is a free service that will send e-mail on your behalf to the appropriate network administrator. Abuse.net at www.abuse.net invites you to forward spam to system managers who can and will (hopefully) act on the messages. Free spam filters and other resources are also available on these sites. Take a look at Junkbusters (www.junkbusters.com) as well. These sites contain lots of information and links to resources that can help you fight the good fight against spammers.

Q. I'm trying to send an e-mail to my brother who uses CompuServe and has one of those numerical CompuServe e-mail addresses, like 478394,637—though that's not his actual address. I added @compuserve.com to his address, but it still isn't being delivered. What am I doing wrong?

A. You're doing the right thing adding @compuserve.com to the numerical address, but you also have to change the comma to a period when sending Internet e-mail to a CompuServe user. A comma is an invalid character in an Internet e-mail address, so that's why the e-mail is undeliverable. Format the address as follows and you won't have any problem: 478394.637@compuserve.com.

Q. Can I get a virus from reading an e-mail?

A. The answer to this question used to be an unequivocal "no way." While it's still true that you can't get a virus by just looking at an e-mail, many e-mail programs support HTML (Hyptertext Markup Language), which is a fancy way of saying it's e-mail that looks like a web page. Scripts, which are little, executable programs, can be embedded in a web page or in HTML e-mail. You're safe unless you have your e-mail program configured to automatically execute scripts in a web page. Better safe than sorry, Mr. Modem recommends that you review your e-mail settings or preferences, and if the option is presented, elect plain-text only.

The nasty folks who launch virus attacks are very cagey individuals. Someday, thanks to these modemized miscreants, it may be possible to contract a virus just by reading an e-mail message. It hasn't happened yet, but knowing that's the Holy Grail for perpetrators of viruses, it's probably just a matter of time. The best defense is always a good offense, so practice safe computing at all times, and be wary of the dangers that lurk within cyberspace.

Having said that, it really boils down to how lucky you feel. Remember the line from the Dirty Harry movie, "Do you feel lucky, punk? Well, do you?" The odds are small that you'll ever be the victim of a virus if you accept HTML e-mail, but there always is a chance.

Q. Sometimes I receive warnings from my e-mail program about potential viruses when I get file attachments. Is there any way I can screen files before I get them to be sure they don't contain any viruses?

A. You can't check a file before you actually download it, but you do need virus-checking software to check incoming e-mail attachments. Your virus-checking software will reside on your computer and can check any incoming files.

The most important thing to remember about using virus-checking software is that it can only check for viruses that it's programmed to check. Many new viruses arrive on the cyber scene each month, so it's important—I dare say it's crucial—that you update your virus-checking software regularly, at least once a month.

Two of the most popular virus-checking programs are McAfee's VirusScan (www.mcafee.com) and Norton's AntiVirus (www.symantec.com). Both McAfee and Norton offer a free, 15- or 30-day trial version of their software, as well as a service that will automatically download and install updated virus "definitions" on a regular basis. You also have the option of visiting either site to download and install updates at any time. McAfee's VirusScan retails for approximately $30, and Norton's AntiVirus is available for approximately $40.

Not only is it important to check every attachment you receive by e-mail, but it's equally important to virus-check every disk you put into your PC.

Whichever virus-checking program you decide to use will permit you to change the default settings so you don't receive warnings about possible viruses every time you download a file or open an attachment. Mr. Modem's recommendation is this: Don't do it. That reminder, as annoying as it might be at times, may save the data on your hard drive some day. Always practice safe computing. The more reminders, the better.

Q. I received a picture file (.JPG) as an attachment, but when I clicked it to see the picture, I got a virus and never did see any pictures. How is that possible?

A. Unfortunately, some files aren't what they appear to be by their file extensions. A .JPG file is usually a graphics file. But sometimes nasty people do bad things to good files so you have to be sure that what you're attempting to view is really a .JPG file, in this case.

To know for sure what types of files you're encountering, turn on the file extensions view in Windows. To do this, click **My Computer** ➢ **View** ➢ **Folder Options**. Click the **View** tab, and unclick the **Hide File Extensions For Known File Types** box under **Files and Folders**. What you may discover is that that .JPG file is actually a program, or .EXE, file, which could be a dastardly virus waiting to ambush you. For example, if somebody named a file `picture.jpg.exe`, and you didn't have your file extensions turned on, all you would see is `picture.jpg` and assume (incorrectly) that it was a harmless graphics or picture file.

For a list of the most frequently encountered file extensions and the programs needed to open them, send an e-mail to `filetypes@MrModem.net`. You'll receive a free, fact-filled article about file types. So much information that I guarantee you'll lose interest within the first few paragraphs or I'll double your money back!

Q. I received an e-mail that warned me about a new virus that's making the rounds. I sent the warning to some of my friends but was told that it was just a hoax. How can I tell whether something is true or is a hoax?

A. There are four red flags to be aware of that most online virus and other hoax messages contain:

- A great sense of urgency. These messages usually have Subject lines written in ALL CAPS with lots of exclamation marks: "URGENT!" "WARNING!!!!"

- Dire consequences. You will be warned of dire consequences that will result if you do not pay heed to the message and thus fall victim to the digital scourge. Dire consequences include loss of all data, destruction of your hard drive, corruption of files, killing of houseplants, etc.

- Request for distribution. You'll be encouraged to e-mail everybody you know about the alleged virus. The perpetrator of the hoax will prevail upon your desire to protect others by helping him or her spread the word.

- Authentication. Most hoax messages are "authenticated" by a quote (fictitious) from an industry leader, a government source, or a well-known CEO of computer-industry company. Sometimes "authentication" comes in the form of something more personal: "My brother-in-law, who is an executive with (*insert company name here*), just got this information from their parent company" etc. It's all phony-baloney, but it sounds impressive.

Don't fall for it! Before you forward a warning to your friends or colleagues, take a minute and visit any of the following sites to investigate further:

Computer Virus Myths and Hoaxes www.vmyths.com/

Hoax Warnings www.datafellows.fi/news/hoax.htm

McAfee's Virus Information Library http://vil.nai.com/villib/alphA.asp

Urban Legends Reference Page www.snopes.com

You're also welcome to send a copy of the suspect message to me at MrModem@home.com. I'll be happy to check it out and get back with you. I've been on the Internet since 1988 and have yet to see one such e-mail that was legitimate.

For additional information about online hoaxes, send a blank e-mail to hoaxes@MrModem.net.

Q. When I delete an e-mail that has an attachment, am I also deleting the attachment?

A. It depends on your e-mail program and how it handles file attachments. With some programs, when you delete an e-mail that arrives with an attachment, you're only deleting the e-mail. Think of it as you would receiving a package by U.S. mail that has a cover letter with it. You can throw away the cover letter, but that won't dispose of the package.

In these instances, the attachment typically goes into a separate folder automatically, when your e-mail arrives. When you double-click the attachment icon that may appear at the bottom of an e-mail, you're opening the attached file wherever it may be residing on your hard drive. The file attachment will usually be found in a subfolder of your e-mail program.

(To determine where your e-mail program stores received file attachments, see the following question and answer.)

Once you know where file attachments reside on your computer, you can use Windows Explorer (**Start** ➤ **Programs** ➤ **Windows Explorer**) to navigate to that folder and view and/or delete and/or move any of the file attachments displayed.

However, if your e-mail program keeps file attachments in your Inbox without routing them to a separate folder as explained previously, be forewarned: If you delete an e-mail that arrived with an attachment, you will be deleting the accompanying attachment as well—or sending it to a Trash folder (not Windows Recycle Bin) where it can subsequently be retrieved up until the point when you empty the trash.

Q. How can I find out where my attachments are located? I see the little icon on incoming e-mail that says I have an attachment, and it tells me the filename, but where does it go? I assume it's on my hard drive someplace.

A. Yes, it's on your hard drive, in a subfolder or subdirectory associated with your e-mail program. The folder may be named Attach, Files, Incoming Files, or something of that order.

Here's an easy way to determine where your attachments are located: The next time you receive an attachment, note the filename. Let's assume for this example that the filename of the attachment is FINDME.TXT. Once the e-mail arrives, minimize or shut down your e-mail program, click **Start** ➤ **Find** ➤ **Files and Folders**, and then proceed with the following steps:

1. In the **Named** field, type **FINDME.TXT**.

2. Leave the **Containing** field blank.

3. In the **LookIn** field, make sure it shows your C drive—or whatever the letter designation is for your primary hard drive. For most of us, it's the C drive.

4. Click **Find Now** to begin the search. The search result will display the path to the FINDME.TXT file. For example, it may be something like C:\Program Files\Eudora\Attach\Findme.txt or C:\Program Files\Netscape\Users\ Yourname\Mail\InBox\Attach\Findme.txt.

The path will vary depending on the e-mail program you're using. Just read the path from left to right and you'll be able to determine which folder contains attachments received. Double-click the folder to open it, and be sure to delete any attachments that you're not familiar with. Do *not* open or launch any attachments without scanning them for viruses first. The data you save may be your own.

Deleted attachments will be moved to your Recycle Bin, so be sure to delete them from the Recycle Bin, or empty the Recycle Bin, by right-clicking the Recycle Bin icon on your Windows Desktop and selecting **Empty Recycle Bin**.

Q. Sometimes I write an e-mail and click **Send**, but I don't think it's actually sending the message. I'm using Outlook Express. Could my e-mail be going somewhere else before leaving my computer?

A. That's probably exactly what's happening, particularly if you're composing your e-mail while offline—not connected to the Internet. In that instance, your e-mail is stored in your Outbox, which serves as a holding area until you are connected to the Internet.

To make sure any messages you write while offline are sent, first establish your connection to the Internet. Once you're online, click **Tools** ➤ **Send/Receive** or **Send All**. Either action will send any e-mail stored in your Outbox.

Q. Can I get a virus from downloading a .JPG, .GIF, or .TIF file from a website? I know executable files (.EXE) and Microsoft Word macros can contain virus threats, but I worry about things that seem harmless, like a picture file, containing a virus as well.

A. Image files like .JPG or .GIF files do not actually execute, or launch, like an executable (.EXE) file does. Instead, a viewer program (often part of a web browser) reads data in these files and converts it to what you see on your computer screen. If someone planted a virus program in such an image file, the viewer might stop or display a garbled picture, but the virus itself would not be able to cause any harm. If viruses could spread through pictures, looking at images on web pages would no longer be safe, and that is clearly not the case.

Q. Most of the junk e-mail messages I receive contain an offer that if I don't want to continue receiving future mailings all I have to do is hit **Reply** to be removed from a mailing list. I've done that, but it doesn't seem to work, so I keep doing it every time I get another e-mail. Any suggestions?

A. Junk e-mail, called spam, is a growing problem because of the growing number of insensitive louts (spammers) who just don't seem to understand that if everybody sent out junk mail, the efficiency of e-mail would be destroyed. It's either that they don't understand or they simply don't care. Bah, humbug!

For some unscrupulous spam-heads, part of their ruse is to ask you to reply to be removed from their mailing list that you probably didn't ask to be on in the first place. It's tempting, but don't reply!

Replying just confirms that your e-mail account is functioning, and you may receive more spam as a result of replying. There are cyber creeps who do nothing but send out spam in an effort to generate responses so they can then sell lists of authenticated e-mail addresses to others, who will then send out more spam. It's a vicious circle.

Instead of replying to junk e-mail, send your junk e-mail to SpamCop, located at `http://spamcop.net/`. SpamCop is a free service that will send e-mail on your behalf to the appropriate network administrator. Abuse.net at `www.abuse.net` invites you to forward spam to their system managers, who can and will (hopefully) act on the messages. Take a look at Junkbusters (`www.junkbusters.com`) as well. These sites contain lots of information and links to resources that can help you fight the good fight against spammers.

Also, visit `www.cauce.org/`, which is the website for the Coalition Against Unauthorized Commercial E-mail. The fight against spam is alive and well!

If you use an e-mail program that has the ability to create filters, such as Eudora Pro or Netscape Messenger, every time you receive an unsolicited e-mail, create a filter for that e-mail address. Use your filters to route incoming spam directly into your trash bin. In the future, any e-mail arriving from that e-mail address will go directly to the trash, and you won't even see it. You'll never be able to rid yourself of all spam, but with some concerted effort, you can make a dent.

Spam, unfortunately, is a part of life on the Internet today. Putting spam into some hopefully meaningful perspective, overall I'd rather receive spam than junk snail mail via the postal service. At least spam isn't killing trees, and a quick stroke of the **Delete** key is the perfect spam-killer.

For additional information about fighting spam and additional resources, send a blank e-mail to spam@MrModem.net.

Q. How do I create a filter to sort my e-mail when it arrives?

A. A filter can be thought of as a personal valet that tends to your mail and processes it in a manner that you specify. For example, you might want e-mail that arrives from one particular individual to be moved into a separate mailbox or to play a sound when it arrives. You might want e-mail that arrives from another individual or several individuals to receive a higher priority or appear in a different color in your Inbox.

What you can do with filters will be dictated by your e-mail program. Some e-mail programs, such as Eudora, have very sophisticated filtering capabilities; other e-mail programs may have something less or may not provide the ability to create filters.

To create a filter for incoming messages using Netscape Messenger:

1. In the **Messenger** window, click **Edit** ➤ **Message Filters**.

2. In the **Message Filters** dialog box, click **New**.

This will display the **Message Filter Rules** dialog box, where you will enter information necessary to define your filter, following these steps:

1. Enter a name for your new filter.

2. Select the **Match** option you want by using the drop-down menus to choose filtering criteria. (For example, select **Sender** if you want your filter to be on the lookout for messages received from a particular sender.)

3. Click **More** to add additional filtering criteria. (Hint: If you get carried away and include too many filtering parameters, click **Fewer** to remove some of your handiwork.)

4. Then, using the drop-down menu, select the filtering action you want to occur, such as **Move To Folder** (you'll have an opportunity to select an existing folder, or click **New Folder** to create a new mail folder), **Change Priority**, **Delete**, etc.

5. Enter information about your new folder in the **Description** field, if you wish, or click **OK** to create the filter.

To create a filter using Eudora:

1. Select **Make Filter** from the **Special** menu to display the **Make Filter** dialog box.

2. In the **Match Conditions** area, select the criteria that will determine whether or not a particular message will be acted upon by your new filter.

3. Select **Incoming** or **Outgoing** so your filter knows where to watch for a message. (Note: You might want to filter outgoing messages to automatically segregate all messages sent to a particular person or business in a separate folder.)

4. After selecting **Incoming** or **Outgoing**, you can choose one of three *content* matches: **From**, **Any Recipient**, or **Subject**. This further instructs your filter what to be watching for. If you select **From**, you'll be prompted to enter a name or e-mail address. If you select **Any Recipient**, you'll be prompted to include a name or e-mail address that will appear in the **To:** or the **cc:** field. Click **Subject** to have your filter keep an eye open for messages containing a specific subject.

5. The **Action** area is where you select what action you would like performed on a given e-mail that meets the requirements you previously designated. Here, you can select **Transfer To Existing Mailbox**, **Play Sound**, **Print**, etc. Use the dropdown menu to select the filtering action item or items you wish to use.

6. When you have all your criteria entered, click the **Create Filter** button. You can also click the **Add Details** button to add additional filtering criteria.

Filters are called *rules* in Outlook, and here's how you create them:

1. Click **Tools** ➢ **Rules Wizard** ➢ **New**.

2. You will then be asked, **What Type Of Rule Do You Want To Create?**, and you'll be presented with several options. For our example, let's select **Move New Messages From Someone**.

   That will bring up the **Rules Description** dialog box, where you should click **People Or Distribution List**.

3. At this point, you will have the opportunity to go into your address book and select the name or names of individuals whose messages to you will be filtered or processed in a particular way. After selecting the name or names, click **OK**.

   You will receive a confirmation, **Apply This Rule After The Message Arrives From** *(Name Of Person)*.

4. Click **Next** ➤ **Conditions** ➤ **From People Or Distribution List**.

5. At the bottom, click **Move To Specified Folder**.

6. This will open a drop-down menu that will display existing folders on your computer. Select the folder you would like any incoming messages from the designated individual or individuals to be moved into.

7. Click **OK**.

8. Click **Next**.

9. Click **Finish**.

Q. With all the spam that's flying around the Internet, are there any organizations that are trying to do something about it?

A. Because spam is such a serious and growing problem, several organizations exist that do a great job trying to help stop the rising tide of spam. To learn more about these organizations and what you can do to help fight spam, visit any of the following websites:

Coalition Against Unauthorized Commercial E-mail www.cauce.org/

Getting Rid of Spam www.thisistrue.com/spam.html

Network Abuse Clearinghouse http://www.abuse.net

Spam Cop www.spamcop.net

Q. I've read about sites where you can register your e-mail address as a "no spam" address. Supposedly, spammers run their bulk mailings through these databases and remove the addresses that have requested no spam. Are these legitimate? How can we be sure that these sites will not misuse the addresses they receive?

A. Some of these sites are merely collection points run by spammers to obtain valid e-mail addresses. Registering at these sites could actually result in an increased amount of spam or unsolicited commercial e-mail. Even if these registries are run by well-meaning people, most spammers probably wouldn't use them anyway.

When it comes to spam, embracing a big-picture perspective can be helpful: Spam is annoying; there's no question about that, but it truly is part of the Internet experience. There is nothing you can do to avoid it completely. I receive thousands of e-mail messages every week, and of those, several hundred are spam. I could spend hours every day forwarding spam messages to ISPs or various websites that attempt to ferret out the spammers, but how practical is that? We each have to decide for ourselves how stirred up we're going to permit ourselves to become over spam. Personally, I shrug it off and simply hit the **Delete** key. Ninety-nine percent of the time I can spot spam just by its subject line and delete it without even looking at it. The more you use e-mail, the easier it will become to recognize spam from the subject line alone. Paraphrasing the popular belief, you *can* judge an e-mail by its cover.

Having said that, if you want to do your part to help eliminate spam, you can forward spam you receive to your ISP. Most ISPs have an "abuse" address that you can use for this purpose. (For example, if your ISP is MindSpring.com, you can address an e-mail to `abuse@mindspring.com` and forward your spam.) The recipient ISP may or may not do anything about it, and in fairness to the ISP, it comes down to a matter of what's practical and what kinds of resources an ISP devotes to attempting to combat something like spam.

Q. Every now and then I receive X-rated or other pornographic materials by e-mail. Is there anything I can do to prevent this?

A. Not really. Whether the material received is X-rated or simply annoying get-rich-quick schemes, spam is very difficult to stop because the senders can hide their identity by using anonymous remailing services. Visit `www.emailabuse.org` for more information and additional tips. Whatever you do, never respond to spam of any type. Doing so will only validate your e-mail address, and the result will likely be even more spam.

Q. I was visiting with a friend who showed me a colorful e-mail set-up. Somehow, e-mail coming in from different people was color-coded, making it easy to spot e-mail from a particular person. Can I do that with Outlook Express?

A. Color-coding incoming e-mail is accommodated in some manner by most e-mail programs, and Outlook Express is no exception. In Outlook Express, you can color-code a particular *thread* or subject line of messages.

The first step is to designate a message or thread to watch. From your Inbox, select the first, or *parent*, message, then on the toolbar click **Message ➢ Watch Conversation**. A small pair of spectacles will appear next to all the messages of a "watched" conversation.

To color-code this watched conversation, click **Tools ➢ Options ➢ Read**. At the end of the **Highlight Watched Messages With The Color** line, select the color you want, then click **OK**. Next time an e-mail arrives that's part of that thread, it will appear in your Inbox in living color.

Q. How can I search my e-mail? I'm always trying to find an old e-mail but never have any luck. Any tips?

A. It depends on what e-mail program you're using, of course, but let's take a look at the three biggies:

Netscape Messenger has a search feature that will help you find the e-mail message you're looking for. Inside the Message Center, click **Edit**, then select **Search Messages**. When the **Search Messages** dialog box appears, click the down arrow under **Search For Items In**, and select the mail folder that you want to search.

Next, click the down arrow in the first two search fields to select your search criteria, and enter your keyword(s) in the text box. Click the **Search** button and any messages that match the criteria will appear in the window.

Outlook Express users, click **Edit ➢ Find ➢ Message**, which will present the **Find Message** dialog box. Enter your search criteria in the appropriate field(s), such as **From:**, **To:**, **Subject:**, **Message:**, **Received Before (Date):**, **Received After (Date):**, and click **Browse**.

Eudora users, click **Edit ➢ Find ➢ Find Messages**. Enter your search criteria in the appropriate fields, and select your search location (folders, mailboxes, etc.). Click the **Search** button to launch your search.

Q. What happens to e-mail after I've received it and deleted it. Is it vaporized from the face of the earth?

A. Not quite. Even after you've received a message and deleted it, the message doesn't vanish. Many Internet Service Providers archive e-mail for some period of time—years even. These archives can be subpoenaed under certain circumstances. How's that for comforting news? The same holds true for messages sent and received at work, particularly if you're on a network. So although you may hit the **Delete** key, the message still exists in the company's mail system.

For e-mail at home, be sure to determine whether your e-mail program actually deletes the e-mail from your computer or simply moves it to a trash bin or similar folder. If it moves it to a trash bin, don't forget to periodically empty the trash.

Q. I use Internet Explorer for my e-mail program. When I receive an e-mail from somebody that has some special effects or formatting, I'd like to be sure that my replies back to that person use the same formatting. Is that possible?

A. The e-mail program that's part of Internet Explorer is called Outlook Express. The good news is that Outlook Express will format replies in the same format as the e-mail received.

To set up Outlook Express so that your message replies are sent in a format that the originator's mail can read, from the main Outlook Express screen, click **Tools ➢ Options ➢ Send**. Then place a check mark in the **Reply To Messages Using The Format In Which They Were Sent** check box. Click **OK** to exit.

Q. I'm using a web-based e-mail service, but I've been told that an Internet Service Provider–based service is "safer." Is that true?

A. Web-based e-mail resides on a mail server (computer) just like Internet Service Provider–based e-mail. Web-based servers are considered more visible and, therefore, might theoretically be more attractive to cyber-terrorist attacks. That's the theory, anyway. Personally, I wouldn't lose any sleep over it. Use whatever service you're most comfortable using.

Q. I'm using Outlook Express for my e-mail program. Is there a quick way to print an e-mail message without having to go through the toolbar menus?

A. There sure is. The fastest way to print an e-mail message is to right-click within the message itself, then select **Print** from the menu that appears. This works with all versions of Outlook, by the way.

Q. Can I send a recorded message through e-mail?

A. As long as you have the ability to record the message and save it as a sound file, you can send it as an attachment. Just be sure the person you're sending it to has the ability to listen to your message. Using an offline analogy, if you record a message on a mini cassette tape and send it to somebody, they'll need to have a mini cassette tape player in order to hear what you recorded. So if you record a message and convert it to a .WAV file format and send it via e-mail as an attachment, the recipient will need to be able to play .WAV files. Most current computers can, but it's always worth checking with your intended recipient first.

Q. I'm looking for a device that just checks e-mail and that I can take with me when I travel. I don't want to spend the money to buy a computer, but aren't there some units that will do what I want?

A. Take a look at MailStation by Cidco (www.mailstation.com). It costs $99.99 plus $9.95 per month for the e-mail service. All you do is plug the device into a phone line and you'll be able to check and send e-mail. Their latest version, the Mivo 300 will allow you to send and receive attachments, something earlier versions could not do. A similar e-mail device worth checking out is the MailBug (www.mailbug.com). Both devices also provide an e-mail address book to store frequently used e-mail addresses.

Q. Several members of my family receive e-mail using my e-mail account. Is there a way to sort the mail in Outlook so I can quickly see what e-mail was received for each person?

A. You can sort your e-mail by using the **View** option. Click **View** ➢ **Current View** ➢ **Sent To**. This will sort messages by the name of the recipient. This is a very handy option to use if you're trying to locate a particular e-mail or to sort and delete junk e-mail as well. You can view your e-mail sorted by subject, date received, and other criteria.

If you would like to permanently change the way your e-mail is sorted or would like to create a customized presentation, click **View** ➤ **Current View** ➤ **Define Views** ➤ **New**. Here, you can be as creative as you wish and experiment with different views. The **View Description** box describes your customized view as you create it. Add or delete conditions to create the precise view you want.

Click an underlined word in the **View Description** box to select a viewing option or to enter a numerical value, where requested.

Select **Show** or **Hide** if you would like to display or hide messages that meet your customized view conditions.

Creating customized views is fun. If you get carried away and find that one of your view creations causes messages to disappear, just return to the **Show/Hide** settings and adjust accordingly.

E-mail can run, but it cannot hide.

Mr. Modem's E-mail Tips

- Make your subject lines meaningful. An e-mail with a cryptic subject line, such as "Help!" or "Question," will sometimes be ignored because it's too vague. Your subject line should give the recipient an inkling of what the e-mail is about.

- Typing in ALL CAPS is considered shouting online and is best avoided—unless you're intending to shout (e.g., "ARE YOU LISTENING?").

- Apply the 24-hour rule: Wait at least 24 hours before sending an e-mail written in anger. Read it once more before sending it. The regret you save may be your own.

- If you're sending an e-mail to many people, use the **bcc:** field to hide recipient e-mail addresses. (Note: AOL users who don't have a **bcc:** field should place addresses to be hidden in parentheses, with each address separated by a comma. For example: (MrModem@home.com, MrModem@TheBeach.com). This will hide these addresses from recipients.)

- Use your virus-checking software to check attachments before opening or launching them.

Mr. Modem's Recommended Websites

Disappearing E-mail   Determine how long e-mail remains accessible to the recipient. Only works with Outlook at the time of publication. Free.

    www.disappearing.com/

E-mail Forwarding Service   Simply fill out a form and your e-mail will be forwarded to the e-mail account of your choice.

    www.re-route.com/

E-mail Return Receipts   Works like the related feature offered by the U.S. Postal Service, only it's free. Receive proof of e-mailing and proof of delivery.

    www.returnreceipt.com

E-mail Stripper   This simple web-based resource will remove those annoying >>> symbols that are inserted when an e-mail has been forwarded many times. Copy-and-paste the message into this web form and click the **Strip It** button. Presto, cleano!

    http://www.geocities.com/cj1alt/tools/unix-bracket-stripper.html

E-mail Test   Test your e-mail's capabilities by sending an e-mail to testhtml@wopr.com. By return e-mail you'll receive an HTML-formatted e-mail message that will let you know whether your e-mail program is capable of displaying HTML and various other formatted text.

Everything E-mail   An excellent source for basic information on how to use e-mail more productively.

    http://everythingemail.net

World E-mail Directory   Access to an estimated 18 million e-mail addresses.

    www.worldemail.com/

Browser Basics and Beyond!

This chapter explores answers to questions about Internet Explorer, Netscape Navigator, Opera, browser settings, preferences, toolbars, downloading, installing, updates, cookies, bookmarks, security, tips, and tricks.

Q. What is a web browser?

A. It's a software program, downloadable from the Web, that allows you to look at pages on the World Wide Web. Web pages are created using a computing language called HTML, or Hypertext Markup Language, and possibly other computer languages as well. A browser reads that language and translates what it reads into text and images that you can then view on your computer monitor. Browsers have a **Location** or an **Address** field or area where you can type in a web address, or URL, such as `www.MrModem.net`. Entering the address and pressing the **Enter** key will instruct your browser to transport you to that particular web page address.

Q. How much should I expect to pay for a web browser?

A. Not a penny! Both Netscape Navigator and Microsoft's Internet Explorer are free for the downloading. You can download Netscape from `www.netscape.com/computing/download/` or Internet Explorer from `www.microsoft.com/downloads/`.

How Suite It Is

Before we meander deeper into the heart of browser territory, let's clear up a source of confusion surrounding the names associated with Netscape: the company and the software. The company that originally graced us with its fine software product is Netscape Communications Corporation (frequently referred to as *Netscape*), which has since been acquired by America Online (frequently referred to as *AOL*).

Its suite of software programs is Netscape Communicator (frequently referred to as *Netscape*). The four programs are all rolled into one luscious package designed to provide everything you need to get the most out of your new Internet lifestyle. Netscape Communicator includes:

- Netscape Messenger, for e-mail
- Netscape Newsgroup Reader for newsgroups
- Netscape Composer, for designing and editing Web pages
- Netscape Navigator, for browsing the Web; also referred to as *Netscape*

Q. Sometimes when one website is taking forever to download, I'd like to be checking out another website. Is there a way to do that, or can I only check out one site at a time?

A. There's nothing worse than waiting for a site to ooze onto your screen. While you're waiting, there is a way to use that time more productively: by opening a new window and surfing to other sites. In Netscape Navigator, select **File ➢ Open Page**, and type in the URL (address) of another website to visit. If you're using Internet Explorer, it's **File ➢ New Window**, or the keystroke combination **Ctrl + N**. If you have both Netscape and Internet Explorer on your computer, you can even use both browsers at the same time!

Q. Many web pages have links to other websites. I'd like to print a list of links from a particular web page for future reference. Can that be done?

A. It can if you're using Internet Explorer 5. To print a table of links, go to the web page that contains the links you'd like to print. Select **File ➢ Print** from the menu bar to open the Print dialog box. At the bottom of the screen, select **Print Table Of Links** and click **OK**. Internet Explorer will print the web page and, at the end, includes a table that lists the URL (web address) associated with each link that appears on the page. This is a very handy, though little-used utility feature.

Q. I'm using an older computer, so I don't have lots of power or disk space for huge programs like Netscape Navigator or Internet Explorer. Are there any other web browsers that can help me surf the Internet, or am I out of luck?

A. While Netscape Navigator and Microsoft's Internet Explorer receive most of the headlines, there is another excellent web browser that's a svelte 2.24MB fully installed, and it will run happily, even on a 386SX with 8MB of RAM. The browser is called *Opera*, and it has many of the same features enjoyed by Netscape and Internet Explorer users. Opera is available for both Windows 3.1 and 95/98/NT. One fun feature of Opera is its Mouse Gestures. These mouse gestures which allows you to perform additional tasks and functions unique to Opera. For example, holding down the right mouse button while sliding your mouse downward will open a new window. There are also a number of "mouse gesture" movements specific to wheel mice.

You can download a free version, which is supported by advertising that appears throughout the program, or you can purchase an advertisement-free version for $39. Whatever you decide, I think you'll soon agree that Opera is the greatest thing since sliced bread.

Happy surfing!

Q. You mentioned Opera as an alternative web browser. I started using it and I'm very happy with it, but I wonder whether I can fill in forms automatically with my e-mail address, phone number, etc.?

A. Opera offers lots of features despite its small size, and the ability to fill in forms is one of those features. Go to the **Preferences** menu, select **Generic/Personal Information**, and fill in your personal information. The next time you encounter a form that requires any of the personal information you have provided, simply right-click in the text field, and select the appropriate text to insert from the menu presented.

Q. I removed Netscape from my notebook computer and installed Opera to free up some hard drive space. I don't always have room to use a mouse with my notebook, and the little pointer device that my notebook has is difficult to maneuver. Can I use keystroke combinations with Opera to navigate?

A. Just like its big-boy cousins Netscape Navigator and Internet Explorer (IE), Opera also provides keystroke alternatives for just about everything you would otherwise do with a mouse. For example, pressing the **F8** key moves your cursor to the **Address** field; typing **Ctrl + F2** opens your Hot List—which is the Opera equivalent of IE's Favorites or of Navigator's Bookmarks. For a complete list of Opera's keyboard commands, press **Ctrl + B**.

Q. When I search for something on the Internet, I get my search results and then go to a website from the links provided. When I do that, the word or term I was searching for is sometimes difficult to find on the web page. Any help would be appreciated.

A. When the information you want is hidden somewhere on a long page, you can use your browser's **Find** command to locate the word or phrase you're looking for. From your browser's toolbar, click **Edit ➢ Find**, or use the keystroke combination **Ctrl + F**. Either one will bring up the **Find** dialog box. You can also find recurring instances of your search term by using the **Find Next** option in the **Find** search box.

Q. I'd like to remove Netscape from my computer, but a warning comes up telling me that removing it may impact one or more registered programs. Now what?

A. When you install a software program using Windows, it's automatically entered into the Windows Registry. This "registration" is what allows you to double-click a filename, for example, and have the correct program launch automatically. The message you're seeing indicates that you'll no longer be able to double-click a file associated with Netscape and have that program start automatically—which, of course, is exactly what you'd expect after removing it.

While that all sounds very hunky-dory, bear in mind that you may not be able to open .GIF, .JPG, .HTML, or other graphics files after you bid a fond farewell to Netscape, unless you have another graphics program installed on your computer. Windows contains a program called Paint, which is a no-frills kind of graphics program that will work, but just be aware that removing Netscape (or Internet Explorer, for that matter) may have some trickle-down effects.

To learn more about registering programs in order to automatically open files, send a blank e-mail addressed to `filetypes@MrModem.net`. By return e-mail, I'll send you lots of additional information about file types, what those cryptic three-letter file extensions mean, what programs were used to create the files, how to associate or register programs to open them, and where to find those programs.

Q. I can't decide whether I should use Internet Explorer or Netscape. Is one better than the other?

A. Mr. Modem enjoys a good dither as much as the next person, so to accommodate my dither-prone propensities, I have both Microsoft Internet Explorer and Netscape Navigator installed on my computer. (Okay, I confess, I also have Opera on my computer. And, yes, I'm a member of Browsers Anonymous, but I keep telling everybody it's not a sickness—it's a lifestyle! I can stop using any one of them any time I want. I really can. I swear.) Both programs are similar—though I'm sure the good folks at Microsoft and Netscape might take exception to that. If Netscape releases a new feature, before you know it Microsoft releases something similar for Internet Explorer—and vice versa.

Statistically, more people use Internet Explorer than do Netscape, but it really boils down to a matter of personal preference. I lean toward Internet Explorer, though I'm told a visit to a competent orthopedist will resolve that problem.

Q. What's the difference between a web browser's memory cache and its disk cache?

A. Memory cache (pronounced "cash," not "cach-ET" or "cash-AY") is an area of your computer's memory (called RAM, or random access memory) that retains data only as long as you're running your browser; disk cache retains data (such as websites previously visited) on your hard drive, so it remains after you exit your browser and even after you disconnect from the Internet.

Q. How important is it to clean out my browser's cache after using the Internet?

A. Some surfers might not know that when they visit web pages, their browser loads those pages into a special area of their computer called a cache. It does that to speed up the process of visiting the same web page in the future. When you visit a website, your browser will check the URL (address) of the web page against the URLs stored in cache. If it finds a match, the page stored in cache will be displayed on your monitor, rather than downloading a fresh copy of the page. After visiting many sites on the Web, it's a good idea to clean out or purge your cache to prevent unsightly cache build-up. You know how people talk. To purge you... these steps for your browser of choice:

- Netscape 4.*x* and 6.*x*: **Edit** ➢ **Preferences** ➢ **Advanced** ➢ **Clear** ... (Clearing memory cache is a good idea also, which you can do by ... ... the **Clear Memory Cache** button.)

- Internet Explorer 4.*x*: **View** ➢ **Internet Options** ➢ **General** ➢ **Delete Files**.

- Internet Explorer 5.*x*: **Tools** ➢ **Internet Options** ➢ **General.** In the **Temporary Internet Files** area, click the **Delete Files** button.

Q. I use Netscape Navigator and wonder: If I delete my History file, is that going to cause any problems?

A. Not for me. Okay, okay, Mr. Modem is just yanking your cable. The History file is a text file that records the addresses of all websites previously visited. You determine how long you want Netscape to retain a log of your cyber travels by clicking **Edit** ➢ **Preferences** ➢ **Navigator**. You will see a field where you can enter the number of days to retain that history, along with a **Clear History** button.

Clearing your history in this manner is harmless and much easier than entering a witness relocation program, as Mr. Modem did many years ago. (Come to think of it, I probably shouldn't have mentioned that.) I keep pages in my History file for 14 days.

Retaining your web-browsing history for a week or two can be helpful should you wish to revisit a website at a later date but can't remember the URL. If you think you might want to revisit a site, however, it's a good idea to bookmark it rather than rely on your History file, the contents of which will expire after whatever period you decide is appropriate.

Q. I know that Internet Explorer keeps the websites I visit in its History file. How can I clean out that history or delete everything that's in it?

A. You can empty your History folder in Explorer 4.*x* or 5.*x* by selecting **Internet Options** from the **View** or the **Tools** menu and then clicking the **Clear History** button on the **General** tab. In older versions of Explorer, the button is located on the **Navigation** tab of the **Options** Menu.

Netscape 4.*x* and later users, click **Edit** ➢ **Preferences**, then the **Clear History** button. Click **OK** to exit.

Q. Can I adjust the number of days that my browser stores websites I've visited in its History files?

A. You can keep as much history as you'd like, but for most Internet users, a week or two should be plenty. The default setting is seven days. To customize the number of days your browser retains its history, follow these simple steps:

Netscape Navigator users, click **Edit ➤ Preferences**. Next, click the **Navigator** tab and change the value in the **Pages In History Expire After ___ Days** field. Click **OK** when you're finished.

Internet Explorer users, click **Tools ➤ Internet Options**, then click the **General Tab**. In the **History** section, change the value of the field labeled **Days To Keep Pages In History**, and click **OK**.

If you would rather not retain any history of where you've been on the Web, just enter a value of zero in the **Pages In History Expire After ___ Days** field of Netscape Navigator or in the **Days To Keep Pages In History** field of Internet Explorer.

Q. I know my browser's History file contains a record of the websites I've visited, but is there any way to add this file to my Bookmarks and/or Favorites?

A. If you're using Netscape Navigator, type **about:global** in the **Location** address area, then press **Enter**. Your History file will appear as a web page. This file will contain links to every component (including individual graphics) of every web page you have visited during the period your History file is recording pages. The default is seven days.

To bookmark this page, click **Bookmarks** and select **Add Or File Bookmark**. Your new bookmark will be labeled **Information About The Netscape Global History**.

The ability to import the History folder into Favorites is not available to Internet Explorer users. Your Internet Explorer History folder can be found at C:\Windows\History. To view your History folder, press Ctrl + H within Internet Explorer.

Q. How can I delete previously visited web addresses from my browser's drop-down address window?

A. These addresses reside in your browser's History file, so how you remove them will vary depending on the browser you're using. If you're using Netscape Navigator 4.*x*, click **Edit** ➤ **Preferences** ➤ **Navigator**, then click the **Clear Location Bar** button.

For Internet Explorer, Versions 4.*x* or 5.*x*, click **View** or **Tools** ➤ **Internet Options** ➤ **Clear History**.

Q. Do I need a separate dialer program to establish my connection to the Internet for each browser I want to use?

A. Multiple dialers aren't necessary. You can run Internet Explorer, Netscape, Opera, or any other browser program using one dialer. Think of it as a two-step process: First you establish your connection to the Internet, then you decide which browser you would like to use. So launch your dialer, then once you have your connection to the Internet, minimize your dialer window, if it doesn't minimize automatically, and launch your browser of choice. When minimizing your dialer window, if you receive a prompt that asks if you want to shut down your connection, be sure to click **No**. With your dialer program out of the way, you'll be ready to dive into the Internet surf and have some fun!

Q. How can I have the time and date appear on web pages that I print?

A. Using either Netscape or Internet Explorer, click **File** ➤ **Page Setup**. If you're using Netscape, check **Date Printed** under **Footer**, and your printouts will include the date and time.

If you're using Internet Explorer, you can have the time and date printed in either the header or footer. You'll have to enter the proper codes in the Header or Footer box, but they're very simple to enter. If you want the time and date, type **&t &d** in the appropriate text box for either Header or Footer. You might want to leave a few spaces between the codes to separate the time and date on the printed page. It may take a little experimenting and printing of a few test pages, but in short order you'll have the time and date information just the way you want it. It's a good idea to do a test print before you attempt to change settings. Many times the date and time will appear on any web pages printed automatically.

Q. I keep getting trapped on web pages that use frames. How can I look at the material displayed inside a frame, but in a full-screen window?

A. When you encounter a web page that is divided up into small windows or compartments, each one of those windows is called a frame. To bust out of a frame, right-click anywhere within the frame, and select **Open Frame In New Window**. When you're finished, just close down that window and you'll be back to your "framed" view.

Q. My connection to the Internet is very slow. Is there anything I can do to speed things up, other than buying a new computer or a new modem?

A. One of the easiest ways to indulge your need for speed is by turning off your browser's graphics capabilities. Downloading graphics can sometimes cause even the fastest connection to feel like you're trying to suck molasses through a straw.

Just one word of caution before you toggle off your graphics: Some sites will be impossible to navigate without graphics because their navigational components *are* graphics. In other words, if the ability to navigate a website is dependent upon your ability to click certain graphical images, and those images no longer appear because you have your graphics turned off, well, you've got big problems, my friend. However, if you do encounter that situation, you can simply turn your graphics back on, then click the **Reload** or the **Refresh** button on your browser.

In Netscape 4.*x*, select **Edit** ➢ **Preferences**, and select **Advanced**. Remove the check mark in front of **Automatically Load Images**.

In Netscape 6.*x*, select **Edit** ➢ **Preferences** ➢ **Advanced** ➢ **Images** and place a check mark before **Do Not Load Any Images**.

In Internet Explorer 4.*x*, select **View** ➢ **Internet Options** ➢ **Advanced**, and uncheck **Show Pictures**.

In Internet Explorer 5.*x*, click **Tools** ➢ **Internet Options, Advanced**. In the **Multimedia** area, uncheck one or more of the **Show Pictures**, **Play Animations**, **Play Videos**, or **Play Sounds** check boxes.

 If the **Show Pictures** or the **Play Videos** check box is not checked, you can still display an individual picture or animation on a web page by right-clicking its icon and then clicking **Show Picture**. If the pictures on a web page are still visible after you clear the **Show Pictures** check box, you can hide them by clicking the **View** menu and then **Refresh**.

Q. Sometimes it takes forever for one page to load. Is there any way to speed things up?

A. There are a number of techniques and software programs available to help speed up the process of loading pages onto your screen. One of the simplest ways to make your web surfing more efficient is to open a second browser window so you can read one page while waiting for the second page to load.

Using either Netscape Navigator or Internet Explorer, open a second browser window (or more) by pressing **Ctrl + N**. If you want to follow a link but don't want to leave the page you're reviewing, right-click the link in question and select **Open In New Window**.

Q. What's the difference between the **Refresh** and **Reload** buttons on web browsers?

A. Netscape Navigator's toolbar has a **Reload** button, while Internet Explorer's has a **Refresh** button. The purpose of either button is the same: to redisplay the current page. Clicking **Reload** or **Refresh** downloads the entire page again from the web server. If you want to be sure you have the latest version of a particular web page, click **Reload** or **Refresh**, depending on the browser you're using.

Q. I'm having difficulty reading the small print on some websites. Is there a way to make the text bigger, or is it a problem caused by my browser?

A. You can change font size using Netscape Navigator or Internet Explorer faster than you can say, "What is this, an eye test?" In Navigator 4.*x*, click **View ➢ Increase Font**. In Navigator 6.*x*, click **View ➢ Text Size** and select the appropriate font size.

Internet Explorer 4.*x* users, click **View ➢ Fonts**, then adjust the font size. Internet Explorer 5.*x* users, click **View ➢ Text Size**, then select the appropriate font size from **Smallest** to **Largest**.

Q. When I'm looking at web pages, is there any way I can see more of a page? Half my screen is filled with buttons and toolbars. I just want to see what's on the web page.

A. If viewing web pages on your monitor feels like you're looking through your automobile's windshield with the sun visor blocking your view, there is a way to expand your digital horizon without those pesky navigational doodads cluttering up the netscape.

To hide your toolbars, using Netscape Navigator, click **View** ➤ **Show**, or **View** ➤ **Toolbars** (depending on the version of Netscape you're using) then select the appropriate toolbar or toolbars to hide. Selecting the toolbar will place a check mark next to it. If there's a check mark, the toolbar is visible; remove the check mark to hide the toolbar. There are three toolbars to choose from in Netscape 4.*x*: Navigation, Location, and Personal. Netscape 6.*x* has Navigation, Personal Toolbar, and Taskbar. You can display or hide any or all of them.

If you're using Internet Explorer 4.*x* or 5.*x*, select **View** ➤ **Full Screen** to remove all toolbars. You can remove or add individual toolbars by clicking **View** ➤ **Toolbars**.

Q. When I'm through with an Internet session and I close down my browser, I continually forget to disconnect from the Internet. That causes my connection to ultimately time out and disconnect. Is there anything I can do to avoid that?

A. You could put a yellow sticky on your monitor that says "Don't forget to log off!" But an easier approach would be to let Internet Explorer remember to do it for you. This only applies to IE 5, but you do have the option of terminating your dial-up connection when you close Explorer. This can be either very helpful or extremely annoying if you occasionally close your browser by accident.

To enable this feature, click **Tools** ➤ **Internet Options** ➤ **Connections**. Highlight the name of your Internet connection, then click the **Settings** button. In the **Dial-Up Settings** area, click the **Advanced** button. Check the **Disconnect When Connection May No Longer Be Needed** box, then click **OK** in each of the three open dialog boxes to make your exit.

Netscape Navigator users: Break out the yellow stickies or tie a piece of string around your finger to help you remember to disconnect: Navigator doesn't have a similar "timed" disconnect feature.

Q. I've been reading about something called "Boolean operators." I know they have something to do with searching for information on the Internet, but every time I read an explanation, I don't understand it. Can you help?

A. In my book, *Mr. Modem's Internet Guide for Seniors* (www.MrModem.net), I provide an in-depth explanation and several examples of *Boolean operators* at work. Quoting myself (which is about as tacky as it gets), "Boolean operators are nifty little words that can refine searches and thereby improve your search results."

"Boolean operators include AND, OR, NOT, IF, THEN, and EXCEPT. When using these words in conjunction with a search program, called a search engine, include Boolean operators with your search terms before clicking the **Search** button and launching a search. For example, 'pets NOT snakes' will return references to pets, but excluding references to snakes as pets. At least that's the theory."

When using any search engine, be sure to look for and read any advanced search tips or techniques available for that specific search program. You'll usually find a link that says "Advanced Search" or "Search Help" associated with each search engine.

Q. I'm concerned about my privacy and how much information my browser is revealing about me when I visit websites. Is there any way to prevent my browser from sharing any information about me?

A. Some website servers (computers) do collect personal information from your browser. There are a few things you can do to prevent that either temporarily or permanently. For example, you can remove your e-mail address, your login name, your real name, and any other personal information from your browser settings.

In Internet Explorer 5.*x*, click **Tools** ➢ **Internet Options**. Select the **Content** tab and choose the **My Profile** button. From each tab, delete the information from the fields that you don't want sites to have access to, then click **OK**.

Netscape Navigator 4.*x* and later users can remove their personal information by clicking **Edit** ➢ **Preferences**, clicking the **Mail & Newsgroups** section, and selecting **Identity**. Remove the information from the fields you don't want to reveal, then click the **OK** button.

With this information removed, intrusive servers (computers) will only see your ISP address and its geographical location.

Q. I know that cookies are not generally bad things, but I still don't like it that cookies are placed on my computer by some websites. How can I prevent a website from placing anything on my computer?

A. There's a great deal of misinformation in circulation about cookies, what they are and what they do. For the most part, cookies are a good thing, and they personalize your web surfing, allowing sites to greet you by name, or remember your previous settings on a customized welcome page, for example.

In answer to your question, you can disable cookies completely or elect to be notified before cookies are placed on your computer. I recommend the latter setting because most reputable websites deploy cookies for good purposes. I have my browser set to accept all cookies, though periodically I do review my cookies folder and either delete specific cookies or delete all my cookies and start over again. That's the easiest approach. If you toss all your cookies, the next time you visit some websites you will have to log in again or reconfigure any personalization settings that may have been lost by nuking your cookies.

Internet Explorer 5.*x* users, click **Tools** ➤ **Internet Options** ➤ **Security**. Under **Select A Web Content Zone To Specify Its Security Settings**, select **Internet**. Then, under **Security Level For This Zone**, move the slider bar to **High**, **Medium**, **Medium Low**, or **Low**. A description of each setting is provided. I have mine set to **Medium**.

Internet Explorer 4.*x* users, click **Tools** ➤ **Internet Options**, then click the **Advanced** tab. Scroll down to the **Security** category. Under the **Cookies** subheading, check either the box labeled **Disable All Cookie Use**, or if you would rather be prompted before accepting cookies—my recommendation—check the box labeled **Prompt Before Accepting Cookies**, located under the **Cookies** subheading.

Netscape Navigator 4.*x* and later users can make their cookie preferences known by clicking **Edit** ➤ **Preferences**. Then click the **Advanced** category and, under **Cookies**, select **Accept All Cookies** or **Disable Cookies**, or elect to be prompted before accepting a cookie by placing a check in the box to the left of **Warn Me Before Accepting A Cookie**.

To learn even more about cookies, send a blank e-mail addressed to `cookies @MrModem.net`. By return e-mail, I'll send you additional information about cookies and possible cookie concerns.

Q. I'm trying to print a web page, but the page is displayed in frames and it's driving me crazy. How can I print out just the content of one frame?

A. Frames can be a royal pain in the ASCII, particularly when you're trying to print a page. If you don't do it correctly, you'll print the wrong information, or the frame you want will end up being blank. To print the contents of a frame, place your cursor in the frame you would like to print. Then right-click the frame and select **Print** from the menu that appears. This works with most current browsers, but some earlier versions may still present a problem.

Q. How can I save my bookmarks?

A. Websites you have previously visited and saved to your Bookmarks (Netscape Navigator) or your Favorites folder (Internet Explorer) are just as important to back up as your data files on your hard drive.

Using Netscape Navigator, locate the `bookmark.htm` file (**Start ➢ Find**), and copy it to a disk. The file resides in the same folder as your browser, typically `C:\Program Files\Netscape\Users\` and then the name of your personal folder.

With Internet Explorer 4.*x* or higher, your Favorites folder is located under `C:\Windows` and can be copied as you would any other Windows folder; i.e., locate the folder, right-click, and select the appropriate action (**Copy**, **SendTo**, etc.) from the menu that appears.

Q. My bookmarks are a mess. I've got hundreds of them, all in one long list, and now I can't find anything. How can I organize my bookmarks?

A. The specifics of what you do varies and depend on whether you're using Netscape Navigator (Bookmarks) or Microsoft Internet Explorer (Favorites). There are also a few minor variations depending on the version of the program you're using. In the spirit of completeness and verbosity, I'll cover both programs, current versions, starting from the point where you're looking at a web page on your screen.

Netscape Navigator: Create a bookmark by clicking the **Bookmark** menu bar item. Choose **Add Bookmark** or **Add Current Page,** or drag the bookmark icon to the **Bookmarks** button and drop it in the folder of your choice.

To tame your wild bookmarks, go to **Bookmarks**, then select **Edit** or **Manage Bookmarks**. You will be presented with a tree-like structure where you can move, delete, rename, and edit bookmarks.

Internet Explorer: Create a bookmark by choosing **Favorites** from the menu bar, then select **Add To Favorites**. You will be prompted to indicate where you would like to stick your shortcut or bookmark. (Be nice!) If you click **OK**, it will appear on the main bookmarks list. You can also select a folder in which to place a favorite URL (or web address), or create a new folder.

To manage your bookmarks, go to **Favorites** on the menu bar, and select **Organize Favorites**. You will then be face-to-face with the **Organize Favorites** dialog box, where you can move, rename, delete, or bask in the glow of your well-organized bookmarks.

Q. I want to install Netscape on my new computer, but even with my 56K modem it's going to take a very long time. Is it possible to obtain a CD of the program without buying a full commercial version?

A. The good folks at Netscape thoughtfully make a CD available for only $5.95. To order the CD, go to http://cd.netscape.com. First-class postage is included for orders within the U.S. Extra-cost delivery options are available as well.

Internet Explorer enthusiasts can also obtain a CD by calling 1-800-485-2048 or by visiting www.microsoft.com/windows/ie/offers/default.asp. For $10, you'll receive the CD and the Internet Tools package.

Q. Whenever I launch my browser, the first page displayed is the home page of my Internet Service Provider. Is there some way I can change that to bring up something more interesting? I feel like I'm being forced to watch a commercial every time I go online.

A. You can change the default start page very easily and set it to any page your little modem desires. The process varies slightly depending on whether you're using Netscape Navigator or Internet Explorer.

If you're using Netscape Navigator 4.*x* or later, go to **Edit ➤ Preferences**. Then click **Navigator** in the left directory tree. In the **Location** field to the right, under **Home Page**, type in the URL (web page address) for the page you'd like to be your start page. Alternatively, you can navigate to the actual web page first, then click the **Use Current Page** button.

If you're using Internet Explorer, go to **View** (or **Tools** in Version 5.*x*) ➤ **Internet Options**. Under the **General** tab (named after General Zachariah Tab of Civil War fame), enter the URL of the page you'd like to be your start page. Alternatively, you can navigate to a particular web page, then click the **Use Current Page** button.

Q. How can I save a picture I see on the Web?

A. You can harvest just about any graphic or other image by placing your mouse cursor on the graphic you would like to save, right-clicking, and then selecting **Save Picture As** or **Save Image As** from the menu that appears.

You can save the picture in its original format as displayed on the Web, or you can change its file type by changing the **Save File As Type** setting at the bottom of the dialog box. Click the down arrow to view a list of alternative file types. Select a file type, rename the file, and designate the location to which you want to save the file in the **Save In** field. Click the **Save** button to save the file.

Copyright laws do apply to web-based materials, so use caution before copying anything you see on the Internet. A delightful graphic or essay or other material you may be interested in copying is the result of somebody's hard work. Saving an image for personal, non-commercial use will generally not be a problem, but it's always best to read the copyright language associated with any website or web-based material and obtain the appropriate permissions first.

Q. I'd like to share a link or URL with a friend, but some of these web addresses are so darned long and complicated, it's almost impossible to copy them. Is there an easy way to share web addresses?

A. Trying to copy a long URL without making a tpyo—particularly when the address is filled with strange-looking text characters—is next to impossible, I agree. An easier way to do that is simply to right-click a link and select **Copy** from the menu presented.

Next, open your e-mail program, and address an e-mail to your friend. In the body of the e-mail, place your mouse cursor at the location where you would like to insert the URL, right-click, and select **Paste**. Voila! The URL will pop right into the body of the e-mail, 100 percent typo-free.

Q. Is it possible to create a shortcut from the Windows Desktop to a particular web page?

A. You can create a shortcut to a web page from the Windows Desktop very easily. Navigate to the web page to which you would like to create a shortcut. Right-click anywhere on the page.

Select **Create Shortcut** from the menu that appears. Presto! An icon leading to that location will appear on your Desktop for one-click navigation to that specific web page in the future—assuming you have a connection to the Internet at the time, of course.

Q. How often should I update my browser software?

A. Regardless of the browser you're using, it's a good idea to visit its home base website to make sure you have the latest updates. Many times, bug fixes called *patches* will be available to repair a recently discovered problem. On occasion, an improved or enhanced feature may be made available as well. I'd recommend checking for updates at least once a month—with this caveat: There's no strategic advantage to being on the bleeding edge of technology. Though I haven't seen a warning from the Surgeon General to this effect, it's been my experience that bleeding-edge technology *can* cause headaches. So whenever a new update or upgrade is released, it's a good idea to hold off and let the release be used for awhile until you're sure it has a fairly dependable track record. Once you have had occasion to read a few reviews about it (or you're welcome to ask me for my two cents), then it might be worth installing.

You can visit the main Internet Explorer web page at `www.Microsoft.com/windows/ie/`. Product Updates can be accessed by clicking **Start** ➢ **Windows Update** on your computer.

Netscape enthusiasts can visit `http://home.netscape.com/download` and select **Smart Update**. Netscape's Smart Update feature can automatically retrieve updates, if the feature is enabled.

To enable or disable Smart Update, click **Edit** ➢ **Preferences** ➢ **Advanced** ➢ **Smart Update**. Select **Enable Smart Update** to turn it on. Select **Require Manual Confirmation Of Each Install** if you want to be notified each time Smart Update springs into action.

To uninstall a Smart Update item, select the item you wish to uninstall from the components displayed, then click the **Uninstall** button.

Q. I've tried looking in several books for help with my browser, but I haven't been that happy with any of them. Any suggestions?

A. The help provided within your browser itself is both excellent and convenient. Just click the **Help** menu to see what's available to you. It's a matter of personal preference how you use the help available. I prefer the **Index** view, which functions as a book's index with hundreds of words listed. Click a word and you'll be presented with the associated help information. You'll also have the ability to enter a word or phrase to search for in a **Look For** or **Type In Keyword To Find** field.

Q. When looking at websites, only a portion of the web page displays in my browser. It's all there, but it's too big, and I have to scroll left and right to see what I think should appear without scrolling. What's causing that and is there a way to fix it?

A. It could be your monitor's resolution settings. Colors and pictures that are grainy, or if you're required to do a lot of scrolling, could indicate that these settings aren't the best they could be. Most websites are designed for viewing with a screen size at least 800 by 600 pixels and a resolution of 256 colors.

To check or change your display settings, click the **My Computer** icon on your Desktop and select **Control Panel**. Double-click the **Display** icon and click the **Settings** tab. Under the **Colors** section, choose **256 Colors** from the drop-down menu.

In the **Screen Area** section, move the slider bar to the right until it indicates a screen size of 800 by 600 pixels. Click the **OK** button and restart your browser. Try different settings until you determine what works best for you.

It's also possible that a poorly designed website could be the source of the problem. A competent and conscientious website designer will design a site so it displays well in a variety of web browsers (and versions of those browsers), as well as on different platforms (Windows, NT, Mac, Linux, etc.) and on different-sized monitors at various resolutions. So if you occasionally encounter a site that doesn't "fit" your monitor, it's probably a website design issue.

Q. I am now using Netscape Navigator and I find it a lot better than the browser that came preinstalled on my computer. How do I change Netscape to be my default browser?

A. When you open Netscape Navigator, a dialog box should appear, asking if you want Netscape to be your default browser. If this dialog box doesn't appear, you need to tweak your Netscape preferences file, `prefs.js`. Your `prefs.js` file is located in **Program Files** ➢ **Netscape** ➢ **Users**. If you can't find it, launch a search using the Windows **Find** command, located under the **Start** menu. When you locate the file, open it using WordPad, Notepad, or any other text editor.

Scroll through your `prefs.js` file to the line that reads `user_pref("browser.wfe.ignore_def_check", true)`. If the value—the last word in that line—is *true*, Netscape won't display the default dialog box. If the value is *false*, it will always check.

If, on the other hand, you've been using Netscape Navigator and decide that you'd like Internet Explorer to be your default browser instead, you can reset your Internet Explorer settings to their original defaults, including your choice of default browser, without changing any Netscape settings.

Accomplishing this is as easy as 1-2-3:

1. From the **Tools** menu, click **Internet Options**.
2. Select the **Programs** tab.
3. Click the **Reset Web Settings** button.

If you would like to be asked if you want Internet Explorer to be your default browser, click **Tools** ➢ **Internet Options** ➢ **Programs** and place a check mark next to **Internet Explorer Should Check To See Whether It Is The Default Browser**.

With those three steps completed, the next time you launch Internet Explorer you will be asked if you would like IE to be your default browser. Regardless of your decision, it's always nice to be asked.

Q. I'm using Internet Explorer 5.*x*, but whenever I click the **Back** button, I always return to the same sign-up page of a particular website—the name of which I won't mention. I was thinking the problem was a cookie that was bringing me back to that page. I deleted my cookies file, but it's still happening. I'm stumped. Any ideas, Mr. Modem?

A. The page you keep returning to is one that's probably stored as a temporary Internet file. The original intention of having pages stored in that manner is to make return visits faster—as opposed to having to download the same page from the website each time you revisit. Sounds like this one page has a real good grip on you, though. The best way to break free is to clean out your temporary files and start with a clean slate.

To clean out your temporary files, click **Tools ➢ Internet Options**. On the **General** tab, click the **Clear History** button. (For readers using Netscape Navigator, click **Edit ➢ Preferences ➢ Advanced ➢ Cache**, then clear your memory and disk cache.)

Q. I've been told I can assign URL keyboard shortcuts for Internet Explorer. How do I do this?

A. Assuming you're using Windows, click the **Start** button located in the lower left-hand corner of your screen. Choose **Favorites**, and then select the link to which you want to assign a shortcut. Right-click that link and choose **Properties**. This will launch a *(Name Of Selected Favorite) Properties* window.

Click the window's **Internet Shortcut** tab—if available—and then on the **Shortcut Key** entry field.

Type a letter into the field. (For instance, for Mr. Modem's website, www.MrModem.net, you might choose the letter *M*; this will assign the keystroke combination Ctrl + Alt + M to launch my website.)

Click the **Apply** button to finish.

The next time you want to visit a site to which you assigned a shortcut key, just press the keystroke combination and you'll be there!

Q. Can I download and use Microsoft's Internet Explorer even though I access the Internet through America Online?

A. You sure can. You can use America Online's "version" of Internet Explorer, or you can use a "plain vanilla" version of IE or Netscape, downloaded from the Microsoft or the Netscape website (www.microsoft.com/downloads/ for Internet Explorer or www.netscape.com/computing/download for Netscape Communicator, which includes Navigator, the web browser).

Once you download and install either browser (explained in excruciating detail in *Mr. Modem's Internet Guide for Seniors*, www.MrModem.net), you'll have an icon on your Windows Desktop available to launch the program. Using either browser with AOL is very simple.

First, establish your connection to the Internet with AOL.

Once your connection is established, minimize your AOL window, and double-click your Internet Explorer or your Netscape Communicator icon to launch either program.

You won't see any of the usual AOL language, advertisements, etc. because you're not using AOL's "version" of either browser at this point. Instead, you're using AOL to connect to the Internet, so in this instance, AOL is simply acting as your Internet Service Provider, and you're free to use any software you wish to access the Internet.

Of course, America Online owns Netscape, so it's probably just a matter of time before an AOL "version" of Netscape appears on the cyber scene, as well.

Q. Sometimes I can't find files after I download them from a website. Is there a special folder for downloaded files in my browser that perhaps I'm not aware of?

A. Through the years I've downloaded hundreds of files from the Internet and have yet to lose one of them—a remarkable feat considering I misplace my car keys several times each week. The reason I never lose downloaded files is because I always download files to my Windows Desktop.

Next time you download a file and you're prompted to designate a location to which the file will be saved, select **Desktop**. Once the download has completed, you'll have a new icon for the file you downloaded located on your Desktop that will be easy to spot. From your Desktop, you can then install, copy, delete, or move the downloaded file to a better location by launching Windows Explorer (**Start ➢ Programs ➢ Windows Explorer**).

Q. When downloading a file from the Internet, is there any way to see the actual percentage of download completed? I usually just see a progress bar that gives some inaccurate guesstimate of how much longer it's going to take for the file to download.

A. Once the download begins, try minimizing the download "progress" window. It should display the percentage of the file that's transferred when the window is minimized on the Taskbar. If you're downloading from an FTP (File Transfer Protocol) site, you'll see the actual file size transferred.

Mr. Modem's Browser Tips

- Use the **Tab** key to move forward through the links (URLs) on a Web page. Press Shift + Tab to move backward through the links.

- Instead of using your **Back** and **Forward** buttons to navigate between linked pages, try opening a linked page in a new window. To do this, right-click a link, and select **Open In New Window** from the menu displayed. When you're finished reviewing the linked page, just close that new window and you'll be right back where you started.

- To find a particular word or a phrase on a web page, press **Ctrl + F**, and enter the word or phrase.

- You don't always have to type in the http://www preface in the **Address** field of a dot-com address. Instead, try typing the word itself; i.e., instead of typing http://www.sybex.com, just type **sybex**. It doesn't always work, but if it does with your browser, it can save a few keystrokes.

- To determine which version of browser you're using, with your browser open, click **Help ➢ About Communicator** or **About Internet Explorer**.

Mr. Modem's Recommended Websites

Browsertune   Tests to determine whether your browser's most essential functions are working properly and whether your Internet connection is up to speed. Nothing to download or install, plus it's free!

    www.browsertune.com/bt2kfast/

BrowserWatch   Information about browsers, plug-ins, and breaking news in the browser industry. A complete list of different plug-ins and browsers allows you to quickly and effortlessly find the plug-ins or browsers you want.

    http://browserwatch.internet.com

Internet Explorer Products Download   Accessories and plug-ins from Microsoft. Download and install them directly from this location.

    www.microsoft.com/windows/ie/download/default.htm

Netscape Netcenter   Download the most current version of Netscape and a host of Internet tools. Lots of related links to visit as well.

    www.netscape.com/computing/download/

Life Online

Home Is Where You Hang Your @

This chapter focuses on answers to questions about connecting to the Internet, using modems, understanding Internet Service Providers, and downloading files, as well as helpful information about cookies, domain names, viruses, and more.

Q. My Internet Service Provider boots me off the Internet when I leave my computer idle for too long. It wouldn't be so bad, but if I'm downloading a large file, sometimes I get disconnected during the download. Is there any way to keep the connection alive?

A. "Stayin' alive, stayin' alive," our polyester mantra of the 1970s, has evolved into "stayin' online, stayin' online" in the new century. There are several things you can do to attempt to keep your connection alive. One of the easiest ways is to set your e-mail program and/or browser (in the case of Internet Explorer) to automatically check for e-mail every so many minutes. This is a feature of almost every current e-mail package. To begin, look under your program's **Options** or **Preferences** settings.

For Netscape Messenger, click **Edit** ➤ **Preferences** ➤ **Mail & Newsgroups** ➤ **Mail Servers**, then click the **Edit** button under **Incoming Mail Servers**. Enter the number of minutes (I'd suggest five) in the **Check For E-mail Every ___ Minutes** field.

With IE 5/Outlook, click **Tools** ➤ **Internet Options** ➤ **Connections** ➤ **Settings** ➤ **Advanced**. Make sure there is no check mark by **Disconnect If Idle For ___ Minutes** and no check mark before **Disconnect When Connection May No Longer Be Needed**.

Several software programs are also available to keep your connection; Stay Connected, by Inkline Global, is one such program that resumes broken connections automatically for all dial-up networking ISPs. Works with all major ISPs including AOL 6.0 and below, CompuServe 2000, Netzero 3.1.2 and below, MSN, Prodigy, AT&T WorldNet, and more. They offer a 21-day free trial. After that, it's $20 to register. You can download the program from `www.inklineglobal.com/products/sc/index.html`.

An even more cost-effective option is to download and run the free version of RealPlayer (`www.real.com`). Under the RealPlayer program heading **Presets**, you can choose an Internet radio station to listen to while you work or surf. RealPlayer will continue playing whatever station you choose, enabling you to walk away from your computer and never lose your connection to the Internet.

Two other "stay connected" programs worth taking a look at include:

- Wake Up (`http://members.tripod.com/robertlmoore/Download.html`) keeps you connected by sending packets of data, according to your specified period of time. Resides in your System Tray and can be easily enabled/disabled.

- Stay Live 2000 (`www.gregorybraun.com/StayLive.html`) keeps your Internet connection active by periodically sending a small packet of data to one of the many atomic clocks maintained by the U.S. Government, thus preventing your ISP from dropping your connection due to inactivity.

Q. I'm moving to a new house a couple of miles away and wondered if I need to inform my ISP of my new telephone number and whether this move will affect my e-mail address or Internet connection?

A. There is no need to notify your ISP of your new telephone number. As long as you haven't moved into an area where the call to your ISP will be a long-distance call, you'll be able to hook up your computer in your new house and log in, same as you did in the old 'hood. Just be sure to notify your ISP of your new mailing address. You wouldn't want to miss an invoice.

Q. My phone company sent me some information about high-speed access to the Internet using an ISDN line. What is it, and is it worth the extra money?

A. Integrated Services Digital Network, or ISDN, lines are becoming increasingly popular. An ISDN connection operates at speeds up to 128,000bps, which is about four times faster than a 28.8Kbps modem and about twice as fast as a 56Kbps modem. It's also more reliable. ISDN lines afford high-speed surfing by changing the way modems and telephone lines work together. Instead of your modem translating digital computer data into an analog format, which is required by most telephone systems, an ISDN line permits data to remain in its native digital format so that it moves faster and with fewer errors.

If you only use the Internet occasionally, it probably isn't worth the additional expense; however, if the Internet is becoming an increasingly significant part of your life, as it is for millions of people worldwide, the increased speed and reliability may well be worth it. Rates can vary widely, so be sure to do some comparison shopping. Check out `www.getspeed.com` to find out what high-speed Internet access is available in your area.

Q. When I use a search engine and then visit one of the sites that comes up, sometimes it seems like the site has nothing to do with what I was searching for. Why does the site come up as a search result?

A. If you located the site by entering a keyword as your search term, that word appears somewhere on the web page displayed. Rather than reading through screens of text to find your search word, try your browser's **Find** command. You can launch your browser's **Find** dialog box by pressing **Ctrl + F**. It will quickly search the page and highlight your keyword.

Here's a nifty searching tip: When entering a search phrase, surround it with quotation marks to further narrow your search. For example, using the Excite! search engine (www.excite.com), a search for *pancakes and sausages* will return 13,205 results, or hits. Break out the Alka-Seltzer! The same search for *"pancakes and sausages"* will return a svelte 341 hits.

Why the difference? Searching without using quotation marks searches for any of your search words appearing anywhere on a web page; using quotation marks searches for an exact match of the words or phrase entered.

Q. I'd like to have my own website, but how can I find out whether the name I want for my address is available?

A. The name you're referring to is called a *domain name*. It's the part before the dot-com. With millions of domain names registered, it's increasingly difficult to find a domain name—particularly a dot-com (.com)—that is available.

There are a number of places where you can search for the availability of a domain name, as well as register a domain name. Several of the more popular domain registration sites include Network Solutions (www.networksolutions .com), Internet Domain Registrars (www.registrars.com), and All-Domains.com (www.alldomains.com).

Once you find a domain that you want to register, you can pay for it online, using your credit card. Registering for the first two years is $70, and you can register the name for several years at a time. Before you can register a domain name, you'll need a host for your web pages, or at least a temporary location where you can place the domain name while you find a web host. A *web host* is a business or entity that provides the computer upon which your web pages will reside.

Here's how it all works: When you visit a website, you're accessing data and information that resides on a host computer—because it *hosts* information—sometimes referred to as a *server*. It's called a server because when you type a web address into your browser, your computer sends out a request to that address to display the web page or information requested. The host computer then *serves* the requested information to your computer, which is called the *client*. So there's a *host* computer and a *client* computer. (Fascinating, in an eye-glazing, mind-numbing kind of way, isn't it?) Most web hosts will also register a domain name for you. Visit `www.webhostlist.com` for more information about locating a web host.

 One word of caution: Before registering your domain name with a service, always read the terms of the registration to be sure that the name you register cannot be "reclaimed" by the service. In other words, you want to be sure that once you register the name of your choice, it's yours until you decide to relinquish it.

Q. Is there any way to avoid those aggravating pop-up windows when surfing the Internet?

A. Try one of several software programs that are dedicated to killing pop-up (called "interstitial") advertisements as they appear.

My favorite is POW! Just run this simple utility while browsing on the Net, and when one of those nasty pop-ups—well, pops up, POW! will automatically close it for you. You can configure POW! to close any new pop-ups that you encounter automatically. Download POW! from `www.analogx.com/contents/download/network/pow.htm`.

Another of my preferred personal pop-up pulverizers is PopUp Killer. This free Windows program keeps a vigilant eye out for pop-ups. When they appear, PopUp Killer closes them automatically. It also memorizes pop-up activity to prevent them from appearing the next time you return to a pop-up–bearing website.

PopUp Killer also has the ability to download a catalog of known pop-up windows so the software knows to suppress them before you even get to one of them.

The software is free, though the author will cheerfully accept donations and suggests a nominal $7 as an appropriate amount if you wish to continue using his program. You can download PopUp Killer from `http://software.xfx.net/`.

Q. I'm having trouble with my modem connecting to the Internet. I read in an online discussion group that Windows 98 has a utility program that can do some modem troubleshooting. Can you tell me where to find this program?

A. Thank heavens for online discussion groups! Some of the best-kept secrets are shared in these areas. Windows 98 does have an interactive modem troubleshooting utility. To access it, click **Start** ➤ **Help** ➤ **Contents**. Then click **Troubleshooting** ➤ **Windows 98 Troubleshooters** ➤ **Modem**. Answer the dozen or so questions—they're easy yes/no type questions—to start the diagnosis. You may not be able to resolve your problem, but using this built-in troubleshooter may shed some light on the difficulty and at least get you headed in the right direction.

Q. I'm trying to find a newsgroup for a particular hobby of mine, but I don't understand the whole newsgroup hierarchy of alt., bit., comp., etc. groups. Isn't there a way just to search by topic without all the mumbo-jumbo?

A. In the old days of the Internet, knowing the hierarchy of Usenet newsgroups was very helpful for locating a group with a particular focus. It's still a good thing to know—right up there along with the Dewey Decimal System, as a matter of fact. But there are easier ways than memorizing lists of cryptic newsgroup hierarchies. Point your browser to `http://groups.google.com/`, enter the topic or topics you're looking for in the **Search Discussions** field, and let Google look through more than 100 million newsgroup articles dating back to 1995.

Q. When I ask a question in any online discussion group or forum, what is an appropriate amount of time to wait before checking back for an answer?

A. It varies by the group or forum you're participating in. Some online discussion groups are very busy with lots of people joining in the discussions. In those types of groups, you may receive an answer to a question within minutes. In other groups that don't have many participants, it can take days or weeks, or sometimes you'll never receive a response.

When joining any online discussion group, it's a good idea to *lurk* before jumping in, in order to get a sense of the group and its participants. You'll get a feel for how quickly questions are answered and what the general tone or ambiance of the group is, as well. Most online discussion groups have a FAQ, or Frequently Asked

Questions, file available that may provide background information about the group, message posting guidelines, and what you can expect.

Depending on the technology employed by the discussion group, you may be able to post a message and request an e-mail notification when a response has been received. That will save you the trouble of checking back frequently only to discover that you're being ignored. If that happens, don't take it personally; I've been ignored by some of the most popular discussion groups on the Internet.

When you do receive a response, be sure to acknowledge the response and thank the person or persons who took the time to answer your question or share their opinions.

Q. How can I keep track of when new things arrive on the Internet that I might be interested in?

A. There are more than 35,000 websites arriving on the Web each month, so keeping tabs on new arrivals can be a bit challenging. There are several free, e-mail–based services that let you choose topics you'd like to be informed about. Then, when anything new appears on the Web, you'll receive an e-mail notification with a link to the particular Web site. My personal favorite is Tracerlock at `www.tracerlock.com`.

Q. Is it true that when I visit websites they can put something on my computer without my permission and can see what's on my machine?

A. You're referring to cookies, and the answer is a definitive yes and no: A *cookie*, which is a small file, can be placed on your computer; but that cookie won't permit anybody to see what's on your hard drive. Myths abound about cookies, but the truth is that most cookies are harmless. For example, a cookie may remember how you configured certain settings on a website, which saves you the trouble of having to configure something again on a return visit.

A cookie is responsible for the insincere-yet-friendly, personalized greeting you may receive when returning to a previously visited website. Your Netscape browser will have three cookie settings available to you: **Accept All Cookies, Reject All Cookies**, and **Ask Before Accepting Cookies**. I recommend the **Ask Before Accepting Cookies** setting because it's always nice to be asked.

Internet Explorer users, you can select from a variety of security settings that will restrict or permit cookies to be placed on your computer.

Additional information about configuring your browser settings for cookies can be found in Chapter 2.

When I visit reputable, well-known websites, I'm always comfortable accepting cookies. All things considered, cookies really do enhance our web-surfing pleasure.

Q. How can I find out what cookie files have been placed on my computer?

A. To see what cookies have been placed on your computer, Netscape users should locate the `cookie.txt` file and use any text editor program (such as Notepad) to take a peek. Mac users should look for the `MagicCookies.txt` file. Netscape stores cookies in the `C:\Program Files\Netscape\Users\`*yourusername*`\cookies.txt file`. Internet Explorer stores cookies in the `C:\Windows\Cookies` folder.

If you want to know when a site is about to drop a cookie on you, you can instruct your browser to alert you to that fact.

If you're using Microsoft's Internet Explorer 4.*x*, go to the **View** menu and choose **Internet Options**. Click the **Advanced** tab and scroll down to **Security**. Under **Cookies**, select either **Disable All Cookie Use** or **Prompt Before Accepting Cookies**.

If you're using Internet Explorer 5.*x*, click **Tools**, then **Internet Options**, and then the **Security** tab. Select the **Internet** zone, then, using the little slidey thing (sorry for the technical terminology), adjust the level of security by reading the descriptions that accompany each level. **High Security** disables all cookies; **Medium Security** prompts you before accepting "potentially unsafe content," including cookies.

In Netscape Navigator 4 and higher, select **Preferences** from the **Edit** menu, then choose **Advanced**. Choose either **Disable Cookies** or **Warn Me Before Accepting A Cookie**. Netscape's cookies reside in `C:\Program Files\Netscape\Users\`*Yourname*, and in the `cookies.txt` file. If you delete `cookies.txt`, it will regenerate itself the next time you encounter a cookie intending to take up residence on your hard drive.

If you're teetering on the bleeding edge of technology and using Netscape 6.*x*, click **Tasks ➤ Privacy And Security ➤ Cookie Manager**. When you visit any website, you can select either **Allow Cookies From This Site** or **Block Cookies From This Site.**

For more information about cookies, send a blank e-mail to `cookies@MrModem.net`. You'll receive an article by return e-mail, with my compliments.

Q. When I arrive at a website and I'm asked to register, is that a good idea or bad idea?

A. Some websites request that you register by entering your name, while others request a bit of additional information. Many times your name is requested for personalization purposes, such as greeting you by name the next time you return to the site. Many sites like to obtain information from visitors with no ulterior motive attached, and there is no charge for this type of registration. If any site asks for information that you're the least bit uncomfortable providing, the answer is simple: Don't provide it.

Q. How much should I expect to pay for access to the Internet?

A. You can expect to pay anywhere from $15 to $25 per month for unlimited access through a local or national Internet Service Provider, or ISP. The monthly charge typically appears on a credit card—preferably your own. Other ISPs may provide you with a monthly billing. If you prefer to pay annually, ask about any discounts that might apply to the Year-in-Advance plan. Some providers offer toll-free telephone number access, which is ideal if you travel, but be sure to find out whether there's a surcharge or additional cost for using their 800 number to access the Internet.

Be sure to check out free Internet access services as well. Most free services are supported by advertising, so you may be required to view advertisements placed on incoming and outgoing e-mail, participate in surveys, or endure other potentially intrusive annoyances.

Also, be aware that there's an emerging trend away from free services as a result of the dot-com meltdown. Many previously free services are now either charging a fee or limiting the service provided, so be sure to carefully review any offers, particularly those that sound too good to be true.

NetZero (`www.netzero.net`) is an ISP that offers a variety of Internet services and access ranging from free to fee-based.

For information about additional free Internet Services Providers, check out the Free E-mail Providers Guide (`www.fepg.net/`).For more information about other Internet freebies, send a blank e-mail to `freebies@MrModem.net`. You'll receive information by return e-mail, and the price? Well, it's a freebie, of course!

Q. My connection to the Internet works pretty well, but sometimes, for no apparent reason, the connection is just dropped. I've called my ISP, but they say everything is fine at their end. Any ideas what could be wrong?

A. It's impossible to say what's wrong without knowing more about your setup, but here are some possibilities worth exploring. First, if you have call-waiting on your phone line, disable it. You can set your modem to dial the disable code (*70, in most exchanges) as part of your dialing process.

Another possibility is line noise or static. If you hear noises when talking on the phone or experience problems with frequent disconnects, call your phone company and tell them you're having problems receiving faxes. They're sometimes more sympathetic to that than modem problem reports, and the fix is the same.

It's also possible that your modem or the one you're dialing into at your ISP isn't working properly.

Since your problems are intermittent, your ISP or your telephone line is probably the culprit. To further isolate the cause, try a different modem, force your modem to run at a lower speed as a test, or send your ISP e-mail suggesting they may have a bad modem. They will probably deny it, but it's worth attempting to bring the possibility to their attention.

Q. I've heard that whenever I visit a website, my address is recorded somewhere on the site. How much can somebody learn about me from this information?

A. When you visit any website, you are leaving a trail of cyber breadcrumbs behind you in the form of your IP (Internet Protocol) address, which is actually a string of numbers separated by periods (e.g., 298.35.26.14). How much information is obtainable depends where you get your IP address. (Never get your IP address from a man selling them from the back of a '68 Chevy along with Elvis paintings on black velvet.)

If you dial into an ISP (Internet Service Provider) for access to the Internet, you are probably assigned a dynamic IP address that will only reveal the identity of your ISP. Permanent IP addresses are assigned by large companies to employees with full-time connections, and also by some high-speed access providers. These IP addresses could be used to identify both the company and the individual user, but not what you had for breakfast or what's green and fuzzy and growing in the vegetable bin of your refrigerator.

Q. How do I find out my IP address?

A. Everyone connected to the Internet has an IP, or Internet Protocol, address for identification. Most Internet Service Providers maintain a pool of addresses and assign them automatically as you dial in. This is called a dynamically assigned address. To find out your IP address for a given session, from the **Start** menu, select **Run**, type in **WINIPCFG**, and click **OK**. You probably won't do anything with this information, but it's not unlike times when I open the hood of my car; I have no idea what I'm looking at, but it makes me feel very auto-savvy to look at the engine and nod approvingly. I think it's a "guy thing."

Q. How can I keep track of all my usernames and passwords when I log on to websites?

A. Anyone who's signed up for a couple of subscription services or registered with a number of websites has run into this problem. A wonderful little program called Gator (www.gator.com/) will fill out registration forms and order forms, as well as remember all your passwords, User ID numbers, and login names. Best of all, it's free!

Q. What's the best way to access the Internet?

A. America Online, CompuServe, and Prodigy are utilized by many people as their point of access to the Internet, though my preference is to connect via a local Internet Service Provider, or ISP. To find an ISP in your area, look in the business or computer section of your local newspaper or the Yellow Pages, or ask for a recommendation from your favorite computer store. If you have friends or family already on the Internet, ask them about their access provider (especially their level of satisfaction with that provider). Also, visit The List site at `www.thelist.com`, where you can search for an ISP by country, city, state, or area code. Another excellent website for ISP shopping is `www.webisplist.com/`, provided by CNET Web Services.

There are also a number of free Internet Service Providers available to you. These free services are usually supported by advertising, which may be placed on your incoming and outgoing e-mail messages or appear during visits to websites. For more information about these free services, you can search more than 1,400 free Internet-based providers in more than 85 countries by accessing the Free E-mail Providers Guide (`www.fepg.net/`). Included are free e-communications services, such as Internet Service Providers, e-mail services, fax, long-distance calls, voice-mail, online storage, etc.

Q. If I'm on America Online, am I really on the Internet?

A. America Online is a proprietary membership network, so it's more accurate to say you go *through* AOL to get to the Internet. AOL, CompuServe, Prodigy, and other similar services are called *gateways* to the Internet. In other words, your modem dials in and connects your computer to AOL (or any other gateway). Once connected, you can then access web pages residing on host computers located throughout the world; that's what most folks refer to as being on the Internet.

Q. If I want to print a web page and I press the **Print Scrn** key on my keyboard, nothing happens. Why the [expletive deleted] won't it print?

A. Probably your attitude. Have you hugged your computer today? Go ahead, give it a little hug. Now, assuming a life-altering attitude adjustment has occurred, the reason **Print Scrn** (or **PrtSc**, or **Print Screen**) won't work is because **Print Scrn** just copies the image to your Windows 95 or 98 Clipboard. You would then have to jump-start your word processor, Paint, or a similar program, import the Clipboard image (by selecting **File ➢ Open**, and then selecting the file), then print.

There is, however, a quickie way to print a screen that's active (meaning, where your cursor is happily pulsating): Hold down the **Alt** key while pressing the **Print Scrn** button, and the window or frame where the cursor is positioned will print faster than you can say, "Holy [expletive deleted], the printer is jammed again!"

Q. I've seen **Download Now** buttons or links on different websites where I can get a file or software program, but I've been afraid to click it, not knowing what to do next. What happens when you download a file from the Internet?

A. When you start to download a file from a website, your browser needs to know what to do with it and where to put it. A message will appear on your screen asking if you want to save or open the file. Choose **Save**. You'll then be prompted where to save the downloaded file on your computer. I always recommend downloading to your Windows Desktop. Once the download is complete, you'll be able to locate the file or program easily, then install it or move it to a more appropriate location.

Q. When I download files from the Internet, I'm usually given a variety of download site options. I know I'm supposed to pick the site that's closest to me geographically, but sometimes that's too slow. How can I tell which of these sites is fastest?

A. There's a wonderful free program called Dipstick that can determine the speeds of different download-site connections. Just drag and drop download links onto the program's Desktop icon to determine the best option for you. You can download Dipstick from `www.klever.net/kin/dipstick.html`.

Q.

Is it safe to use my credit card on the Internet?

A.

Fear of the unknown is a very human characteristic, so there is a natural tendency to believe that it's extraordinarily risky to use a credit card on the Internet, particularly if you haven't done so previously. It's really not, though. Until you've tried it and observed firsthand that your next Visa bill won't reflect Concorde tickets to Paris or Louis Vuitton golf bag purchases, it can be a bit intimidating.

Using a credit card online is actually less risky than giving out your number over the phone to an unidentified operator or transmitting your credit card by fax, where you have no idea how many people have access to your information at the receiving end. It's also less dangerous than leaving your signed credit-card receipt for dinner on a table in a restaurant. Yet most of us do these things daily with nary a second thought.

Fact: There has yet to be a single documented case of an individual having his or her credit card "stolen" while transmitting the information over the Internet. If any reader knows of an incident that can be verified with documentation, please contact me at MrModem@home.com. A free, autographed copy of my book awaits the first such documented case, presented and confirmed. (What did you expect, a million dollars?)

When providing personal information of any type, online or off, common sense should always prevail. If you have any doubts about the reliability of a merchant, don't transmit your credit card number electronically. It's that simple. Apply the patented Mr. Modem "heebie-jeebie" test: If it gives you the heebie-jeebies, don't do it.

When you're ready to try shopping online, start slowly, with a small purchase. Buy yourself a treat! The risk is minimal, and the convenience is wonderful.

When you decide to venture into the great cybermall, bear in mind the following helpful points:

- Shop for brand names sold by merchants you know and trust.

- Avoid ordering from online merchants that do not display a telephone number, street address, or other form of offline contact. Call the phone number. Does it sound like a legitimate business, or do you get the sense that whoever answers the phone doesn't have a clue what you're talking about?

- Never purchase from a spam (unsolicited) e-mail unless you know the merchant and recognize the sender's e-mail address as legitimate.

- Print a copy of your completed order form before submitting your order.

- Use common sense! Listen to the voice of your inner modem: If anything makes you uneasy during the ordering process, *do not place the order!*

For more information about using credit cards online, send a blank e-mail to plastic@MrModem.net.

Q. What can a brand-new user like me expect when first entering a chat room?

A. Excellent question, but it's a lot like asking, "What can I expect if I walk into a building?" Just as it depends on which building you enter, so does it depend on which chat room you enter. The best advice I can offer is to expect the unexpected. The ability to communicate anonymously with others occasionally brings out the worst in a few people. Some will use provocative language or attempt to be controversial.

Chat sessions can be a little disorienting at first—at least until you get your "chat legs." When you first enter a chat room, you may be dazed and disoriented by all the conversations and cross-conversations scrolling by quickly. Think of it as a big conference call or an ongoing party where lots of people are engaged in conversations.

If you just *lurk* for a while (read what's going on without participating) and watch the conversations scrolling by, you'll soon get a sense of what's going on, and it will slowly become less overwhelming than it might have appeared at first glimpse. What you're seeing are multiple conversations occurring at the same time.

Every chat room will display a list of the people who are logged in to that chat room, so you can get a sense of how many people are present. Remember, too, that your username or chat handle will appear on that list seen by other participants, so don't be surprised if somebody says hello to you. Before each person's comments, the "speaker's" username appears, so it's like reading a moving script:

```
WebHead: Hi guys!
MaryS: Hi, WebHead.
PuterMan: What's happenin'?
WebHead: Not much.
```

The conversation is not always as scintillating as the preceding example.

If somebody says hello and you're comfortable responding, go right ahead. To respond, you'll type your response in a small window that appears on your screen and then press **Enter** to move your words from your computer into the chat room. There is no right or wrong time to jump in, so when you're ready, dive right in!

If you wish to speak to a particular participant, start your comments with the person's username, as shown in the preceding example.

Most chat room participants are friendly folks who are happy to lend a helping hand. If you see an abbreviation or acronym and you don't know what it means, just ask.

If you cross paths with somebody whose language offends you or is rude, just leave. Don't respond; just leave. You can limit your exposure to offensive material by visiting chat rooms that have a particular focus. If it's a chat room for seniors, needlepoint enthusiasts, or golfers, the odds are heavily in your favor that you won't encounter any *homosapienus idiotus*.

Q. Why do some web addresses begin with "www" and some don't?

A. Historically, the "www" in a web address served as a destination command from your computer to the Internet's World Wide Web or www. For example, if you wanted to go to MrModem.com in days of olde, you would have to type `www.MrModem.com`. So the one-word answer to your question is, "Tradition."

As time and technology evolved, today most of us are accessing the Web as opposed to other areas on the Internet. For that reason, the "www" in many cases is assumed, so there is no reason other than the above-mentioned tradition, to add "www" to the host name. To test this out, type into your browser's Address field, `http://www.MrModem.com`, then try `http://MrModem.com`. Both addresses will take you to the same destination.

Q. New area codes were just added in my state, so I now have to include an area code to connect to the Internet. How can I add the area code so my modem dials it automatically?

A. Ten-digit phone numbers are rapidly becoming the norm in many parts of the U.S. Fortunately, this is one inconvenience that is easily accommodated by your Windows Dial-Up Networking, if you follow these steps: Start by double-clicking the **My Computer** icon on your Desktop, then double-click the **Dial-Up Networking** icon.

Highlight the connection for your ISP, right-click, and choose **Properties**.

Enter the area code in the **Area Code** field, and place a check mark by the **Use Country Code And Area Code** box.

Q. When I'm on the Internet, sometimes my husband will pick up a phone in another room to make a call. By the time I scream "I'm online!" it's too late and I've lost my connection. Is there any way to prevent that, short of having another telephone line installed?

A. *Internetus interruptus* is a phenomenon experienced in many households today that is easily resolved. Several gizmos called exclusion devices are available. The $35 Proto-Share II (`www.prototel.com`) is one such device. If you're online and hubby picks up an extension, the Proto-Share II will keep your online connection from being interrupted.

An easily avoided but related annoyance is getting bumped offline when an incoming telephone call causes call-waiting to signal you. The two call-waiting beeps can, and usually do, disrupt and terminate your Internet connection.

You can, however, disable call-waiting while you're connected to the Internet by inserting *70, (star symbol, 7, 0, comma) before the telephone number your modem dials to establish your connection. The *70 disables call-waiting, and the comma forces your modem to pause for one second and allow the new dial tone to begin.

After you conclude your Internet session, your call-waiting service will be automatically enabled (active) again.

 The prefix *70, is used in most areas of the U.S., but check with your telephone company to be sure it's correct for your area.

If you're using the Windows Dialer, to insert *70, in the dialing field, click **My Computer ➤ DialUp Networking**. Right-click the name of your Internet Service Provider or Internet account, and select **Properties**. Click the **General** tab, then, in the **Telephone Number** field, enter ***70,** (including the comma) followed by the number your modem would usually dial to establish your connection to the Internet. Click **OK**, and back your way out to your Desktop.

Q. How can I look at what websites my kids have visited? I'm using America Online.

A. You'll find a listing of the last 25 sites visited displayed on the drop-down list in the Keyword box. That's located at the top of the screen, just below the Toolbar, in the large white box where you would enter a Keyword or web address. If you click the down arrow located to the right of this box, you'll see a list of the previous places visited. Click any item in this list to revisit the site or web page. Each time you visit a new site, the oldest item on the list scrolls off. You can delete this history by clicking **My AOL ➤ Preferences**. Click the **Toolbar** button and you'll see an option to clear the History.

Q. Do you think there will ever be any control over what information is available on the Internet?

A. In a word, no. Information that is accessible on the Internet can originate from anywhere in the world. That fact alone makes legislation or meaningful control of any kind impossible. For example, if gambling is prohibited in your community, you can easily access a web-based casino, lose your home and car, ruin your life, yet never leave the comfort of the house you used to own. Cool, huh?

"How is that possible?" you ask while fondling the digital dice. A host computer upon which the virtual casino resides may be located within a jurisdiction where gambling is legal; further, that host computer may be located in a foreign country, so local laws would be neither applicable nor enforceable at the host location.

In order to control, monitor, or regulate what you have access to on the Internet, the control would have to be implemented at the user end—on your computer or at the Internet Service Provider (ISP) level. And that's simply not going to happen.

There are software programs available that will block access to X-rated sites, for example, but, once again, that type of software is installed and implemented by the user or the ISP.

Q. I received an e-mail regarding a petition filed with the FCC that, if granted, would force CBS to discontinue *Touched by an Angel*, and that all Sunday worship services being broadcast on radio and television would be stopped. Is this true?

A. This is just another one of the thousands of e-mail–borne hoaxes that are designed to stir the passions of community-spirited Internet users like you. Cyber hoaxes generally share four common characteristics that make them easy to spot:

- A prediction of dire consequences if you do not act.

- A call to action, usually in the form of a request, to "Forward this to everybody you know."

- A great sense of urgency, typically manifested by multiple exclamation marks!!!

- Some form of authentication or corroboration by a high-falootin' muckety-muck, such as a Pentagon official, the chairman of Intel, or the U.S. Postmaster General. It's all a bunch of high-tech hooey.

Before helping out the perpetrators by passing along any message of this type, visit a site such as www.vmyths.com or www.snopes2.com and verify for yourself that it's a hoax. Even easier, e-mail me at MrModem@home.com and I'll be happy to check it out and report back to you promptly. For additional information about online hoaxes, send an e-mail to hoaxes@MrModem.net. Leave the Subject line and body of the e-mail blank and you'll receive the information by return e-mail.

Q. I'd like faster access to the Internet, but I'm not sure what options are available to me in my location. Is there any way to find out other than by checking with each individual access provider?

A. There sure is! Just visit www.getspeed.com. Enter your zip code, street address, and telephone number (or use your zip code if you're uncomfortable providing the additional information) and Getspeed will tell you if you have access to DSL, cable modem, satellite, or wireless service in your area.

Q. I've tried shopping online, but, personally, I think it takes too much time visiting a variety of sites in order to find the best price for an item. Is there a more efficient way to comparison shop online?

A. Comparison shopping by using a shopping agent or website to help you find the best prices available is becoming increasingly popular. My personal favorite is my-Simon (`www.mysimon.com`). Just select the item or items you're interested in and Simon will return a list of websites that sell the product, as well as provide pricing information. If you see something that looks interesting, with a click of your mouse you will be transported directly to the site and the specific item. All shopping agents function in generally the same manner. Additional price-comparison websites include PriceSearch (`http://price-search.net/`), PriceComparison (`http://pricecomparison.net/`), and PriceScan (`www.pricescan.com`).

Happy comparison shopping!

Q. I've been reading about all kinds of bad things that can happen because of an e-mail virus called *I Love You*. I'm afraid to use e-mail for fear of getting it. What can I do?

A. Viruses are a fact of life online today, but here are three tips that will keep you safe:

- Make sure you're using a virus-checking software program and that you update it regularly—at least once a month. My personal favorite is McAfee's VirusScan (`www.mcafee.com`), but Norton's AntiVirus (`www.symantec`) is excellent as well. If you're not sure how to update, visit the home page of your antivirus software manufacturer.

- Never, never, never, never—am I making myself clear—*never,* double-click (or launch) any e-mail file attachment until you scan that file with your virus-checking program. Moms, dads, and kids of all ages can transmit viruses, so it's better to be safe than sorry.

- If you receive an attachment, before you do anything with it, contact the sender and ask if he or she intended to send the file attachment to you. This is an important step because some viruses infiltrate e-mail address books, and infected files are attached to every outgoing e-mail—unbeknownst to the sender. So always contact the sender of any attachment received and ask if the attachment you received was sent intentionally.

Treat all computer files downloaded from the Internet, and especially all file attached to e-mail, as potentially dangerous. Open one without confirming that its contents are clean and you're playing digital roulette.

Q. I'm planning to buy a new external modem for my computer running Windows 98. Should I consider a USB modem?

A. Definitely! If your computer has one or more USB (Universal Serial Bus) ports, installing hardware, including modems, is a snap. With your computer turned off, plug in the new device to your USB port, power up, and let the Hardware Installation Wizard do the rest. Because communication with your computer is faster through a USB port than an older serial port, or COM (communications) port, you'll generally receive better overall performance from a USB modem.

Q. How can I stop my modem from squealing? It's driving me crazy, and my husband gets annoyed when he hears me going online in the middle of the night.

A. It used to be embarrassing enough getting caught standing by the sink, spoon in hand, enjoying an up-close-and-personal visit with Ben & Jerry in the middle of the night. Today, it's even worse getting caught going online at 3:00 A.M. thanks to a digital squealer. I've tried everything from smothering the speaker with a pillow to coughing loudly in hopes of masking the noise. The only thing the coughing accomplished was awakening Mrs. Modem, who would then say, "What's with all the coughing? Are you okay?" Oh, the irony of it all.

Squeal-stiflers, take heart! To turn down the volume on your modem or silence it completely, check your modem configuration in two areas. First, click **Start ➢ Settings ➢ Control Panel**, then double-click **Modems**. Select your modem, click the **Properties** button, and move the speaker volume slider thingie (technical term) all the way to the left. Then click **OK**, then **Close**. Close the Control Panel folder, and return to your Windows Desktop.

The next time you log on in the middle of the night, relax, and enjoy the sound of silence.

Mr. Modem Loophole: If the preceding steps do not result in additional quiet time, it's possible that your modem's settings are overriding the changes you made. I just hate it when that happens. If this is your digital dilemma, consult your modem manufacturer for instructions specific to your particular modem. Your modem vendor probably has a website, so make that your first stop, and look for a FAQ (Frequently Asked Questions) file. The answer as it relates to your specific modem may only be a mouse-click away.

Q. I only have one phone line, so when I'm online I'm missing phone calls. Is there any way around that, short of paying for a second phone line?

A. You might consider trying one of the web-based call-waiting services that handle incoming calls while you're online. CallWave (www.callwave.com) is a downloadable program that installs an Internet answering machine and plays a preprogrammed outgoing message to your callers. Once a caller leaves a message, it is replayed through your computer speakers. The service is free, but a small banner ad appears in the CallWave notification window whenever you're online.

An alternative is Internet Call Manager (www.internetcallmanager.com), which acts more like caller ID. Incoming phone numbers appear on your screen, permitting you to make a few choices on the spot: Instruct Internet Call Manager (ICM) to ignore the call, or with a fast mouse-click, you can transfer the caller to your ICM web-based voice-mail or to a prerecorded message that says you will return the call shortly. You can also answer the call, in which case ICM will terminate your Internet connection and forward the call to your telephone. With the exception of a few fee-based options ranging from 25¢ to $1 per use, this is a free service, so expect a banner ad to appear whenever a call comes in.

Both of these services are for Windows only and require that you activate the "busy-call forwarding" feature with your local telephone company, which should cost approximately $1 to $3 per month. CallWave and Internet Call Manager can activate that service for you.

Q. Some of my friends told me that I should be using a surge protector with my computer. If so, why?

A. A combination surge protector (sometimes referred to as a surge suppressor) and UPS, or uninterruptible power supply, is highly recommended. A surge protector will insulate your computer from power spikes that are common in most homes and offices.

An *uninterruptible power supply* device is really a back-up battery that protects your computer and its data from power failures. Different UPS systems have different capacities, but the better ones will supply power to your computer for approximately 30 minutes after a power failure. If a power failure occurs, the device will beep or flash in hopes of getting your attention so you can then save your work and shut down your computer.

Some UPS devices have an additional feature that will actually shut down your computer for you. This can be a lifesaver because a UPS isn't going to be much help if it detects a power failure, starts beeping at you, and then loses power in approximately 30 minutes—if you're not around to hear the beeps. To protect against a sudden shut-down due to power loss, some UPS units have software that will shut down your computer after a designated period of time, saving any open files in the process.

Surge protector and UPS systems can be purchased at most computer stores or other electronics retailers.

Q. Is there a way to monitor my Internet connection? Sometimes things appear to hang up—nothing happens, then all of a sudden it's like a data dam breaks and images and pages download quickly. I know it might just be heavy traffic on the Internet, but I'd like to keep an eye on my connection. Any ideas?

A. You might consider trying a small program called NetMonitor that keeps an eye on your Internet connection and shows, in graphical fashion, kilobytes received and sent. It also has a "keep alive" function that prevents your ISP from pulling the plug on you for inactivity. You can also run a test to determine your connection speed. For more information or to download this free program, visit `www.modem wizard.com/netmonitor.html`. And tell 'em Mr. Modem sent you. On second thought, there's no sense asking for trouble.

Q. I heard you on a local radio station talking about a device that isn't a computer but that checks for e-mail. I didn't hear the beginning of the show, so I missed the name of the product.

A. The device is called MailStation, by Cidco. It weighs just two pounds, measures 10 inches by 7 inches by 1 inch, and costs $99.95. E-mail service costs $9.95 per month.

It's a good news/bad news situation, however. The bad news is that you must use their monthly service even if you already have an Internet Service Provider. The good news is that checking e-mail from home or on the road has never been easier. Complete information is available on the MailStation website (www.mailstation.com).

A similar e-mail product is the MailBug, which, coincidentally, costs $ $99.95 (what are the odds?) and $9.95 per month for e-mail service. Additional information is available at www.mailbug.com.

Q. Is there any way to speed up searches on the Internet? Sometimes it takes forever for one page to load.

A. Whining always helps any situation, so you're half-way home! There are actually a number of techniques and software programs available to help speed up the process of loading pages onto your screen. One of the simplest ways to make your web surfing more efficient is to open a second browser window so you can read one page while waiting for the second page to load. In either Netscape or Internet Explorer, open a second browser window (or more) by pressing **Ctrl + N**. If you want to follow a link but don't want to leave the page you're looking at, right-click the link in question, and select **Open In New Window**.

Q. I'm not that comfortable using a mouse. Is there a way to navigate the Web using my computer keyboard?

A. Yes, just about every mouse-based action has its equivalent keyboard-based short-cut for use with either Internet Explorer or Netscape Navigator. Following are a few examples for Internet Explorer.

Keystroke	Action
Tab	Moves forward through items or fields on a web page
Up arrow	Scrolls toward beginning of current page
Down arrow	Scrolls toward bottom of current page
Shift + Tab	Moves backward through items or fields on a web page

Keystroke	Action
Page Up	Scrolls toward beginning of page a screen at a time
Page Down	Scrolls toward bottom of page a screen at a time
Enter	Activates the current link
Home	Moves to top of a page
End	Moves to end of a page
Esc	Stops downloading a page
Backspace	Goes to the previous page (like using the **Back** button)

Use the following keystroke shortcuts with Netscape Navigator.

Keystroke	Action
F1	Activates Netscape Help
Ctrl + 1	Opens Netscape Navigator
Ctrl + 2	Opens Netscape Messenger (E-mail)
Ctrl + 3	Opens Netscape Message Center
Ctrl + 4	Opens Netscape Composer (for creating web pages)
Ctrl + Tab	Cycles through all open windows
Ctrl +]	Increases font size
Ctrl + [	Decreases font size
Ctrl + A	Selects all web page components, including graphics
Ctrl + B	Displays Bookmarks

For a comprehensive list of keystroke commands for Internet Explorer and Netscape Navigator, send a blank e-mail to `keystrokes@MrModem.net`. You'll receive the information by return e-mail.

Q. I've started a home-based business and could use some help with some of the basics. I've always been commercially employed, so while exciting, it's also terrifying now that I'm the boss. Any websites you can recommend that might be helpful?

A. Congratulations! You're entering one of the fastest growing segments of the working population, home-based businesses. Due in large part to the Internet, reaching potential customers on a worldwide basis has never been easier, and thanks (again) to the Internet, informational resources and help abound! Check out the following:

- EntreWorld (`www.entreworld.org`) is a wonderful informational resource for entrepreneurs. Information is grouped by stages of business development.

- The National Association for the Self Employed (`www.nase.org`) with 320,000 members, offers a wealth of information as well as keeping tabs on small-business issues in Washington.

- AllBusiness.com (`www.allbusiness.com`) offers a variety of resources, including access to more than 250 free business forms and links to a number of additional free business-related resources on the Web.

- Microsoft's bCentral.com (`www.bcentral.com`) is a treasure trove of information and resources for the small business owner.

- Lastly, BizMove.com (`www.bizmove.com`) is a small-business knowledge base containing hundreds of pages of practical information.

Q. My grandchildren are on the Internet and I'm concerned about the material they're coming in contact with. Is there any way to filter out some of the raunchier content they're likely to encounter?

A. Internet Explorer 5.*x* (`www.microsoft.com`) has what's called the Content Advisor. This feature let's you screen inappropriate Internet content by controlling the type and degree of sex, violence, bad language, etc. that can be viewed. To configure this feature, select **View** ➢ **Internet Options**, and click the **Content** tab. Click **Enable** in the **Content Advisor** area, create a password, then select the levels of permissibility for language, nudity, sex, and violence.

Unfortunately, there will always be inappropriate material accessible on the Internet, but the Content Advisor is certainly a step in the right direction for parents and grandparents everywhere.

A number of software programs are also available to help filter out what is generally considered to be offensive or inappropriate material. Several of the more popular ones include:

- Net Nanny (`www.netnanny.com/`) gives parents control over what is being accessed from your computer. Incremental steps permit you to relax "strictness standards" at your discretion. Net Nanny provides registered users with free "can go" and "can't go" site lists to download into Net Nanny screening databases. Net Nanny costs approximately $40.

- CYBERsitter (`www.cybersitter.com`), winner of *PC Magazine* Editors' Choice Award for 2000, permits selectable blocking of websites, newsgroups, chat rooms, and mail by filtering the offensive addresses.

  A "content recognition" system recognizes even new sites and prevents access. A 10-day trial version is available for download; to register, the program costs approximately $40.

- CyberPatrol for Home (`www.surfcontrol.com/products/`) is a software program that helps parents keep kids safe online. Empowers parents to make their own choices about children's online experiences. Download a free 14-day trial version, then register, or purchase a copy for $49.95, including 12 months of filter updates.

For an excellent review of available content-control software and filtering systems, visit `www.getnetwise.org/tools/`.

There are also a number of child-friendly sites, where content is screened to ensure safe surfing. Child-friendly sites include `www.yahooligans.com`, `www.pbs.org`, `www.ajkids.com`, and `www.nick.com`.

For parents concerned with their children's online safety, have your children read, understand, and agree to a list of online safety rules or rules of engagement. One of the best I've seen is located at `www.safekids.com/kidsrules.htm`.

Mr. Modem's Online Tips

- Most software downloaded from the Internet is in zip (compressed) format. Be sure you have a program on your PC for unzipping (decompressing) these files. You can obtain the popular WinZip program from www.winzip.com.

- If web pages are only partially downloading, press **Ctrl** + **Alt** + **Del**, which will bring up the **Close Program** dialog box. Review the list of programs currently running. If you see two copies of Netscape or Internet Explorer listed, highlight one of them, and click **End Task**.

- Pause for a second when typing in a URL either in Explorer or in Netscape and it will automatically finish the address for you if you've visited the site before.

- To import Netscape Bookmarks into Internet Explorer 5, click **Favorites** ➢ **Organize Favorites** ➢ **Import**. Browse to your Netscape Bookmark file (bookmark.htm), and click **Open**.

- Want to use your Internet Explorer Favorites in Netscape? In IE 5, click **File** ➢ **Import And Export**. Follow the **Import/Export Wizard** instructions, then click **Export**. Choose where you want to save the file, and give the file a name. IE will create an HTML copy of your Favorites, which can then be used by Netscape Navigator via **File** ➢ **Open**, or rename it bookmark.htm and use it as your Netscape Bookmarks.

Mr. Modem's Recommended Websites

Blink   Organize and store your bookmarks online; access them from anywhere, using any web browser.

> www.blink.com/

BugNet   Heralded as the world's largest supplier of bug fixes, with more than 500 new software bug fixes available on this site each month.

> www.bugnet.com

CatchUp   Don't you just hate it when you think you have the latest version of a software program and then you discover a file or website that requires a newer version? Have no fear, CatchUp automatically finds what you need to keep your PC up-to-date by analyzing the programs on your hard drive and generating a customized list of updates available, including download sites!

> www.catchup.com

ISPcheck   One of the quickest, easiest ways to locate an Internet Service Provider.

> www.ispcheck.com

Virus Myths and Hoaxes   Learn about the myths, the hoaxes, the urban legends, and their implications.

> www.vmyths.com/

Deciphering Netspeak:
Terms and Definitions

S o much terminology, so little time! In this chapter, I'll take the gobbledygook out of the geekspeak and explain computer- and Internet-related terms in plain ol' English.

Q. My friends all seem to be talking about the Internet, but what is it?

A. It may be helpful to think of the *Internet* in terms of our telephone system: There are millions of telephones loosely connected together, and all you have to do is dial a number to talk to your next-door neighbor or somebody located on the other side of the world. Substitute computers for telephones, let your modem do the walking instead of your fingers doing the dialing, and that's the essence of the Internet. These connected computers—yours, mine, and millions of other people's—can "talk" to each other by exchanging information or transferring data from one computer to other computers.

Q. Are the Internet and the World Wide Web the same thing?

A. The *World Wide Web* is part of the larger Internet. The snooze-inducing definition of the World Wide Web is "a distributed heterogeneous collaborative multimedia information system." And if that doesn't make you lose interest in the whole thing, I don't know what will.

Setting highfalutin technical language aside, think of the Web as a vast library, with every book located just a mouse-click away. A friendly, helpful librarian is always available to you through your web browser software, typically either Netscape or Internet Explorer. Click the **Search** button, enter a word or phrase to search for, and in seconds the results of the search will be displayed on your screen.

Because the Web is so easy to use, an estimated 600,000 new users join the online lifestyle each month. I hope you're one of them!

Q. What's the difference between a home page and a website?

A. Continuing our library metaphor, imagine a *home page* as the cover of a book, with the pages of the book being the underlying website. A home page provides information about the site and its contents. A website is simply a collection of related web pages.

Q. Everybody is always talking about "cyber" this or "cyber" that. What does *cyber* really mean?

A. There's no agreement about the true origin of the words *cyber* or *cyberspace,* except that everybody agrees that Al Gore had nothing to do with it. Author William Gibson, in his 1982 book *Neuromancer,* is generally recognized as having introduced the term *cyberspace,* referring to that Rod Serlingesque dimension of time and space where data resides while in transit. Others believe the term *cyber* comes from the word *cybernetics* and is a prefix attached to everyday words to add a computer, electronic, or online connotation. One school of thought believes that the word *cyber* comes from the Greek *kybernetes,* which I believe is a small pastry that Internet purists traditionally consume while reading e-mail. (I could be wrong on that.)

Q. When people talk about clicking a link, what exactly is a link?

A. A hypertext *link* is actually a shortcut to another web page. Links typically appear as blue, underlined text. When you encounter a link anywhere on the Web, your cursor will change shape as it passes over the link. If you use your mouse to click the link, you will be presented with another web page containing related information.

Q. What does the *http* stand for that appears as a prefix to every website address?

A. Hypertext Transfer Protocol is the method used to transfer HTML documents across the Internet. HTML stands for Hypertext Markup Language and is the language or computer coding used to create web pages. When you see *https* at the start of a web address, you have accessed a secure server, which will encrypt or scramble data to prevent it from being read by unauthorized eyes. At least that's the theory. The HTTPS protocol is frequently used for transmitting credit card information or other particularly sensitive materials.

Q. What is a FAQ?

A. A frequently seen acronym (FSA) on the Internet that stands for Frequently Asked Questions, *FAQs* are documents that answer common questions about a topic, such as how to utilize a certain website feature or how to get the most out of certain software. When you visit a website for the first time, look for a FAQ button or link, and click it to obtain more information about the website.

Q. What is a search engine on the Internet?

A. A *search engine* is a program that resides on the Web that makes it easy to find websites and other information by performing keyword and other searches. Think of a search engine as a giant library card catalog. Some of the most popular search engines are AltaVista (`www.altavista.com`), Yahoo! (`www.yahoo.com`), Lycos (`www.lycos.com`), and WebCrawler (`www.webcrawler.com`).

Q. What is an Internet newsgroup?

A. *Newsgroups* are Internet-based discussion groups, sometimes referred to as forums. To participate in a newsgroup, users post public messages, and other participants respond or offer additional opinions, using the newsgroup functions of Netscape, OutLook Express, or dedicated newsgroup software, such as FreeAgent (`www.forteinc.com/agent/freagent.htm`) or Gravity (`www.microplanet.com/`). There are over 20,000 newsgroups covering every imaginable topic and many topics you don't want to imagine. Most newsgroups are not moderated in any manner; therefore, no topic or verbiage is off limits. For this reason, some newsgroups are not for anybody easily offended. So don't say I didn't warn you.

Q. I'm hearing about something called a USB that's supposed to make hooking up printers, etc. much easier. What is it, and how is it supposed to work?

A. In the old days of computerdom, you would connect your printer to a printer port, your modem to a serial port—where you plug in something—and on and on it went. The Universal Serial Bus, or USB, is designed to support a variety of devices by letting you plug them in to one USB port hub. For example, if you plug a four-port hub in to a Windows 98 computer USB port, you instantly have four additional ports in which to plug in or attach any of the preceding devices or a scanner, CD-ROM, Zip drive, digital camera, joystick, etc.

Q. I was shopping for a new monitor, but I'm confused by the term *dot pitch.* Can you explain that in English?

A. If I recall correctly, I believe Dot Pitch was an actress in the silent screen era, but, then again, I could be wrong. Okay, okay, Mr. Modem is just yanking your cable. *Dot pitch* is a measurement of how closely pixels (the little dots that make up the images that appear on your screen) are packed together. The closer the pixels, the sharper the picture will be. You want a monitor with a dot pitch of no higher than 28. The lower the number, the more closely spaced the dots are. A dot pitch of 26 is, therefore, preferable to 28. Photographic images look great even with a dot pitch above 28, so always test the sharpness of a monitor's display with text instead of graphics.

Q. I heard somebody refer to a "snail mail" address. What is that?

A. *Snail mail* refers to your regular postal address. Because e-mail is so fast, other land-based mail is often referred to as "snail mail."

Q. Can you explain what cookies are?

A. *Cookies* are small files placed on your computer when you visit certain websites, usually for personalization or customization purposes. Myths abound about cookies, but the truth is that if you accept a cookie you're not permitting people to access your hard drive, your clothes closet, or root around your medicine cabinet. Most cookies remember how you configured certain settings, for example, thus preventing you from having to configure something again on a return visit, or cookies will permit a website to greet you by name on a return visit.

Your browser software will have three settings available to you, something like **Accept All Cookies**, **Reject All Cookies**, or **Ask Before Accepting Cookies**. I suggest the latter setting if you're unsure about cookies. With this setting selected, you'll have an opportunity to decide whether to accept or reject a cookie based on the website you're visiting at the time. If you're visiting a reputable, well-known website and not looking at pictures located on somebody's dormitory room server, I'd be very comfortable accepting any cookies available. All things considered, cookies really will enhance your web surfing pleasure.

Q. What is an Easter egg?

A. An *Easter egg* is a hidden feature inserted within a software program by the developers, usually just for fun. It could be a special keystroke combination that shows a list of the programmers' names, an undocumented command, a hidden game, or a graphical display. Easter eggs are not software bugs, since they're put there on purpose, and they are always harmless.

They exist because programmers have a strange sense of humor, typically work in confined spaces, and drink large quantities of caffeinated beverages. To discover what Easter eggs you have lurking within your computer, visit The Easter Egg Archive at `www.eeggs.com`.

Q. I just got my first computer, and one of the manuals refers to a file extension. I'm not sure what that is. Can you help?

A. You bet! A *file extension* refers to the three letters or characters that appear after the period, or dot, in a filename. For example, on a file named `readme.txt`, the letters *t-x-t* compose the file extension. Extensions let us know what kind of file we're looking at. For example, an .EXE (short for *executable*, but pronounced ex-EE) file extension tells us that the file is a program of some type or that some action will be performed if we double-click or launch the file.

If you're not seeing file extensions, your default Windows setting is configured to hide file extensions. You can change that by following these steps:

1. Click **My Computer** ➤ **View** ➤ **Folder Options** ➤ **View**.

2. Make sure there is no check mark by **Hide File Extensions**.

3. Click **OK** when you're done.

For more information about file types, file extensions, and the programs needed to view specific file formats, send a blank e-mail to `filetypes@MrModem.net`. Information will be e-mailed to you within minutes.

Q. What is an autoresponder?

A. An *autoresponder* is an e-mail utility that automatically sends a reply in response to an e-mail message it receives. An autoresponder allows a person to request information about a product or service via e-mail and receive a response back automatically. If you send a question to an online tech support e-mail address, you may receive a response back within minutes acknowledging receipt of your e-mail and providing additional information. The e-mail you receive is generated by an autoresponder.

Autoresponders can send information in response to a blank e-mail sent to a specific e-mail address, or more sophisticated autoresponders can be configured to inspect the incoming message for key words or phrases and vary its reply accordingly.

To see how an autoresponder works, send an e-mail to `cookies@MrModem.net` and you'll receive an article I wrote about computer cookies. You don't have to write anything on the subject line or in the body of the e-mail itself.

Q. What is a mailing list?

A. A *mailing list* is a method of distributing topical news and information by e-mail sent to a list of recipients. There is no charge for signing up for a mailing list, and the act of signing up is called *subscribing*. To subscribe, you typically enter your e-mail address into a web-based form or send an e-mail containing specific wording to a designated e-mail address. If you subscribe to a mailing list, you may receive hundreds of messages each day or receive as few as one mailing per month, depending upon the popularity of the list.

Many high-volume lists offer a digest format, which bundles many messages into one, sent once a day. In the process of subscribing to a mailing list, you will be advised what the average number of e-mails generated daily is. Depending on the number, you may elect to subscribe to the digest format.

To find a mailing list of interest to you, visit `www.liszt.com`, with more than 100,000 mailing lists to choose from.

Q. I've heard people say they are subscribing to a listserv, but what the heck is a listserv?

A. The technical definition of a *listserv* is an automatic mailing list server that manages additions and deletions to electronic mailing lists. But Mr. Modem's eyes roll back in his head when he hears technical definitions, so let's just say that a listserv is a way to correspond with groups of people about a particular topic via e-mail. When you subscribe to a listserv, the automatic mailing list server places you on an electronic mailing list. You will then receive e-mail each time a listserv subscriber sends e-mail to the listserv. There is no charge for subscribing to a listserv. (Mailing lists are also called *listprocs* and *listservs*.)

Q. What's the difference between a music file that's a WAV file and one that's an MP3 file?

A. The *WAV* file format for storing sound in computer files was developed jointly by Microsoft and IBM. Smart cookies that they were, they then built the ability to play these files into Windows 95/98, making it the standard for sound file formats on personal computers. WAV sound files have a .WAV extension and can be played by virtually all Windows programs that support sound. On the downside, however, because these are not compressed or compacted files, they can be very large.

MP3 files, on the other hand, use an audio compression technology that allows the files to be compacted, but without distorting the sound. MP3 files have an .MP3 file extension and require special software, called a *player*, in order to listen to them. Because of compression, an hour of near CD-quality audio can be downloaded in five minutes or even less with a high-speed Internet connection. For more information, visit www.mp3.com.

Q. My new computer has a DVD drive that replaces my old CD-ROM drive. What's the difference between a DVD and CD? Will my CDs still work in the DVD drive?

A. Depending who you talk to, *DVD* stands either for Digital Versatile Disk or for Digital Video Disk. I'll cast my vote for Digital Video Disk—not to suggest they aren't versatile, however.

Think of DVD disks as very high-capacity CD-ROMs. A CD has a capacity of approximately 650MB (megabytes, or million bytes), while a DVD has the capacity to hold anywhere from 4.7 to 17GB (gigabytes, or billion bytes) of data. One DVD disk can hold nine hours of studio-quality video, 30 hours of CD-quality audio, or 47 years of scratchy, old radio broadcasts.

Your CDs will function fine in your DVD player because the drive is "backward compatible." Your DVD disks will not function in your CD player, however.

Q. What's a vCard?

A. A *vCard*, short for Virtual Card, is a digital business card that you can add to your outgoing e-mail messages so that recipients can automatically place contact information into their address books. A vCard attached to your outgoing e-mail will arrive as an attachment that the recipient can then double-click to open.

Though the ability to attach a vCard exists in many e-mail programs, very few people use it. Go figure. For more information about vCard and products using vCard, visit www.imc.org/pdi/pdiprodslist.html.

Q. What's the difference between a portal and a search engine?

A. A *search engine* is a website that lets you search other websites by using keywords or phrases. For example, you might search for "aardvarks as pets" which will retrieve a list of links to websites that provide information about the suitability of aardvarks as pets.

A *portal* is a website that contains a search engine as well as many other services, such as e-mail, shopping, categories of websites, etc. Portal publishers would like you to make their portal your home page or starting point of all web excursions.

Examples of search engines include www.google.com and www.goto.com; portals include www.yahoo.com and www.altavista.com.

Q. What are .JPG and .GIF files?

A. These are both graphics file formats. *.JPG* (pronounced JAY-peg), stands for Joint Photographic Experts Group. .JPG, or JPEG, represents a widely accepted, international standard for compression of color images.

.GIF (pronounced Gif—as in "gift") stands for Graphics Interchange Format and is a standard for digitized images created in 1987 by CompuServe.

Files created in both .GIF and .JPG format can be viewed with Netscape, Internet Explorer, or Microsoft's Paint program. For a complete listing of file formats and the programs needed to view them, send a blank e-mail addressed to `file-types@MrModem.net`. You'll receive information by return e-mail.

Q. I've heard the term *bandwidth* used in connection with the Internet. What is it?

A. Information or data on the Internet flows much like water through a garden hose. If you only want to water your plants, the amount of water that flows through a typical garden hose should be just fine. But if your house catches fire, the fire department won't use your garden hose because the amount of water flowing through the hose won't be sufficient to put out the fire. If you think of water as data, think of the size of the hose as *bandwidth*. (Sounds like one of those IQ test questions: "Air is to granola as sawdust is to beryllium. True or False?") Just remember this: The greater the bandwidth, the greater the amount of data that can be transmitted.

Q. I'm new to computers and don't understand something called *RAM*. I know that I'm supposed to have it, but what is it?

A. *RAM* (random access memory), sometimes referred to as "memory," is arguably the single most important element contributing (or not) to your computer's overall performance. RAM is actually a temporary storage area your computer uses to hold the things (programs or files) that are currently open or being used. In other words, if you launch your word processing program, it loads into RAM so you can use it. Think of it as removing a stapler or other object from a desk drawer and placing it on your desktop. As long as it's there it's easily accessible, although it's taking up space. If you keep piling things on top of your desk, pretty soon you'll run out of room.

If you are computer shopping and trying to decide between a higher processor speed, such as 500+ MHz (megahertz) or more RAM, err on the side of more RAM.

Q. Bits and bytes confuse me. Can you explain which is which—in English?

A. A *bit* is the smallest unit of data recognized by a computer, with the possible exception of keyboard lint. There are eight bits to one *byte*, and a byte is a character, such as the letters *A* or *B*.

When driving, we measure our speed in terms of miles per hour, or mph; when computers move data, the speed is quantified in bits per second, or bps. So a 56,000 bps (or 56Kbps, which stands for kilobits-per-second) modem can transmit about 7,000 characters per second, which is approximately four pages of text. (56,000 divided by 8 equals 7,000.)

Q. What is an intranet?

A. An *intranet* (different from Internet) is usually the reference to a corporate off-shoot of the Internet. Functionally similar to how the Internet works, the office intranet is isolated and secure, like a little world existing apart from other networks. Some intranets have no connections to the outside world; others have connections guarded by various security measures.

Q. I've heard of an intranet, but lately I've been hearing about something called an extranet. What is it?

A. Mr. Modem believes you should never leave home without a spare net, so an extranet is always a handy thing to have around. Just a little digital humor. The Internet is intended for public access, and the *inter* prefix means "between" or "among" networks in this context. An intranet is sometimes referred to as an internal Web and is a platform for delivering information to members within an association, for example. Some companies and organizations want to provide access to information for a limited number of customers or members, and to accomplish that objective the concept of the *extranet* was born. It's not open to the public as the Internet is, nor is it closed to the outside world as an intranet generally is. Instead, an extranet provides certain individuals limited access to specific materials or other information.

Q. I read an article that talked about Internet2 but didn't explain what it is. Can you explain it?

A. Internet2 is a high-speed version of the Internet. At this time it's only accessible by government agencies, universities, and a few corporations. Think of Internet2 as a testing ground for new technologies. For more information about Internet2, visit `www.internet2.edu`.

Q. My son gave me his old computer and said that it might need to have its BIOS upgraded. I'm clueless. What's a BIOS?

A. *BIOS* (pronounced BYE-ose) is an acronym that stands for Basic Input/Output System. It's really just a set of instructions that reside on a computer chip. These instructions tell your computer, among other things, what devices are connected to it, such as keyboard, monitor, external drives, etc., each time you start (boot) your computer.

You might have to upgrade your BIOS if you're planning to add new technology—like a USB port or some other technology that wasn't around when your computer was built. If you're not planning to add anything, you may not need to upgrade the BIOS. Use your computer for a while to determine whether it satisfies your needs. If so, you may be home free.

If you do decide that your son was right and it's time to upgrade the BIOS, don't panic! Consult your computer manufacturer for specifics, but, these days, upgrading the BIOS is generally as easy as installing a piece of software to upgrade the "flash" memory chip that contains your BIOS.

Q. What is the "Java" I see referenced on websites?

A. *Java* is a programming language for creating small applications (programs), or applets, that load onto your computer when you visit certain websites. These applets most generally provide animation and some type of interaction with the user. Java has really changed the look of websites in a dramatic way. Sites that used to be boringly static are now teeming with activity. So much activity, it can give you a headache.

 JavaScript, which has absolutely nothing to do with the Java programming language—though the two are often confused—is a scripting language invented by Netscape that is embedded into the HTML (web page) code of a document.

Q. What is encryption, and how does it work?

A. *Encryption* is a means of encoding or scrambling a message or document to make it unreadable by unauthorized eyes. Most encryption systems use two "keys," which are really nothing more than very complex numeric codes to encrypt and decrypt messages. Let's say I want to send you an e-mail that contains very sensitive information—so sensitive, it's susceptible to chafing. I would use a "public" key (coding created by software) to scramble the message, and you would use a secret "private" key to unscramble it. As long as you never share the private key with anybody else, any message scrambled by me and sent to you would be unreadable by any third party. PGP (Pretty Good Privacy) is one of several encryption programs on the market. A trial version of this program is available at www.pgp.com.

Q. What does the term *lurking* mean as it relates to the Internet?

A. *Lurking* refers to watching an online discussion without participating. Though it sounds like a pejorative term that conjures up disturbing images of trench coats and school playgrounds, it's really quite the contrary. It's a very good idea to lurk when you first enter any online discussion in order to get a feel for the tone and tenor of the discussion under way. Just as you wouldn't walk into an ongoing meeting and instantly begin talking as soon as you enter the room, so it is with online discussions. If you encounter a discussion on a message board, in a chat room, or in a newsgroup, just observe the discussion for a little while until you have a sense of what the topic is and who the participants are. Once you're comfortable, jump in and have fun!

Q. I've seen the term *legacy technology* used in computer-related publications. What does it mean?

A. The wild and wacky world of computers is continually spawning its own vocabulary, and *legacy tech*, or *legacy technology*, are among the latest buzz words. Legacy tech refers to old or obsolete hardware and software that we just can't bring ourselves to remove or throw away, usually because we paid too much for it. By the way, if anybody is interested, I have a lovely monochrome monitor….

Q. My phone company keeps sending me information about DSL phone service that promises high-speed Internet access. It refers to different types of DSL lines like ADSL, SDSL, etc. Do I need to be concerned about the letters associated with DSL lines?

A. *Digital Subscriber Lines* transmit data through regular phone lines at a much faster pace than is possible with "normal" analog phone lines.

DSL is available in several varieties, each with a different connection speed. Two levels of DSL service are the most popular, ADSL and SDSL. *ADSL* (asymmetric DSL), features faster download speeds—obtaining information from the Internet, for example—than upload speeds. *SDSL* (symmetric DSL) means download and upload speeds are equal. ADSL is the most popular DSL and is generally priced between $50 and $70 per month. SDSL, because it is bi-directional, is priced higher than ADSL, generally between $130 and $200 per month. Options vary with each provider, so be sure to investigate thoroughly.

To find out what high-speed Internet access options are available in your area, visit www.getspeed.com.

Q. I just read a Consumer Reports test on a computer I was interested in buying, and the report refers to the "clock speed" of the computer. What's clock speed? I assume it's something other than minutes and seconds?

A. You assume correctly. *Clock speed* is the speed, measured in megahertz (MHz), at which a microprocessor (chip) regulates and synchronizes its work flow—which is a geeky way of saying "processes information." All things being equal, the higher the clock speed, the faster a processor can process data.

Q. What does "wizzy-wig" mean? I'm not sure how to spell it, but I've heard several people use the term in my office, and I don't want to sound like an idiot by asking what it means.

A. *WYSIWYG* (pronounced wizzy-wig) is short for What You See Is What You Get and refers to the ability to see something on your computer screen as it will appear in print or in its final format. Within the context of designing web pages, an HTML editor software program that creates and displays web pages as they would be seen with a web browser is called a WYSIWYG editor.

Q. When I go to a website and it says something to the effect of "Get the plug-in," what is a plug-in?

A. *Plug-ins* are small software programs that allow your browser to do more than originally created to do. For example, many web pages contain pictures, animation, video clips, sounds, or things that go .BMP in the night. These features are contained within the page as small, proprietary-format files. That's just a fancy-shmancy way of saying that your browser may not be able to recognize and open the file without a little additional assistance.

Plug-ins, such as RealPlayer (`www.real.com`) or Adobe Acrobat (`www.adobe.com`), make it possible for your browser to work with a new type of file without having to use what's called an external helper application or program. Before the arrival of plug-ins, we had to download, install, and configure a separate software program to accomplish tasks that plug-ins handle so easily and conveniently.

When you encounter a "Get the plug-in" message, it's usually a link to the plug-in program itself, so click the link and follow the instructions. It's fast and easy, so give it a try!

Q. I hear the word *streaming* used in conjunction with files on the Internet, like a streaming audio or video file. What is streaming?

A. A *streaming* file is one that can start performing some action on your computer before it has finished downloading or transferring to your computer. In the "old days" before streaming (a week ago last Thursday), you would have to wait until a large audio or video file completely downloaded before you could use it. Depending upon the size of the file and the speed of your connection to the Internet, that could take minutes or even hours. Streaming files are compressed files. Compressed files are smaller in size than uncompressed files and, therefore, download faster. The audio and video are sent as a continuous stream of individual sounds, pictures, or animations and begin playing as soon as the downloading process begins rather than after the downloading process concludes.

Q. What's the difference between a laser printer and an inkjet printer?

A. Besides the spelling (badda-bing, badda-boom), an *inkjet printer* works by spraying "jets" of ink onto a page. Because it's a relatively low-tech way to print, inkjet printers tend to be much less expensive than laser printers. *Laser printers* use laser beams, mirrors, heat—they're more complex technologically but generally print faster and produce cleaner and clearer copies than do inkjet printers.

Q. When I try to print, I'm getting a prompt that tells me I don't have the correct printer driver. What does that mean?

A. A *printer driver* is a program that controls how your computer and your printer communicate with each other. This communication would include allowing you to select between options such as a best-quality mode or faster rough-draft printing. Years ago, every software program needed its own printer driver, but today a single driver, usually supplied by your printer's software, will handle all printing functions for all Windows-based programs. Try reloading the software that came with your printer, or visit the Driver Guide website at www.driverguide.com. This site maintains a massive database of drivers and provides detailed instructions on how to locate and install the correct driver.

Drivers vary in size; some are larger than others. A very small driver is occasionally referred to as a Minnie Driver—but not by anybody who has any sense of shame.

Q. What is a proxy as it relates to the Internet?

A. A *proxy* server is a heavyweight computer that sits between you and the Internet and stores a local copy of all the files and documents that you (and everyone else connected to it) have accessed recently. When your browser software (typically Netscape or Internet Explorer) requests a web page, the proxy server checks to see if it can supply (*serve*) it from its stored or cache files first. It only reaches out to the Internet and retrieves it from the web address (URL) you specify as a last resort.

This method of retrieving web pages reduces the number of times you are forced to compete with all the other Internet traffic trying to access and retrieve the same document or web page.

You can visit sites you've never visited before in this manner, because somebody else might have visited previously and, thus, that site resides on your ISP's proxy server.

Q. I've heard of computer viruses, but what's a Trojan horse? I think it has something to do with viruses, but I'm not sure what.

A. A *Trojan horse* is a program that camouflages itself as a harmless software application. Unlike viruses, Trojan horses generally do not replicate themselves and gobble up your hard drive or computer memory. One common Trojan horse is a program that claims to check your computer for viruses. By doing that, it masquerades as a helpful program, but, in reality, this dastardly digital demon actually introduces viruses into your computer. Oh, the pain. Stick with reputable, name-brand virus-checking programs such as Norton's AntiVirus (`www.symantec`) or McAfee's ViruScan (`www.mcafee.com`). Avoid Big Louie's Viruz-Away.

Q. Some people refer to the number of hits a website receives, and sometimes I hear about visitors to a website. Are "hits" and "visitors" the same thing?

A. The terms *hits* and *visitors* are not interchangeable. A surfer can register many hits during a visit. A hit simply records that an element of a web page (such as a graphic or a button) has been clicked. A single visitor (or even a married one, for that matter) can register as many as 20 or 30 hits while surfing five or six pages, if each web page contains a number of components within it, such as graphics or animations.

Using hits as a measure of traffic to a website is not an accurate measurement. A more accurate measurement is *unique visitors* to a website, determined by individual IP (Internet Protocol) addresses.

Q. What does MMX mean?

A. *MMX* is a computer chip containing an additional set of 57 instructions, all dealing with multimedia tasks. Think of them as a kind of shorthand, allowing one new instruction to take the place of many previous instructions. Intel developed the standard but licensed the technology to its competitors. Virtually all computers now sold in the United States are MMX-enabled.

Q. What is Linux?

A. *Linux* is an operating system that allows computer hardware to run and operate the software programs you love to use. Linux is an alternative to Windows, Unix, or DOS. It's actually referred to as "Unix, the Next Generation." There are many pros and cons surrounding the use of Linux, which was originally developed by a university student named Linus Torvalds. After others began using the program, a friend of Linus dubbed his program *Linux,* which is short for "Linus's Unix." For most average computer users, stick with Windows. Linux has a way to go before it's truly mainstream and a realistically viable alternative to Windows.

Q. I'm interested in online auctions but don't understand the difference between a minimum bid and something called a reserve price. Can you explain the difference?

A. Going once…going twice…. Sure! A *minimum bid* is the lowest amount a seller of an item will accept for a first bid. If you price the minimum bid too high, you might scare away potential buyers. Online auctions encourage sellers to set low minimums.

If you are the seller of an item, by entering a *reserve price* you indicate the minimum amount you are willing to accept for an item. The fact that an item has a reserve price established is made public to the bidders, but the actual reserve price set is kept private. Once the reserve price is met, the auction site indicates that the reserve price has been met, and the seller is notified. Online auctions are great fun. The biggest auction site on the Web is eBay, located at www.ebay.com, but for lots of additional information about online auctions in general, visit www.auctionsonthenet.com. Happy bidding!

Q. What's a Dutch auction online?

A. A *Dutch auction* involves the sale of several identical items at the same time. The highest bidders each receive an item at the lowest successful bid price.

Q. How does a reverse auction work? Does the price keep going down?

A. Exactly! The seller offers an item at a high price, then reduces the price by a fixed amount every day, hour, or minute, until a buyer agrees to purchase the item at the current asking price. "Sold to the bearded author cowering in the second row!"

Q. What is flaming?

A. A flame is a hostile e-mail. When two or more people begin *flaming* each other, the result is referred to as a *flame war*. Sometimes a flame will occur in response to an innocent message that just happens to upset the recipient or the reader of a posted message in a newsgroup or other interactive forum. Other times, Cyber-Morons intentionally flame other people just because they can. Many times, flamers hide behind an alias or an assumed name, masking their true identity.

If you encounter a flamer, the best approach is to ignore the person completely. Don't respond in any manner; just ignore the message completely. People who flame are like small children seeking attention. They frequently say inappropriate or provocative things in hopes of getting a reaction out of others. Ignore them completely and they'll eventually move on. It's no fun for a flamer if he or she cannot provoke a response.

Q. I bought a computer that has a GPS (Global Positioning System) navigational feature. I know it can tell me my location and provide directions to various destinations, but how does it work? No technical talk, please.

A. There are 24 GPS satellites orbiting the earth at an altitude of approximately 11,000 miles. Through a process called triangulation, your *GPS receiver* locks on to and measures the signals of at least three of the 24 satellites to pinpoint its own location anywhere on earth to within a few feet. Your GPS receiver is the hardware part of the equipment necessary to accomplish this amazing feat. The software, called GIS (Geographic Information Systems), is referred to as *mapping software* and works in concert with your GPS receiver. Your receiver reads the coordinates, and the software translates that data into maps.

Mr. Modem's Related Websites

Computer Science Glossary   Includes hardware, software, protocols, acronyms, and units of measure.

> www.info.unicaen.fr/~fournier/glossary/glossary.html

Computer Terminology   More than 3,000 topics and 12,000 linked cross-references.

> http://whatis.com/

NetLingo Internet Dictionary   Includes definitions, acronyms, smiley face interpretations, ASCII art, and more.

> www.netlingo.com/

Technical Encyclopedia   More than 20,000 definitions.

> www.techweb.com/encyclopedia/home

Webopedia   Computer and Internet dictionary.

> www.pcwebopaedia.com/

Web-Based Treasures:
Sites and Software

The Internet is a treasure trove of informational resources that are sometimes difficult to find in the more than one billion web pages accessible today. In this chapter, in response to readers' questions about websites and web-based software programs with a particular focus or function, I share some of my favorite sites as well as free and low-cost software programs that are guaranteed to enhance your surfing experience.

Q. There are so many e-mail hoaxes and scams in circulation; can you recommend any websites that I should use to determine whether something is a hoax or not?

A. E-mail hoaxes, scams, phony virus warnings, etc. are a cumulative thorn in the side of all Internet users. E-mail hoaxes typically share several common characteristics, and the first step in not falling victim to a hoax is to recognize these three signs:

- A great sense of urgency!!!!—usually manifested by lots of exclamation marks.

- A prediction of dire consequences should you fail to heed the warning.

- A request that you be a good CyberCitizen and forward the warning message to all your friends to help spread the word. (Mr. Modem's advice: Don't do it!)

When you forward one of these messages to others, you're playing into the hands of the perpetrators of the hoax. That's exactly what they want you to do, so don't be gullible. Use any of the following sites to check it out first, and chances are you'll discover the message you received is nothing more than a hoax:

- Fraud.org Subject Index (`www.fraud.org/news/subject/subject.htm`)

- F-Secure Corporation's Hoax Warnings (`www.datafellows.fi/news/hoax.htm`)

- McAfee's Virus Information Library (`http://vil.nai.com/villib/alpha.asp`)

- Symantec's AntiVirus Research Center (`www.symantec.com/avcenter/`)

- Urban Legends (`www.snopes2.com/`)

- U.S. Dept. of Energy Hoaxbusters (`http://hoaxbusters.ciac.org/`)

- Vmyths.com (`www.vmyths.com`)

Q. All kinds of public records are available on the Internet, but what about automobile histories? It would be helpful when buying a used car to know about the car's history—not that I don't trust used car salesmen, you understand, but it would be a help.

A. Mr. Modem feels your queasiness. Through the miracle of the Internet, you can launch a lemon check on any car as long as you have the VIN (vehicle identification number). Just go to `http://autos.yahoo.com/auto/cf/lemon.html`, enter the VIN, and the Lemon Check will let you know if the vehicle was a manufacturer buyback (lemon) by searching its database of almost a billion records. There is no charge for this service.

If you need additional information, you can order a full Carfax Vehicle History Report (www.carfax.com) report for $14.95. The full report helps detect salvage history, flood damage, odometer fraud, and any other hidden problems in the vehicle's past. Happy modeming!

Q. How can I find out what my telephone number spells? Isn't there something on the Internet that will translate the numbers into letters?

A. Using your telephone number to spell words can help people remember your phone number. Just be sure to include the numbers themselves in parentheses to help those not so enthused about engaging in a hunt-and-peck phone-dial letter search. Example: WAY COOL (929-2665). (Note: Don't forget to include the area code when creating your telephone number in words.)

Point your browser to the cleverly named PhoneSpell website at www.phonespell.org. Type in your telephone number and possible word combinations will appear.

Q. Software programs are continually being updated, so it's really hard to know when an update is available. Any Internet-based services available to keep track of things like that?

A. You can get software update notifications by e-mail whenever your favorite software is updated. Just register for this free service at www.versions.com.

Q. Is there any way I can check my credit report on the Internet?

A. Equifax, one of the leaders in personal credit reports, is the power behind a service called Privista (www.privista.com). For an annual fee of $29.95, this service will monitor your personal credit report and provide weekly e-mail updates and alerts for any indication of fraud.

Q. I'm having trouble keeping track of all the different usernames and passwords I've created while registering with different websites. Is there any way to keep track of those automatically?

A. One option of keeping track of passwords and usernames is the Mr. Modem Method (patent pending), which involves the use of yellow stickies and Scotch-taped notes around the perimeter of the computer monitor. It's inexpensive, it's functional, and it's colorful. For a more sophisticated, higher-tech approach, try Gator (www.gator.com). Gator fills out forms, remembers passwords and usernames, and disappears when it's not needed. Best of all, it's free!

Q. Any websites you can recommend that show what time it is in different time zones around the world?

A. Here are a couple of timely suggestions: Try the Time Zone Converter at www.timezoneconverter.com. You can use the current computer time displayed on your computer or enter any time you choose. The Time Zone Converter will display the corresponding time anywhere in the world.

Another excellent resource is Local Times Around the World at www.hilink.com.au/times/. This site displays the time for more than 1,500 cities, 177 time zones, and hundreds of countries. If you ever need to make an emergency call to Cousin Louie in Losotho or Uncle Kenny in Kyrgyzstan, check this site so you don't call in the middle of the night. All cities are adjusted for daylight saving time.

Q. Sometimes I don't visit a website for several weeks, but I'd like to know whether anything new is added to the site during the interim. I've heard there's a service that will notify me of any changes on a website. Ever heard of anything like that?

A. You may be referring to the Webspector by Illumix Software, www.illumix.com. This software monitors web pages for content changes, so it really comes in handy if you have favorite sites you would like to keep tabs on. Changes are highlighted so they're easy to spot. Webspector is free for the download. It's almost 3MB in size, so allow about eight minutes for the download at 56Kbps.

Q. With so many new websites appearing every day, I find myself getting overwhelmed and end up visiting sites of little interest to me. Is there any way to keep track of new websites of interest to me?

A. There are a couple of excellent free services that can help you monitor new sites on the Web. Try TracerLock (`www.tracerlock.com/`) or WhatsNu (`www.whatsnu.com`). These services let you choose the topics you would like to be informed about and then will send you an e-mail when anything new appears on the Web.

Q. It's a real pain having several e-mail accounts and having to check each one individually. I've got my primary AOL account and then several other free e-mail accounts. Is there any way to combine them so I can just check one place and get all my e-mail?

A. ePrompter (`www.eprompter.com`) is a free e-mail notification utility program that automatically checks up to eight e-mail accounts. There's a really cool screensaver feature that displays the number of messages waiting for you in each account while your computer is idle, and a rotating tray icon that shows the number of messages for each account when your computer is active. Audio prompts will also alert you when new e-mail arrives.

If you have a dial-up account to the Net, you can configure ePrompter to check for e-mail periodically throughout the day by automatically logging on at predetermined times.

Q. I received a file attachment that has a filename with a .CWK extension. I've never seen that extension before. How can I find out what program is needed to open the file?

A. There are thousands of cryptic, three-letter filename suffixes, or extensions, in circulation today, which makes it next to impossible to know what they all mean. A wonderful searchable database of more than 1,700 file extensions and their definitions is available at `http://extsearch.com/`.

For more information about file types and where to obtain the programs necessary to launch those files, send a blank e-mail addressed to `filetypes@MrModem.net` and you'll receive information by return e-mail.

By the way, your mysterious .CWK file is a ClarisWorks data file.

Q. I'm a college student majoring in sociology. I'm working on a research paper and trying to determine surname distribution (geographically) within the U.S. I've surfed for hours but haven't found anything like that on the Web. Any thoughts would be greatly appreciated, Mr. Modem.

A. Great question! If this doesn't demonstrate to any CyberSkeptics the incredible depth of information accessible on the Internet, I don't know what will.

Hamrick Software provides a surname distribution research database located at `www.hamrick.com/names/`. Just enter a surname (last name) into the Web-based form and a map of the United States showing the distribution of people with that surname within the 50 states will be displayed.

The source of this data is the 1850, the 1880, and the 1920 Census, plus 1990 phone books. The Census data is a sampling of 1 in 100 names, so the 1990 data is the most accurate. Year 2000 Census data will be added when it becomes available.

Q. When I uninstall a program, sometimes it doesn't uninstall completely and some of its files continue to show up in the **Add/Remove** list. How can I delete the remnants?

A. These files are sometimes referred to as orphan or phantom files and can be next to impossible to remove without a little outside assistance. Try a free utility program called Add/Remove Plus, which is available at `www.pcworld.com/fileworld/file_description/0,1458,6477,00.html`. (Catchy URL!) This program works with Windows 95, 98, or NT.

Q. I've got a 56K modem, but I'm just sure I'm not connecting at that speed. Is there some way to get an accurate reading of what my connection rate is?

A. Just point your browser to the free modem-performance test located at `www.toast.net`. No software is needed to take this test. Just click **Free Performance Test** and follow the instructions. You can test your connection speeds for both text and graphics.

A similar free test called the Bandwidth Speed Test is available through Microsoft at `http://msnhomepages.talkcity.com/WindowsWay/diagnostics/modem/modem1.html`.

Q. I'm looking for a website that has a glossary of dental terms but haven't been able to find anything. Any suggestions?

A. Try putting the bite on the Dictionary of Dental Terms located at www.bracesinfo.com/glossary.html. Take a look at the Definitions of General Dental Terms section. It's quite extensive, so be sure to floss after visiting.

Q. I'm interested in genealogy. I know there are a bunch of websites that deal with this topic, but are there any in particular that you would recommend?

A. There are many such sites, most having been passed down from generation to generation. Some of the most popular include Cindi's List at www.cyndislist.com/, Genealogy.com at www.genealogy.com, and The Genealogy Home Page at www.genhomepage.com.

Q. I've tried to capture screen shots using the **Print Screen** key, but the results are never very good. How can I capture what I see on screen so that it doesn't get all reformatted or garbled?

A. Have I got a program for you! SnagIt has been referred to as the utility that Windows forgot to include—and that's a very good description. I wish I had said that. With SnagIt, you can capture an entire screen, a window, or an arbitrary rectangle of screen real estate. SnagIt can also capture menus and perform repeated captures of fixed-sized images, such as icons and buttons.

You can also capture the entire contents of scrolling windows, which is invaluable if you've ever tried to capture web pages or unprintable lists. SnagIt can send any captured image to your printer, the clipboard, a graphic file, or as an e-mail attachment.

You can download SnagIt from www.snagit.com/ and try it out for 45 days. After the 45-day trial period, SnagIt costs $39.95 to register.

Q. My husband and I are fanatics about coupons and always cut them out of the newspaper. I know there are newspapers on the Internet, but are there coupons, too?

A. Absolutely! www.hotcoupons.com delivers local supermarket, entertainment, travel, and other money-saving coupons to you on the Internet. You can even search for coupons by zip code or city. Also, take a look at www.coolsavings.com and www.couponclippers.com, which feature discount coupons in your neighborhood.

Q. This is going to sound like Big Brotherism at its worst, but I own a small company and I think some of my employees are wasting a lot of time on the Internet when they're supposed to be working. Is there any way I can monitor what they're doing online?

A. Dear Big Brother: A software program called WinGuardian (www.webroot.com/chap1.htm), described as an "Employee and Child Monitoring Utility" program, is what you're looking for. This is a password-protected, hidden program that logs all programs, all text typed, and all websites visited. It will display screen shots at periodic intervals, deny access to certain programs, and even e-mail its own log files to a designated e-mail address so you can monitor what's going on even if you're not at the office.

Having the ability to monitor your employees' surfing is one thing, but being fair to your employees is also appropriate, in Mr. Modem's opinion. In the spirit of fairness, WinGuardian has a feature that allows you to set a customized warning to users that their computer usage is being monitored. You can even require users to acknowledge the warning so they can't say they weren't aware that you're looking over their shoulder.

You can try the program for free for 15 days. It costs $39.95 to register after the 15-day trial period.

Q. Somebody told me about a site that contains nothing but clichés. Sounds like fun, but I haven't been able to find it. Can you help?

A. You can bet your bottom dollar I can help. Have you been searching high and low for just the right cliché to tie up some loose ends? Well, every cloud has a silver lining, so even though I might be on my last leg, let's share and share alike to make sure we stay in the groove. You'll find more clichés than you can throw a stick at on this site! Use it or lose it! Have a nice cliché at www.westegg.com/cliche/.

Q. Hey, Mr. Modem, where can I find a list of holidays in foreign countries? We look forward to your column in our local paper. Keep up the good work.

A. Hey, Kind Reader, thanks for your comments! The Worldwide Holiday and Festival Site features information about holidays and other happenings in hundreds of countries around the world. You can party your browser off at `www.holidayfestival.com`.

Q. My husband started using a new stockbroker that I don't have a good feeling about. Is there any way to check up on a broker's background online?

A. Thanks to the National Association of Securities Dealers, you can check up on more than 500,000 registered brokers and determine whether a broker has a disciplinary record. The website address is `www.nasdr.com`. Click the **About Your Broker** link for additional information.

Q. I need to obtain a passport in a hurry in order to take advantage of an unexpected birthday-gift trip to Europe. Are the passport-expediting outfits on the Web legitimate, or are they scams?

A. What a wonderful birthday gift! Mrs. Modem took me to a local mall's food court for my birthday dinner. Not that it wasn't fun, but…. Well, enough about me, let's talk about you.

Yes, indeed, there are a number of web-based enterprises that promise to deliver your travel-ready passport within days. The good news is that most of these services are legitimate; the bad news is you'll pay up to $150 for the service, in addition to the $60 charged by the government.

However, Mr. Modem believes in saving money whenever possible—as does Mrs. Modem, obviously. You'll save enough to have mussels in Brussels if, instead of paying the steep fees of the third-party passport companies, you pay a $35 rush fee directly to the U.S. passport agency. They will mail you your new passport three days after receiving your application. For additional information, visit `www.travel.state.gov` and click **Passport Information**. Bon voyage!

Q. I can't make up my mind which search engine to use on the Web. Any suggestions? I'm using Netscape Navigator 4.

A. Have I got a book for you! My "Internet Search Engines" chapter of *Mr. Modem's Internet Guide for Seniors* (Sybex, $19.99) explores the most popular search engines and provides many search tips for each.

Rather than settle on just one search engine, why not have some fun and play a little digital roulette? Enter two or more words that aren't a web address (URL) in Netscape Navigator's **Location** field. The words will be entered into a random search engine and the results displayed. Sure, it's living on the edge, but isn't that what the Internet is all about?

Lots more information and links to additional search engines are available at `www.mrmodem.net/html/links.html`, or send an e-mail addressed to `search@MrModem.net`.

Q. I attended one of your presentations and you mentioned something about backing up data into cyberspace. Could you explain that a little bit more?

A. Even the most reliable computer is apt to take a nose dive eventually—which is a nice way of saying *crash*. When a computer crashes, it can destroy data. Protecting data is the main reason for *backing up*. Some folks recommend making two, three, or even four sets of backed-up data. I'm an old belt-and-suspenders kinda guy, but personally, I think one backup that's updated daily should be sufficient for most people. If you're more comfortable with additional backups, go for it!

In the past, computer users would back up data on floppy disks, tapes, or other forms of storage media. Today, you can back up your data into cyberspace—on the Internet itself. This kind of off-site storage requires no hard drives, disks, or tapes. Instead, with your backed-up data on the Internet, it's available from any location as long as you have Net access.

The following websites offer Internet-based storage for your data:

- FreeDrive (`www.freedrive.com/`) offers 50MB of storage space for free and is an excellent way to try out remote storage of data.

- @Backup (`www.backup.com`) offers several affordable options ranging from $99 per year (for up to 100MB of space) to $299 per year (for up to 500MB). One handy feature is the ability to schedule automatic backups at certain times of the day or night. You can also obtain a CD-ROM of all your backed-up files for $39 plus shipping and handling.

Q. I'm a writer looking for a website where I can find spellings of technical terms—words that aren't generally in the dictionary. Any suggestions?

A. My favorite dictionary reference site is OneLook Dictionaries, located at `www.onelook.com`. Here you can access more than 700 dictionaries for just about any topic you can imagine—and some topics that you probably don't want to imagine.

Another excellent resource is the Online Dictionaries, Glossaries and Encyclopedias 101 website, located at `http://stommel.tamu.edu/~baum/hyperref.html`. As of the publication date of this book, 163 dictionaries and 443 glossaries are accessible from this site.

Lastly, take a look at `www.dictionary.com`. Here you'll find many specialty dictionaries, glossaries, *Roget's Thesaurus,* a translation service, and more.

Q. I saw an ad for a little device that is not a computer, but it checks e-mail. It looked pretty interesting, and I thought it might be perfect for checking e-mail while traveling. Do you know what I'm referring to?

A. There are several e-mail–only devices available, but two of the most popular ones are MailStation by Cidco (`www.mailstation.com`) and MailBug (`www.mailbug.com`).

MailStation and the Mivo series are devices look like a little keyboard with a small, flip-up LCD screen. There are four models to choose from ranging in price from $99 for the unit, and $9.95/month for Internet access to $129.95 and $12.95/month.

The MailBug is a similar device and costs $99.95—surprise, surprise!—plus $99.95 for a year of access to the Internet for e-mail only. It's déjà vu all over again: Doing the math, that breaks down to $8.33 per month, if you pay for the year in advance. On a month-to-month basis, access is $9.95 per month. Coincidence? Perhaps.

I've tried both products, and both are excellent. Just be aware that you must establish an e-mail account with either MailStation or MailBug, so your e-mail address will be something like `username@mailstation.com` or `username@mailbug.com`. You cannot use an existing e-mail account with either device.

Q. A recall notice just arrived for my car, and that started me thinking about what other recall notices might be around that I'm not aware of. Any place on the Internet where all recall notices are posted?

A. About the closest thing to that would be the SafetyAlerts website at www.safetyalerts.com. (Did you know there were more than 1,000 safety-related product recalls issued in the U.S. in 1999? I didn't either. I think I felt better not knowing, actually.) Sign up for the free SafetyAlerts *Safemail* e-letter to stay on top of issues that might affect the health and safety of you and your family. Archives of previous recall notices are available on the website.

Q. I'm trying to locate an old Army buddy from more than 20 years ago. Any suggestions for websites I should check out?

A. First up, try Military.com at www.military.com. Foxhole friends are just a mouse-click away.

Next, try MilitaryUSA at www.militaryusa.com. This site is dedicated to bringing veterans together for reunions and to helping disabled vets locate former buddies to substantiate claims for veterans' benefits.

Don't overlook reunion-type sites, either, such as www.greatreunions.com.

Last, check out the Missing Friends Network at www.missingfriends.com/ASP/searchall.asp. Here, you can search using the name of your military base, as well as find civilian friends by searching the name of the town you grew up in, the name of your elementary school, high school, or college. Good luck, Soldier.

Q. My husband is going to need full-time care in the near future. I've heard so many horror stories about nursing homes, and I'm not sure where to begin looking. Is there any way I can find out what options are available in my area using the Internet?

A. The CareGuide website (www.careguide.com) provides an excellent means of searching more than 170,000 care providers, homes, retirement communities, and child care and nursing facilities, accessible and listed by geographic location and type of care provided in more than 15,000 cities nationwide.

Q. I had been using Norton's AntiVirus software, and it didn't detect any viruses. Then you recommended McAfee's virus-checking program called VirusScan, and it found "traces" of a virus but no active ones. I switched to McAfee, figuring you knew what you were talking about, but now it detects nothing. So what gives, Mr. Modem?

A. I see the problem: The first mistake you made was assuming that Mr. Modem knew what he was talking about. All kidding aside, my recommendation is to just use one virus-checking program. McAfee's VirusScan (www.mcafee.com) is excellent, as is Norton's AntiVirus (www.symantec.com).

What probably happened is that one virus-checking program detected the other one. In order for a virus-checking program to work, it has to have the virus patterns in its memory to match and report them to you if it finds them. If your virus-checking program doesn't know what it's looking for, it can't locate a virus. When these virus patterns remain in your computer's memory or in a file, they may be detected by another program, but this does not necessarily indicate a virus infection.

Q. I'm looking for a website that I can use to find the spellings of doctors' names. Is there anything like that on the Internet?

A. There are many such sites, but I've found two to be most comprehensive. First there's the DoctorDirectory (www.doctordirectory.com/), which provides a listing of each doctor's name, specialty, address, telephone number, map to the office, board certification, medical school, residency, fellowship, secondary specialty, office hours, languages spoken, affiliated hospitals, health plans accepted, and dogeared, outdated magazines in the waiting room. Virtually every practicing physician in the U.S. is listed.

The second site serves a dual role: It's handy for finding spellings, but it's also useful if you need a doctor yourself and want to be sure you select a board-certified physician. Ambulate to the American Board of Medical Specialties website (www.abms.org/newsearch.asp), which includes a free service to determine the board certification status of any physician.

Q. I like to read some product reviews before I buy something new, but word-of-mouth—what others are saying about a product—is even more useful. Is there some way to do that online other than by trying to find a newsgroup for the product I'm interested in purchasing?

A. Take a look at `www.epinions.com`. This site is a gathering place for users—not professional writers or product reviewers—to get together and share opinions about products and services. You can review opinions on hundreds of thousands of products. Even if you're not looking for a specific product or service, it's still fun just to read what others are saying.

Q. Are there any programs that keep a record or log of what my kids are doing on the Internet? I know programs exist to block their access to some adult-oriented sites, but I'd like to see for myself what they're looking at online.

A. A number of concerned parents have asked about similar programs. A program called WinWhatWhere Investigator will keep an eye on your kids' (and other individuals') computer usage by providing as many as 20 types of reports, including daily or weekly Internet use, keystroke activity, and general computer monitoring.

The program costs $99 and is available from WinWhatWhere Corporation (509-585-9293, or e-mail `www.winwhatwhere.com`).

Q. I spend eight hours a day working at the computer, and it's driving my eyes crazy. I've tried a new monitor, tried changing the monitor's resolution, and tried changing colors and fonts. Despite all that, after two or three hours it's like nothing has changed. Are there any products that can help with something like this?

A. I'm not a doctor, nor do I portray one on television, but experts in the field (Author's Truth-in-Writing Disclosure: I have no idea what experts nor in what field) tell us that Computer Vision Syndrome (CVS) affects millions of computer users. Strictly speaking, CVS is a repetitive stress injury caused by the act of repeatedly refocusing on a computer screen image.

The same unidentified experts compare the repetitive refocusing required while computing to that of squeezing your hand hard 30,000 times a day. (Bonus Worthless Information: If each hand-squeezing sequence requires one second to complete, 30,000 hard hand squeezes would require 8.3 hours. That's a whole lotta squeezin' goin' on.)

Compounding the visual challenges of computer usage, your blink reflex, one of the fastest in the body, is brought to an unnatural standstill when you stare at a computer monitor. Away from a computer, you blink an average of 22 times per minute. While reading, that rate decreases to 12 times per minute. At the computer, however, blinking is reduced to just 4 times per minute, thus increasing tear evaporation and resulting in drier, more irritated eyes.

Some additional or supplemental lighting can help if—and this is a big *if*—it doesn't result in glare on the computer monitor. A product called the Eclipse Computer Light (`www.onetech.net/main.cfm`) claims to correct symptoms associated with eyestrain or CVS by providing the proper amount of light without producing any glare on the screen. The light costs $49.95.

Q. A friend was telling me about a website that lets you create a customized newspaper just for yourself. It isn't the usual home page type of feature where you can get headlines but an actual newspaper that you can create. Any ideas where to look for that?

A. The CRAYON website, `www.crayon.net`, was one of the first sites on the Web to offer customization. The name *CRAYON* is actually a jumbled acronym that stands for Create Your Own Newspaper. If you're tired of clicking through multiple websites each morning to get your daily dish of information, simply decide which ones you want displayed on your own newspaper's front page.

In a matter of seconds, you can create your own environmentally responsible, virtual newspaper. The rain forests thank you.

Q. I know that sites like `www.priceline.com` allow you to bid for airline tickets, hotel rooms, etc. Is it true that there's a site where you can bid for medical services?

A. Kind of makes you wonder where it's going to all end, doesn't it? If you were one of the few, the proud, the queasy who were less than enthused when a kidney went up for auction on eBay recently, have I got news for you! If you thought bowling for dollars was fun, how about name-your-price for cosmetic surgery? That's right, suture enthusiasts, `www.medicineonline.com` is the perfect site to cauterize the cost of those pesky nips and tucks. Once you register online, let them know what it is you'd like—a nose job, lipo, or even LASIK vision-correction surgery—and then surgeons bid to perform your work!

Let's say you want a honker revision. Post your request for rhinoplasty, along with your age, gender, occupation, location, health information, and insurance coverage. Doctors then have 72 hours to start bidding based on their credentials, fees, and location. What a deal! "Yes, that's my final answer, Regis!" A board-certified plastic and reconstructive surgeon with 25 years experience might charge $10,000 for a nose job, but you can shave thousands of dollars off that fee by accepting a bid from Tony "The Bleeder" DeFonzio, who has a neighbor who took some premed courses at Granada Community College. Tony can save you thousands of dollars! No overhead, no anesthesia, and no license translate to big, big, *big* savings for you!

Q. Trying to keep my bookmarks current on two computers isn't as easy as I thought it was going to be. I'm continually copying files between my desktop and notebook computers. Is there an easier way to keep my bookmarks up-to-date on both computers?

A. Clickmarks (`www.clickmarks.com`) is a free service that lets you upload and manage your Netscape Bookmarks and Internet Explorer Favorites. By maintaining your bookmarks on the Web itself, in one location, you can use your web browser from either computer to access and maintain your bookmarks. If you access the Internet using a friend's computer, simply log in to your Clickmarks account and you'll always have access to your bookmarks.

A similar bookmarks-management site is `www.blink.com`. Once you set up your free Blink account, you can share and exchange bookmark links with others. Links can be grouped in shared folders, annotated, discussed, and even e-mailed to non-Blink users. You can designate who will be allowed to view your links, and what editing privileges, if any, others can have.

Q. I installed a new program on my computer that really messed things up in some other programs. I tried uninstalling it, but everything still isn't right. What can I do to get things back to the way they were before I installed the program?

A. Going back in time on your computer is easy thanks to a wonderful software program called GoBack (`www.goback.com`). GoBack provides you the ability to undo errors and system problems on your computer. Have you ever installed a new program or started getting adventuresome with your computer and really messed things up? (You're not alone.) When intrusive "I've really done it this time!" thoughts start creeping into your consciousness and that sinking "Why did I do that?" feeling overwhelms you, have you ever wished you could go back in time and return your computer to the way it was before you unleashed your creative talents? GoBack software can do that and more. You can download and test drive GoBack for 30 days, after which time the software will automatically uninstall itself from your computer unless you register it for $39.95.

Q. A friend told me there's a website that sells hard-to-get tickets for concerts and other events. Do you know which site he's referring to? Is buying a ticket online like this safe?

A. "Psssst! Hey, buddy! Wanna buy two front-row seats for the Spice Girls concert?" Nah, me neither.

Several websites specialize in selling tickets for sporting events and concerts. Some of the more popular sites include www.tickets.com, www.ticketmaster.com, and www.ticketweb.com. Fees, above the face price of the ticket, range from $1.50 to $7 or higher, plus a per-order handling charge. For really, *really* hard-to-find tickets, try www.ticketcity.com.

Comparisons can be made to CyberScalping in that the seller sets the price and adds a per-transaction service fee that at times can be as much as 30 percent of the sale. All of the sites referenced here are considered reputable, and I wouldn't hesitate to buy my tickets for the next Abba concert from any of them. (Oh, what I'd give to hear "Fernando" just one more time.)

Q. When I download files from the Internet, I'm usually presented with a variety of download site options. I know I'm supposed to select a site that's closest to me geographically, but sometimes that's too slow. How can I tell which of these sites is fastest?

A. There's a really neat—and free—program called Dipstick that can determine the speed of download site connections. Just drag and drop download links onto the program's Desktop icon to determine the best option for you. You can download Dipstick at www.klever.net/kin/dipstick.html.

iscovered a web page that looked very interesting but was in French. I didn't see English version of it available. Is there any way to get it translated on the Web?

A. Oui! Point your browser to `http://babelfish.altavista.com/translate.dyn`. Here, you can type in the URL (address) of any web page and select the language you would like to translate from and to (in this case, from French to English); then adjust your beret, sit back, relax, and behold the miracle of the Internet in action! You can also copy and paste text into the translation field and click the **Translate** button. Contrôlez-le dehors! ("Check it out!")

Q. Is there a way to get rid of those annoying Web pop-up ads?

A. Yes, through the use of a free program called POW! It loads into your System Tray (lower-right corner, next to the time display in Windows) and is very simple to use. You can configure POW! to close any new pop-up windows automatically as soon as they appear, or you can vaporize them manually whenever you encounter one.

The more you use POW! the more pesky pop-ups it remembers having encountered in the past and prevents them from reappearing.

The program works with Netscape Navigator 4 or higher or with Microsoft Internet Explorer 4 or higher. Download it from `www.analogx.com/contents/download/network/pow.htm`.

Q. Is there a program that will check my bookmarks for dead links? I have a large bookmark file, and to check the links one by one would take days.

A. Weren't the Dead Links a grunge band out of the Seattle area? I could be wrong.

I don't know of a program that does *precisely* what you're looking for, but Netscape users can use a little-known feature that's part of Netscape Navigator to launch an update on their bookmarks file. Go to **Bookmarks ➤ Edit Bookmarks ➤ View ➤ Update Bookmarks**, and click the **Start Checking** button.

Netscape will examine each bookmark, and if a bookmarked page has changed, it will note the change and update the page.

One word of caution: Mr. Modem is doubtful of the reliability of this updating feature. When I ran it, out of more than 2,500 bookmarks in my `bookmarks.htm` file, the Update Bookmarks feature found only 37 that had changed. That's a suspiciously low number considering that some of the bookmarks are several years old. My suspicions notwithstanding, it's definitely worth a try. You may be pleasantly surprised.

Q. Have you heard of a phone-in service that finds things on the Internet for you?

A. There is a service offered through the `www.iNetNow.com` website that will surf the Internet for you. This service is available to any person who has registered and has been assigned a valid account number. When you can't get to a computer (or don't want to), you can contact iNetNow by calling a toll-free number to obtain any web-based information from stock quotes to sports scores, from news headlines to traffic updates, and from trivia questions to online shopping prices.

Though advertised as a resource for individuals who don't own a computer, it's not without a touch of irony that the registration process itself occurs online. During the registration process you will be required to provide your credit card information. The service is free at the time of publication of this book, but several pricing plans will be introduced in the future.

Q. I've got a bet with a friend that I hope you can settle, Mr. Modem. I said that the Web, despite its millions of web pages, has an end point—a last page, if you will. It's no different than if you were to go into a library and go through all the books one at a time; sooner or later, you'd get to the last book. My friend says the Web is more "circular" and, therefore, has no final page or end point. We've got a six-pack riding on this, so the pressure is on.

 Better split up that six-pack because you're both right. I can hear you saying, "How can that be?"

Here's how: Technically, there is no "end of the Web" because the Web isn't a static medium. The Web is growing at a rate of approximately 35,000 new web pages every week. Because it's continually expanding, if you went through every single web page, as soon as you arrived at what you might believe was the last page, there would be many more pages added.

But, hypothetically, if you could freeze the Web and stop its growth completely, you would end up at the following web page: `http://home.att.net/~cecw/last-page.htm`.

Mr. Modem's Recommended Websites

Google Search Engine   A purist's delight. No stock tickers, weather reports, or current moisture content in the Sahara desert. Search results are based on matches to your queries, as well as what other similar sites have said about previously matched sites. It works like a charm.

> `www.google.com/`

Learn2.com   Heralded as the "Number 1 most-useful site on the Web" by *Internet Yahoo!* magazine.

> `www.learn2.com/`

Merriam-Webster Online   Access to both the collegiate dictionary and the thesaurus.

> `www.m-w.com/dictionary.htm`

OneLook   Access more than 700 online dictionaries!

> `www.onelook.com`

Webopedia   Searchable database of computer and Internet terminology.

> `www.pcwebopaedia.com/`

Paneless Answers to Windows Questions

Windows is fun! If your reaction to that statement is, "How can operating-system software that will probably ruin my life be fun?" then this is the chapter for you! As you read through the following frequently asked questions about Windows, you'll quickly see that, whatever questions you may have, you are definitely not alone.

Q. When I have several programs running at once, I usually minimize the ones I'm not using so they appear on the Taskbar at the bottom of the screen. Is there a faster way to move between programs other than clicking the Taskbar icon of the program I want to return to and then minimizing it again when I move to something else?

A. A little-known feature of Windows called the Task Switcher is the fastest way to move among running programs or open windows. Just hold down the **Alt** key and press **Tab** repeatedly to cycle through all running programs. A small selection box will appear, displaying an icon for each active program or window. A square "frame" around an icon marks it as the active program or window when you release the **Alt** key.

Q. I've been deleting files in order to free up additional disk space, but I'm not seeing any increase in the amount of free disk space available. What's the problem?

A. When you delete files in Windows, they aren't really deleted in the sense that you're freeing up disk space. Instead, you're moving them into your Recycle Bin, where they will reside until you empty the Recycle Bin.

Think of the Recycle Bin as you would a wastepaper basket in your home. If you crumple up a document and throw it in your wastepaper basket, then later in the day decide that you need to take another look at it, you can easily retrieve the document by reaching into the basket and pulling it out. The Recycle Bin serves that same purpose. It's a wonderful safety net should you accidentally or unintentionally ever delete a file.

However, once you take the wastepaper basket from your home, empty it into the dumpster, and the City hauls it away, then it's gone. Similarly, when you empty your Recycle Bin, that's the high-tech version of emptying that wastepaper basket into the dumpster and the City taking it away.

Q. It seems that most adjustments to Windows require accessing the Control Panel. Is there a faster way to get to the Control Panel than by clicking **Start** ➢ **Settings** ➢ **Control Panel**?

A. A two-step method is to double-click the **My Computer** icon located on your Windows Desktop and then to double-click **Control Panel**. At least that saves a click. There is a faster way, however.

Because I access the Control Panel frequently, I found it much easier to create a shortcut to the Control Panel so it's always just a double-click away from my Windows Desktop. To create a shortcut to your Control Panel, click along with Mr. Modem:

1. Right-click anywhere on your Windows Desktop and select **New ➤ Shortcut**.

2. On the **Command Line**, type: **C:\Windows\Control.exe**, then click **Next**.

3. Under **Select A Name For The Shortcut**, type **Control Panel**, then click **Finish**.

Your new shortcut to the Control Panel will appear on your Desktop; just double-click it whenever you need fast access.

If you don't like the look of the default icon associated with the shortcut—and who does?—you can easily change it to something more aesthetically pleasing by following these steps:

1. Right-click your new Control Panel shortcut icon, and select **Properties**.

2. Click the **Change Icon** button.

3. Highlight an icon from the icons displayed, then click **OK**.

 If you don't find an aesthetically appealing icon among the icons displayed, type in **C:\WINDOWS\ SYSTEM\SHELL32.DLL** in the **Filename** field and click **OK** for an additional assortment of icons.

4. Click **Apply**, then **Close**, and the new icon will appear on your Desktop.

Q. Sometimes when I have several windows open, I need to get to my Desktop to find a shortcut, but I can't find what I'm looking for. I admit it, my Desktop is a mess with too many icons, but is there any way to get to my Desktop quickly, or should I just plan on deleting some of the icons that are preventing me from finding what I'm looking for?

A. Cleaning up your Desktop would certainly help, but if you don't want to delete any of your icons, here's a quick way to view your Desktop shortcuts: Leaving all current windows open, click the **Start** button, then select **Run**; type a period (.) in the **Open** field, and click **OK**. A screen with all your Desktop icons listed alphabetically will be displayed, making it easy to access the one you're interested in.

Q. I'm always hitting the **Caps Lock** key by accident. Is there any way to turn it off completely so that it cannot become LOCKED? (See what I mean?)

A. You can't completely block the lock, but Windows does provide the ability to make it squawk at you if you do hit it. Click **My Computer** ➢ **Control Panel** ➢ **Accessibility Options**. On the **Keyboard** tab, place a check in the **Use ToggleKeys** box. Next, select the **General** tab, and clear the check box next to **Turn Off Accessibility Features**.

From this point forward, your computer will beep at you if you press the **Caps Lock**, **Num Lock**, or **Scroll Lock** keys.

 If you don't see the **Accessibility Options** icon in your Control Panel, that means those options haven't been installed from your Windows installation CD. To install them, follow these steps:

1. Click **Start** ➢ **Settings** ➢ **Control Panel**. (Eagle-eyed readers will know that you can also reach the Control Panel by double-clicking **My Computer** ➢ **Control Panel**.)

2. Double-click **Add/Remove Programs**.

3. Select the Windows Setup tab.

4. Place a check mark by **Accessibility**, and click **Details**.

5. Select **Accessibility Options**, and click **OK**.

6. Insert the Windows installation CD in your computer, and press the **Have Disk** button to complete the installation.

Q. When I use the Auto Arrange feature for the icons on my Windows 98 Desktop, everything is too crowded together. Is there any way to change that, short of turning off Auto Arrange and manually rearranging my icons?

A. The Auto Arrange feature positions your icons according to a default grid determined by Mr. Gates & Company. If you want to change the amount of spacing between each icon, place your cursor anywhere on the Desktop and right-click. Select **Properties** ➢ **Appearance**. Under **Item**, select **Icon Spacing (Vertical)**.

Note the starting number that appears in the field to the right. Adjust the number downward to move the icons closer together; increase the number to move the icons farther apart. Click **Apply** to check your adjustments. Next, select **Icon Spacing (Horizontal)**, and repeat the preceding steps.

Horizontal and vertical spacing of icons affect each other, so you may have to fine-tune your number adjustment a few times to get it just right.

Q. I'd like all my Desktop icons to line up on the right side of the screen instead of being scattered all over. I know I can drag them there, but is there a way to do it automatically?

A. You can line up your icons anywhere you'd like on your Desktop. To line them up on the right, for instance, first right-click anywhere on the Desktop, and select **Arrange Icons**. Make sure you remove the check mark next to **Auto Arrange**.

Highlight all your icons by holding down your **Shift** key and clicking each icon, or highlight all of them in one fell swoop by holding down your **Shift** key and clicking the icon that appears in the top-left corner of your screen, and then the icon in the bottom right corner of the screen. Drag and drop the icons to the far right side of your screen.

Next, right-click anywhere on the Desktop and select **Line Up Icons** to straighten them all up neatly and tidily.

Q. For some reason my **Start** button moved to the side of my computer. Can you tell me how to put it back on the bottom where it belongs?

A. The bar that contains the **Start** button is called the Taskbar. Its "home base," or default position, is at the bottom of your screen, but it's movable—as you have discovered. To escort your Taskbar back to the bottom of your screen, place your mouse cursor in any blank or empty area of the bar. While holding down your left mouse button, drag the bar to the bottom of your screen (or wherever you'd like to move it), and release the button. It will snap into place.

If you find that the Taskbar is occasionally in the way, you can easily hide it. Just right-click in an empty area of the Taskbar, click **Properties**, then choose the **Taskbar Options** tab, and place a check mark by **Auto Hide**. Click **OK** to exit. The Taskbar will remain hidden until you move your mouse cursor to the edge of the screen where the Taskbar is normally located. The Taskbar will then magically appear and remain visible until you move your cursor out of the area again.

Q. When I originally installed Windows on a computer that I rarely use, I assigned a password. For the life of me, I can't remember what password I assigned, so I'm stuck when Windows prompts me for the password. Is there a way to eliminate this problem?

A. Lots of us forget passwords, where we leave our car keys, and where we leave our cars in parking garages. I can't help you with the car keys or your car, but there is a way to remove the password you originally created when you installed Windows. This is best attempted if you have some familiarity with DOS. During the boot-up sequence of Windows, press **F8**, and choose **Command Prompt Only**. At the prompt, go to the Windows directory by typing **cd\windows**. Delete .PWL files (your password files) by typing the command **del *.pwl**. No password will be required on your next boot-up.

Type your *old* password in the **Old Password** field. Tab to the **New Password** field, and, leaving the field blank, press **Enter**. Then do the same for the **Confirm Password** field. Next time you launch Windows, you should be footloose and password-free.

If you wish to set a new password, you can do that by following this sequence: **Start ➤ Settings ➤ Control Panel ➤ Passwords**; then click **Change Windows Password**.

If you're more comfortable locating and deleting your .PWL files using Windows Explorer or some other method, use what you're most familiar with, and be comfortable.

Q. What's the difference between using My Computer and Windows Explorer?

A. Both programs are excellent for managing your computer's files—cutting, copying, moving, or deleting them—or accessing hard drives or other devices. My Computer (launched by double-clicking the **My Computer** icon on the Desktop) offers a more simplified view of your computer's internal file structure and setup. This view is often found to be particularly useful to new users.

Windows Explorer (launched by clicking **Start ➢ Programs ➢ Windows Explorer**) presents access to your entire system. Explorer opens with your C drive highlighted in the left pane. The right pane displays the files and folders contained within each folder displayed on the left. For example, after launching Windows Explorer, if you click the Windows folder that appears in the left pane, its contents will be displayed on the right.

You might notice that some folders and drives displayed on the left have a little plus (+) symbol or a minus (–) symbol next to them. You can click the plus symbol to expand the directory "tree" and display more files and folders.

Q. Somebody sent me a file as an attachment, but when I try to open it, I get the message, "This file does not have a program associated with it for performing this action. Create an association in My Computer by clicking **View ➢ Options**." What's that all about?

A. This your computer's cryptic way of telling you that it doesn't know what to do with the file you're trying to open. The *association* referred to means that when you double-click a file with a specific extension (like .TXT or .JPG) the associated software program is launched automatically and is used to open that file. So *association* in this context refers to an assigned connection between files having a particular extension and a specific software program.

Most associations are created during the installation of a program. For example, if you have Microsoft Word installed on your computer and you encounter a .DOC file, your computer knows to use Word to open that file.

In order to associate files with programs, you need to know what programs will open what files. Visit `http://extsearch.com/` if you're unsure of a particular file extension and the program needed to open it. When you find the file extension, note the name of the program needed to open it. For more information about file types and their related programs, send a blank e-mail message addressed to `filetypes@Mr.Modem.net`. You will receive information by return e-mail.

Now that you have determined what the file type is and its associated program, you need to find that program located on your computer. Using Windows Explorer or My Computer, find the file attachment that you received. Hold down the **Shift** key while you right-click the file. That will open a dialog box that invites you to open the selected file with a particular program.

When you select **Open With**, you'll see an alphabetical listing of the programs installed on your computer. Locate the name of the program needed to open the file.

Place a check mark in the box next to **Always Use This Program To Open This Type Of File** so Windows will remember the file association you have just created.

Q. I'm an old DOS guy who just switched to Windows. I hate it. Things were much simpler with DOS. I know how to delete a program under DOS, but I'm told I have to "uninstall" a program under Windows? Why can't I just go to the DOS command line, find the directory (I refuse to call them *folders*), and delete it?

A. Okay, so how do you *really* feel about Windows? (I'm just yanking your DOS prompt.) In the DOS days, installing a program was as simple as creating a directory (called a *folder* under Windows), and launching the .EXE (executable) file to install the program. Fast and simple—the proverbial piece of cake.

Under Windows, a program isn't installed in a nice, neat-and-tidy package. Pieces of a program are scattered throughout your hard drive during the installation process. In order to remove (uninstall) a program, you have to retrieve those scattered bits and pieces, and that's what an uninstaller program does.

Click **Start** ➢ **My Computer** ➢ **Control Panel** ➢ **Add/Remove Programs** to locate your Windows Uninstall program. You'll then see a list of installed programs. Just highlight the program you would like to uninstall, and click the **Add/Remove** button.

Be aware, though, that even the Windows Uninstall program doesn't remove all the tiny fragments that were placed on your hard drive during the installation process. For a more thorough uninstall, consider using a program like McAfee's Uninstaller (www.mcafee.com) or Norton's CleanSweep (www.symantec.com).

Q. I know when I install a new program that it adds new files to my computer. Is there any way I can see exactly what's added or what files are overwritten with newer versions?

A. You sure can! A little-known utility program that is part of Windows is the System File Checker, which has a neato logging feature. (Caution: The Surgeon General advises that use of the word *neato* in public may lead to jeers, taunts, and public humiliation. Do so only at your own risk.) This log will show you precisely which files were added to your computer during the installation and which files were updated with a newer version.

Launch the program by selecting **Start ➢ Programs ➢ Accessories ➢ System Tools ➢ System Information**; select **System File Checker** from the **Tools** menu.

Click the **Settings** button and then the **View Log** button to take a peek at the log.

Under **Log File**, I have mine set to **Overwrite Existing Log**, but you can also elect to append or add to your log files. You'll also have the option to go logless.

Q. I've been trying to copy and paste a link displayed on a web page into a newsletter I'm writing, but every time I click the link to try to copy it, I end up at the website itself. How can I copy a "live" link?

A. Place your cursor on the link and right-click. One of the items on the menu that will appear will be either **Copy Shortcut** (if your browser is Microsoft's Internet Explorer) or **Copy Link Location** (if your browser is Netscape Navigator). At that point, the "live" link will be placed on your Windows Clipboard. Then, navigate to the location where you would like to place the link (your word processing program, for example), right-click, and select **Paste**.

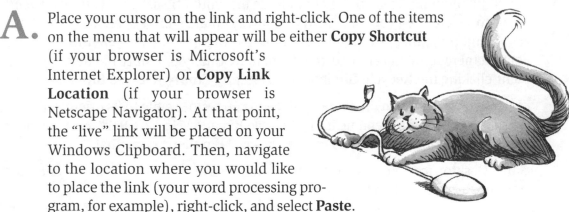

Q. I've tried to obtain telephone support from Microsoft, but there are so many phone numbers that it's confusing and frustrating. Can you help?

A. Microsoft's sheer size certainly makes it easy to get lost in a maze of telephone numbers. In the good old days (as recently as last year), Microsoft maintained a wonderful Personal Support Telephone Numbers directory on its website. But perhaps all the phone numbers overwhelmed the directory, because it no longer exists. Instead, all support-related issues are to route through Microsoft's main customer support number, 800-426-9400.

One of the best-kept secrets for those special times when you're in a technological tizzy and *must* get immediate help for a Microsoft product is their Fee-Based Personal Support service. The cost is $35 per incident, but the service is available 24 hours a day, 365 days a year, and the tech support personnel are wonderful. Call 800-936-5700 for more information or to utilize the service.

Q. I have uninstalled/deleted some programs, but their icons still remain on my Desktop. How do I remove them?

A. What you're experiencing is called the DIOBTMLO Syndrome, which is a shorthand way of saying the "dance is over but the melody lingers on."

Tidying up your Desktop by removing icons is a quick and easy process. Select the icon you wish to delete, right-click your mouse, and select **Delete**. You will be asked if you really want to delete it. If you're sure, click **Yes**, and it will vaporize before your eyes. Icons that display a little arrow in the lower left-hand corner are shortcuts and can be deleted without affecting the underlying program or document.

If it's the program itself you're about to delete, you'll be asked if you really, *really* want to delete the program. (And that always makes my knees weak.) Deleting icons and programs from the Desktop moves them to the Recycle Bin. They will remain there until you either delete them individually or empty the Recycle Bin by right-clicking the **Recycle Bin** icon and selecting **Empty Recycle Bin**.

Unless you've emptied the Recycle Bin, you can restore a file to its original location by right-clicking the filename in the Recycle Bin and selecting **Restore**. For readers familiar with this process, you can safely say, "Bin there, done that."

Some Desktop icons represent Windows programs or folders (such as My Computer and the Recycle Bin) and cannot be deleted.

Q. When trying to connect to the Internet, I get a Windows error message that says "Unable to negotiate a standard set of protocols," and no connection is established. There aren't any suggestions offered with that message, so I'm not sure what to do about it.

A. The protocols being referred to are your computer's protocol for dialing your modem in order to connect with your Internet Service Provider, and your ISP's protocol for connecting to your computer. Your ISP is probably using what's referred to as PPP (Point-to-Point Protocol), and your computer is most likely configured for SLIP (Serial Line Internet Protocol). Fancy technical talk notwithstanding, the result is that a connection (or *handshake*) cannot be established.

To change your computer to the PPP protocol, click **My Computer** ➢ **Dial-Up Networking**, and right-click the icon for your ISP. Select **Properties** ➢ **Server Types**. Below **Type Of Dial-Up Server**, you'll see a field with a little arrow to the right. Click the arrow, and select **PPP: Internet, Windows NT Server, Windows 98**. Then click **OK**, close the **Dial-Up Networking** window, and try connecting again. Chances are, it will connect just fine.

Q. I'm using the Windows dialer to establish my connection to the Internet, but it takes about 30 or 35 seconds to connect. It's a new computer with a 56Kbps modem. Why is it taking so long to connect?

A. When I received your e-mail, I hosed off my old stopwatch and timed three of my computers to determine their average dial-up connection time. All computers are running Windows 98, use 56Kbps modems, and are similarly configured. One computer required an eye-glazing 1 minute and 47 seconds to connect; another required 46 seconds; and the speed demon of the group required 34 seconds. So, based on my exhaustive, comprehensive, and not-remotely-scientific study, your 30 to 35 seconds sounds about right.

 Bear in mind that there are a number of variables that may adversely impact connection times, including the quality of the phone line involved and the amount of traffic on the network also logging in to your ISP.

Q. Is there any way to balance the sound levels of the speakers on my PC? It seems that my left speaker is louder than the right speaker, and there's only one volume control.

A. For a low-tech fix, try a wad of cotton in your left ear. That should help balance the volume. Okay, okay, so you were hoping for something a little more technical, perhaps? Windows 95 does have a sound balance control, but it's not the easiest thing in the world to find. Click **Start** ➢ **Programs** ➢ **Accessories** ➢ **Multimedia** ➢ **Volume Control**. You'll be face-to-face with a dialog box that lets you adjust the volume and the balance of your computer's sound system.

Windows 98 users should look for the little speaker icon in the System Tray (located to the left of the time display). Double-click the speaker icon to display the **Volume Control** dialog box. Among the adjustments and slidey things, you'll see a speaker balance control.

Q. How are icons added to the System Tray, and how can I remove them?

A. System Tray mini icons (or iconettes) are added either during the installation of software programs or by Windows itself. Some icons provide the ability to temporarily or permanently remove or deactivate themselves. To determine what options, if any, are available, try the following three actions on each icon. First, right-click the icon. Next, single-click the icon. Lastly, double-click the icon. One of these actions may result in a **Close**, an **Exit**, or a **Remove** option.

Q. Is there any way to speed up the performance of my CD-ROM? Sometimes searching for information on a CD seems to take forever.

A. You won't be able to dramatically increase your CD's performance, but you can do a few things to help move things along. Click **Start** ➢ **Settings** ➢ **Control Panel** ➢ **System**, and select the **Performance** tab. Then click **File System**, followed by the **CD-ROM** tab.

Move the **Supplemental Cache Size** slider to the right to allow more RAM (memory) for caching data from the CD-ROM drive, or to the left to allocate less. Not very helpful, is it?

So what should you do? It really depends on how you're using your CD and what kind of material you access. For example, CD-ROM–based programs perform better with a smaller cache because they seldom reuse or need to re-access data. For reading continuous data, such as video files, select a higher setting for Optimize Access Pattern. For reading random data, such as searching a CD for specific items, increase the Supplemental Cache Size and decrease the Optimize Access Pattern.

Q. When I attempted to copy a file to a floppy disk using Windows, I highlighted the file, right-clicked, and put my cursor on **SendTo**, but I was given only three options: **Mail Recipient**, **Fax Recipient**, and **Briefcase**. Shouldn't I be able to send the file to my A drive?

A. Usually, the A drive is included as a default SendTo option, but if it's not, that's easy to fix. The SendTo options reside in a folder cleverly named SendTo, which is found in the Windows directory.

Double-click **My Computer**, select your C drive, then double-click the **Windows** folder, and then your **SendTo** folder. You'll probably find it only contains icons for **Mail**, **Fax**, and **Briefcase**.

To add your floppy drive, leave the SendTo folder open, and click **My Computer** again. Click and drag the A-drive icon to the SendTo folder. When you release your mouse button, you will get a message saying that you can't move the icon, but Windows will be delighted to create a shortcut for you. Isn't that thoughtful? Click **Yes** to create the shortcut. You will then have an A-drive icon in your SendTo folder.

The next time you right-click a file or folder and choose the SendTo option, your floppy drive should be listed as one of the possible destinations. You can follow the same process to add additional destinations, such as a backup drive or even a specific folder on your C drive.

Q. I'm using Windows 95 Dial-Up Networking to connect to the Internet, but I'm having trouble getting it to use my regular dial-up phone number and settings as the default. Any suggestions?

A. First, it's not your fault. It's been well documented that Windows 95 is a bit flaky in this area; the good news is that Windows 98 resolves the flakiness.

The dial-up default is pretty well hidden, so just follow these steps: From your Desktop, click **Start** ≻ **Settings** ≻ **Control Panel** ≻ **Internet** ≻ **Connection** ≻ **Settings**. Near the top, you'll see a drop-down menu that let's you select which dial-up connection to use as your default. Make your selection, click **OK**, click **OK** twice again, and you'll be back at the Control Panel. Close the Control Panel and you'll be ready to start dialing for downloads using the telephone number of your choice.

Q. The squeal of my modem is driving me crazy. Is there a way to silence the modem?

A. There sure is! Double-click the **My Computer** icon on your Windows Desktop, then double-click the **Dial-Up Networking** folder icon. Right-click the icon for your dial-up connection (the name of your ISP, most likely). Select **Properties**, then click the **Configure** button.

You should see a **Speaker Volume** control and a slider bar to adjust the volume levels, ranging from **Off** to **Wake-the-Neighbors**.

If you don't see a volume control, click the **Connection** tab, press the **Advanced** button, and, in the **Extra Settings** box, type **ATM0**—that's a zero. ATM0 is a command for the modem to knock off the noise.

If you're an AOL user running Windows, click **Setup** on the **Sign On** screen, then press the **Expert Setup** button. Click the **Devices** tab, and double-click the name of your modem, which will appear on the list displayed. Select a comfortable volume level in the **Speaker Volume** field.

Q. I'm not crazy about the look of the icons that appear on my Desktop. Can I change them?

A. I also found the default icons dull and depressing and decided to break out of the pack. There are actually many icons to choose from in Windows, but they're pretty well hidden. You can smoke them out by right-clicking the icon you want to change, then selecting **Properties** ➤ **Shortcut** ➤ **Change Icon**. Choose from any of the icons displayed, or, in the **File Name** box, type in **C:\windows\system\shell32.dll**. Click any icon that catches your fancy, and back your way out by clicking **OK** until you're once again on your Desktop.

So now that you know the secret, you'll understand why, when anybody asks me if I can change my icons, I always respond, "Icon if I think Icon."

Q. I bought a new computer, and it has Windows 98 on it. Can I still install and run my Windows 95 programs on it?

A. You sure can. Windows 98 is backward compatible, which means just about any Windows 95 program is going to be happy as a clam under Windows 98—which, of course, begs the question of whether clams are really happy, or are they just good-natured bivalve molluscae by nature?

Q. I'm only seeing filenames when I use Windows Explorer, but I want to see file extensions also. How can I change my current set up to show extensions like .EXE, .TXT, etc.?

A. From your Windows Desktop, click **My Computer** ➤ **View** ➤ **Folder Options**. Click the **View** tab, and click to clear the **Hide File Extensions For Known File Types** box under **Files and Folders**.

Q. I attended one of your seminars and noticed, when you were using your computer, that any time you had to click **OK** before continuing, your cursor was automatically positioned over the **OK**. In other words, you didn't have to move your cursor to that location. How did you do that?

A. For years, I found moving my mouse cursor to be exhausting, so, in an effort to prevent MFS (Mouse Fatigue Syndrome), I purchased Microsoft's Intellimouse, available at finer mice supply houses everywhere. One of its most endearing qualities is its ability to "jump" to any selection box automatically.

 As an alternative to clicking the **OK** button, try pressing your **Enter** key instead. It won't matter where your cursor is located, and the result is the same. You can also use your **Tab** key to navigate between data entry fields and buttons.

Q. My computer isn't that old, but it seems slower than it's ever been. One of my neighbors told me that Windows just runs slowly. Should I remove Windows and try something else? I've got something like 5 gigabytes. Shouldn't it be faster?

A. Let's not mix apples and gigabytes here. The 5 gigabytes (or 5 gigs, for those of us who want to sound really cool and don't mind people snickering behind our backs) refers to the size of your hard drive. That's storage space for data—files, programs; most of the things you use your computer for are stored on its hard drive. Hard drives are measured in megabytes and gigabytes. Gigabytes are much larger than megabytes, so if you have a 5GB (gigabyte) hard drive, that's a big 'un.

But the size of your hard drive really doesn't have anything to do with the speed of your computer. It's not unlike the relationship of the size of a car's trunk to the speed of the car: It doesn't have a whole lot to do with it—unless the trunk is filled with cement. But let's not even go there.

One component that *can* affect the speed of your computer is memory (RAM), which is measured in megabytes, or MB. Many people confuse memory with storage space, so you're in good company.

In general, the more memory your computer has, the faster your system will run. If you're using Windows 98, your computer will need a minimum of 32MB of RAM. Sometimes computer manufacturers get real stingy with the RAM, but trying to run Windows with 16MB is not going to be a happy experience. Even better than 32MB of RAM would be 64MB, and if your budget can afford it, go with 128MB.

To determine how much RAM you have, click **My Computer** ➤ **Control Panel** ➤ **System** ➤ **Performance**. The first item listed is **Memory**.

If you decide you need more RAM, contact your computer manufacturer, look in your computer manual to determine the specifics of what you need, or contact a reputable, local computer repair facility.

Q. When I try to open files using WordPad, sometimes instead of seeing text I see a bunch of small squares and what looks like computer gibberish. What do I have to do to convert that into something readable?

A. Not every file you attempt to open is going to be readable. It depends on what type of file it is. For example, an .EXE (executable) file is a program file. If you try to open it with a text editor program such as WordPad, you'll see all kinds of strange characters that you won't be able to read.

Even files created using popular word processing programs like WordPerfect and Word can cause problems. Word, for example, uses a .DOC format. If you create a document using Word 6 that has a .DOC file extension and try to open it using Word 97, you'll be advised that it's a different format. The format used by Word 6 (which can be opened by WordPad under Windows 95) is not the same as the format used by Word 97 (which can be opened by WordPad under Windows 98). Clear as mud, right?

What you're experiencing with the little squares and other characters is caused by your WordPad program not being able to open the files you're attempting to open due to a file format conflict.

Your computer may have the program(s) needed to open the files you're attempting to open, but they may not be *associated* with those file formats.

For a list of the most popular file types and the programs needed to open them, send a blank e-mail addressed to `filetypes@MrModem.net`. You'll receive a free, fact-filled article about file types. So much information that I guarantee you'll lose interest within the first few paragraphs or I'll double your money back!

Q. Whenever I call for technical support, I'm always asked specific questions about my computer's configuration that I can never answer. Is there some way to find out what my computer has—type of modem, CD-ROM speed, etc.?

A. Click **Start** ≻ **Programs** ≻ **Accessories** ≻ **System Tools**, then select **System Information**. Here, you'll find some of your system's information that should get you started. One item not displayed is the size of your hard drive.

To determine the size of your hard drive and the amount of disk space you have available, double-click **My Computer**, then right-click the icon for the drive you're interested in (probably your C drive). Select **Properties** from the menu displayed.

Additional system information is available by pressing the Windows key (it has the little Windows logo) while pressing the **Pause-Break** key. (Hint: The **Pause-Break** key, if your keyboard has one, is usually located in the top, right-hand corner of your keyboard.) This will display the **System Properties** window. Select the **Device Manager** tab, and click the little plus sign appearing to the left of each of the devices displayed for additional information.

Q. How do I make an emergency start-up disk in case my computer crashes sometime in the future?

A. The old Boy Scout motto "Be prepared" has never been more applicable than in the computer era. An emergency start-up disk, also called a *boot disk* (it's short for *bootstrap*), is important to have on hand in order to jump-start your computer if your operating system fails at some point.

To create an emergency start-up disk, place a blank floppy disk in the A drive, and click **Start ➢ Settings ➢ Control Panel**. Double-click the **Add/Remove Programs** icon, which will, not surprisingly, open the **Add/Remove Programs** property box. Click the **Startup Disk** tab near the top, then click **Create Disk**. When your computer stops grinding and wheezing, label the disk *Emergency Start Disk*, and date it. Put it in a safe place, but preferably a place that you'll remember.

Make a start-up disk for each computer you use, and use each computer to make its own start-up disk. In other words, you cannot make a start-up disk on one computer and use it on other computers. If you have more than one computer, be sure to label each start-up disk with the name or identification of the computer that created the disk.

Floppy disks do deteriorate over time (don't we all?), so it's a good idea to replace your emergency start disk at least once each year. With any luck, you'll never have to use it.

Everything You Ever Wanted to Know about Bootstraps

The terms *boot* and *boot disk* in computer parlance derive from the verb *bootstrap,* which derives from the noun *bootstrap,* which probably comes from the Latin *bootus strappus,* for all I know. Regardless, it refers to a loop of leather, cloth, or other material that is sewn into the side or the top rear of a boot to assist in pulling the boot on.

The etiology of the verbs *bootstrap, bootstrapped,* or *bootstrapping* stems from using one's own initiative to accomplish a task without reliance on others, such as one might do in putting on boots. (Too much more of this explanation and we'll all need a good pair of boots.)

A *boot disk,* therefore, refers to the ability to initiate the launch, or start-up, of a computer without relying on other programs or devices. In the case of a computer or hard drive crash, inserting a boot disk into the A drive or floppy drive allows the computer to start (or boot) without interaction with the computer's hard drive.

(This mercifully concludes our superfluous explanation section.)

Q. How can I change the size of my screen's viewing area?

A. From your Windows Desktop, right-click a blank area, and select **Properties**, then the **Settings** tab. On the right side of the window that appears you'll see a slider bar under **Screen Area**. If you click to the right and left of where the slider is set, you can increase or decrease the display area. You'll see a preview of it in the little monitor image that appears in the center of the window. When you find the setting you want, click **Apply** and **OK**.

All settings depicted on the slider bar may not function, even if selected. Your computer's monitor and video card capabilities may impose limitations. It's not unlike the speedometer on my Yugo. Even though *120 mph* appears on the dial, it's just not going to happen.

Q. One of my friends told me that instead of clicking my Desktop icons to launch programs, I can use my keyboard's numeric keypad. Is that true, and if so, how can I do that?

A. Yes, it's true. It's a nifty little trick that will both amaze and irritate the heck out of your friends and family, particularly if you refer to it as *nifty.*

If you rarely use the number keys on your keyboard's numeric keypad, you can put those keys to work as single-click keyboard shortcuts for launching FUAs—Frequently Used Applications.

Start by pressing the **Num Lock** key to turn it on, if it's not already on. Next, right-click an existing Desktop shortcut icon, and select **Properties**. Select the **Shortcut** tab.

Click once inside the **Shortcut Key** field, then press the number key that you want to use to launch that particular program. Click **Apply**, then **OK**. Repeat the above steps for each program.

 For Internet Explorer, because the icon that appears on your Desktop is not a shortcut, you'll have to make a shortcut to the Desktop icon first, then follow the above steps using your new shortcut.

Q. I'm not very good at using the mouse. Is there a way to use the keyboard instead of trying to click the little pictures on my computer to start programs?

A. While most people prefer to click the icons or little pictures that appear on their Desktop to launch a software program, if you prefer to use keystrokes instead of mouse clicks, you can easily create what are called hot keys. To do this, right-click any Desktop icon you would like to create a hot key for, and select **Properties**. Click the **Shortcut** tab, and click once in the **Shortcut Key** field.

Type in the letter or the number you would like assigned to the *Ctrl + Alt* combination. For example, enter the letter **K** if you would like the hot-key combination to be *Ctrl + Alt + K* to launch a particular program. Then click **Apply**, followed by **Close**.

Assigning a hot key will allow you to move quickly to a program at any time, just by pressing your assigned keystroke combination.

Q. I'd like to remove a program from my computer, but a warning comes up telling me that removing it "may impact one or more registered programs." Now what?

A. When you install a software program using Windows, it's automatically entered into the Windows Registry. This registration, sometimes referred to as an *association*, is what allows you to double-click a file and have the correct program needed to display that file launch automatically. Windows accomplishes that by recognizing the three-letter filename extension, such as .TXT, .JPG, or .DOC, and knowing what program is needed to open a file format of that type.

So how does this information relate to your situation? The message you're seeing indicates that you'll no longer be able to double-click a file associated with the program you want to uninstall and have that program start automatically—which, of course, is exactly what you'd expect after removing it.

For additional information about file types and the programs needed to open them, send a blank e-mail to `filetypes@MrModem.net`. You'll receive a free, informative article by return e-mail.

Q. I know that pressing **Alt** and certain number combinations will result in symbols being inserted into documents or e-mail. The only one I know is *Alt + 0162*, which creates the ¢ (cents) sign. How can I learn what other symbols are available?

A. Many special characters can be created within programs running under Windows. If your e-mail program is a Windows-based program, for example, you can insert special characters into your e-mail messages (the same with your word processor, spreadsheet, or other programs).

To create special characters and symbols, follow these steps:

1. Enable the number pad on your keyboard by pressing the **Num Lock** key. (On your keyboard, you will usually see a small light or other indication when the number pad is toggled on.)

2. Hold down the **Alt** key, then, using the numeric keypad, type the number that is associated with the special character you would like to use.

3. Release the **Alt** key.

4. The special character will appear in the location of your cursor.

For example, To type the little ™ symbol (for trademark), as in *Mr. Modem*™, hold down the **Alt** key, type the numbers **0153** using the number pad, then release the **Alt** key. Voilà! (Hint: The little accent over the *a* in *voilà* was created by using *Alt + 0224*.) Have fun!

For a list of special characters, symbols, and the Alt + numbers needed to create them, send an e-mail addressed to `characters@MrModem.net`. By return e-mail, you'll receive more characters than you can shake a † at.

Q. When my computer boots up, there's a lot of text that scrolls by too quickly to read. I'd like to slow that down so I can take a look at it. Is there any way to do that without fouling up the startup process?

A. Somewhere on the right side of your computer keyboard—sometimes near the top, sometimes near the bottom—you'll see the little-used **Pause** key. When you see that text start to scroll by, just press the **Pause** key and you'll be able to freeze the text long enough to read it. Press any key to resume scrolling. This works great for pausing scrolling text during your computer's boot-up sequence, but it doesn't work in all Windows programs.

Scrollin', Scrollin', Scrollin': The Mystery behind the Blur

The scrolling text you see as a blur serves a similar purpose as the dashboard lights that appear when you start your car, which also generally disappear before you have a chance to read the text that appears on the face of each light. The scrolling text on your computer is the result of your computer waking up and checking itself out, identifying peripheral devices (such as printers, scanners, external hard drives, etc.) that may be attached to it, running a virus scan (if you have a virus-checking program installed), checking out its own memory, etc.

All this self-examination is intended to occur without your intervention, so don't be overly concerned that it all flashes by faster than you can read. If a problem is encountered, an unnerving message will generally appear and ruin your day. Until that occurs, consider no news to be good news.

Q. How can I tell how much free hard disk space I have?

A. There are a couple of ways you can check the amount of free (and used) hard drive space, one more colorful than the other. The less colorful method is to double-click **My Computer**; then, from the **View** menu, select **As Web Page**. Next, select the drive you would like to check (probably the C drive) by clicking once on the appropriate icon. The status of your drive (including total capacity, free space, and used space) will be displayed on the left side of the screen. You'll see numbers followed by the letters *MB* or *GB*.

MB stands for megabyte, and GB stands for gigabyte. A gigabyte is a thousand megabytes, and a thousand gigabytes is a terabyte. A thousand terabytes is an overbite, which can be resolved by any competent orthodontist. (It's not nice to groan at Mr. Modem!)

For a more colorful, graphical presentation, follow the same initial steps outlined above, but do not select **View ➤ As Web Page**. Instead, select **View Large Icons**, **Small Icons**, **List**, or **Details**.

Move your cursor to the appropriate drive to select it. Right-click and choose **Properties**. Click the **General** tab. You will see a graphical depiction of your hard drive, the used space appearing in blue and the free space appearing in pink.

You can even select your A drive (floppy drive) to determine how much free space remains on a floppy disk.

Q. My hard drive is almost full, so I know I have to delete some files or programs to free up some additional room. Are there some "throw-away" files or things that I should get rid of first?

A. If your computer is like most computers, there's a fair amount of hard disk space that's consumed by programs you never use and files that you probably don't even know exist.

First, empty the Recycle Bin. Right-click the **Recycle Bin** icon, then select **Empty**. (Deleting files on your computer sends them to the Recycle Bin, where they remain until you empty it.)

Next, jettison all the old *cached* files that Netscape Navigator or Internet Explorer have saved from your previous web surfing. These files are copies of web pages that you have visited and are stored in your browser for faster display on subsequent visits to those sites. Follow either of the following steps:

- If you're using Netscape Navigator 4 or higher, click **Edit** ➢ **Preferences**, then click the little plus sign to the left of **Advanced**, and select **Cache**. Click the **Clear Disk Cache** button, followed by **OK**.

- Internet Explorer 5.*x* users should click **Tools** ➢ **Internet Options**. Select the **General** tab and, under **Temporary Internet Files**, click the **Delete Files** button.

Next, launch a search-and-destroy mission for temporary, or .TMP, files on your hard drive. These are files that you're not using anymore, and even though each one is very small, they can build up over time and consume a lot of hard disk space. Click **Start** ➢ **Find** ➢ **Files Or Folders**. In the **Named** field, type ***.tmp**, and in the **Look In:** field, be sure your C drive (or other appropriate drive) is selected. Click the **Find Now** button and your hard drive will be searched for .TMP files, which will be displayed in the window below where they can be selected and deleted, if they're not currently in use.

We're almost done. Next, go to your Control Panel (**My Computer** ➢ **Control Panel**), click the **Add/Remove Programs** icon, and uninstall any programs you're not using. Games, in particular, can gobble up disk space, so if you've got some oldie-but-goodie games you can remove, you'll free up some additional digital real estate.

Lastly, close all open programs and run Disk Defragmenter. Defragging your hard drive will consolidate data on your hard drive and can free up 15 or 20 percent of your disk space, particularly if you haven't defragmented lately. Click **Start** ➢ **Programs** ➢ **Accessories** ➢ **System Tools** ➢ **Disk Defragmenter**.

Defragmenting can take hours, depending on the size of your hard drive and how fragmented it is. Once you start defragmenting, walk away from your computer, have lunch, clean out a closet, or start construction on that room you've been meaning to add to your home. Trust me, you'll have time. Check your computer an hour or so after starting the defragmenter to see how things are progressing, but remember the old axiom "A watched hard drive never defrags."

Q. When I try to use Disk Defragmenter or Scan Disk, sometimes my computer freezes up or I'll get a message that says the program has attempted to start ten times and failed. What's causing that?

A. If your computer seems to stall when you are trying to defragment or scan the hard drive, chances are good that there's some program running in the background preventing it from completing its chores. Before attempting a defrag or Scan Disk you should close all tasks except Explorer and Systray. You can do this by pressing **CTRL + ALT + DEL** and end each of the tasks you see displayed there.

Q. I'm left-handed and would like to reverse the functions of the left and right mouse buttons. Is that possible?

A. I'm also left-handed, and yes, you can reverse the functions of your mouse buttons. Before you do, though, be sure to do this: If you've been using a computer for a period of time, you're probably fairly comfortable using a right-handed mouse. We southpaws tend to adapt to right-handed devices like scissors, can-openers, and mouses—mice (well, you know). If you've ever tried to use a left-handed scissors or other device, it can take some getting used to, and so can getting comfortable with a left-handed mouse.

If you're sure you'd like to reverse the functions of your mouse buttons so that the left button will act as the right one does now, and vice versa, click **Start ➢ Settings ➢ Control Panel ➢ Mouse**. Look for the **Button** configuration box, and check the left-handed option. Then click **OK**.

 If you share your computer with others, be sure to tell them you've reversed the mouse buttons. Either that or sit back, relax, and wait for the high-tech hijinks to begin! I suspect it would be a lot of fun to see how long it took for a right-handed person to discover that he or she was using a left-handed mouse.

Q. You say in your *Mr. Modem's Internet Guide for Seniors* (www.MrModem.net) book to be sure to obtain the Windows 98 installation CD with any new computer purchased. I was shopping for a new computer and asked about that. The sales person said they don't provide the CD and told me that I could make my own back-up copy of Windows. What should I do?

A. There is an emerging trend among some computer manufacturers to not provide the Windows 98 installation CD in order to save a few dollars. I would not purchase a new computer without obtaining the installation CD. If the store or manufacturer is unable or unwilling to provide it, I would purchase the computer elsewhere.

It may be suggested to you that you can simply create your own Windows installation disks using the built-in Windows utility program for that purpose. Baloney! Windows is a huge program, and to do that would require tons of floppy disks and hours of your time. It's not your responsibility. Obtain the installation CD, or don't buy the computer. It's that simple.

The reason I'm so adamant that you have the Windows installation CD-ROM is this: While using your computer, there may be occasions when you will be prompted to insert the installation CD to install a specific driver file (a program that provides instructions to hardware), to install a new Windows component, or in the event of a system crash. If you need assistance at that time, your friendly salesperson probably won't be around to lend a helping hand.

Q. I'm still trying to figure out what the *Windows* key on my keyboard is used for. Any ideas?

A. The **Windows** key, or **WinKey** (pronounced *winkie* among friends), is located between the **Ctrl** and **Alt** keys on newer keyboards. This key is used in conjunction with other keys to perform certain tasks. I've found that the highest-and-best use for the **WinKey** is in conjunction with the **D** key. Pressing **WinKey** and **D** will close all open windows and take you right to your Desktop. Press **WinKey** and **D** again and you'll return precisely where you were. (This only works with Windows 98.)

Q. When I'm typingg, I keepp getting reppeat characters. I'm not a fast tyypist, and I'm thinkking that mightt be parrt of the probblemm. It'ss veryy annoyiing.

A. Depending on how fast your keyboard's repeat delay is set for, a slight pause in your typing may result in character repetition, such as you're experiencing. To remedy the problem, double-click **My Computer** ➤ **Control Panel** ➤ **Keyboard**. Adjust how much time elapses before characters begin repeating by adjusting the **Repeat Delay** slider—also called "the little slidey thing." Use the test area provided to determine the best rate for your typing speed and watch your repeating-key problem disappearrrrrrrrr. When you find the perfect rate, be sure to click the **OK** button to preserve your new setting.

Q. I bought a new computer, and the three little buttons in the upper-right corner that open and close each window are much too small. Is there any way to increase their size?

A. Those three buttons, formally known (from left to right) as the **Minimize, Maximize/Restore**, and **Close** buttons, can be enlarged by following these steps:

1. Right-click any blank area of your Desktop.

2. Choose **Properties**.

3. In the **Display Properties** dialog box, click the **Appearance** tab.

4. In the **Item** list, select **Caption Buttons**.

5. To enlarge the buttons, click the up arrow on the **Size** box. (You can see your changes in the **Preview** area.)

6. When the buttons are the size you want, click **OK**.

Q. I'm running out of disk space on my computer, so I'm continually getting warning messages about it. I feel bad enough, but do I have to keep being reminded about it every time I start my computer? Is there any way to stop the warnings?

A. Nag, nag, nag. It does get old, doesn't it? Yes, you can get rid of the annoying low-disk-space warning by clicking along with Mr. Modem in the following sequence: **Start Programs** ➤ **Accessories** ➤ **System Tools** ➤ **Disk Cleanup**. You'll be prompted to select the drive you wish to clean up. In most cases, you'll want the default C drive, so click **OK** or change to the appropriate drive.

Click the **Settings** tab. Remove the check mark next to the box labeled **If This Drive Runs Low On Disk Space, Automatically Run Disk Cleanup**, then click **OK**.

Presto! No more warning messages—at least until the next time your disk space runs low—but be sure to keep an eye on your available disk space. You really don't want to run out.

It's also possible that the warning message you're receiving is a virtual memory issue. Sounds very high-tech, but all that means is that if you're running more programs than can cram into RAM (your computer's short-term memory) your computer will allocate a portion of your hard drive and trick itself into believing that it has more memory than it actually has. The hard drive space your computer will commandeer is called a "swap file." This can result in the type of warning message you have received.

To check the size of your virtual memory, right-click the **My Computer** icon, select **Properties** ➢ **Performance** ➢ **Virtual Memory**. The recommended setting is to let Windows manage virtual memory and keep your opinions to yourself. If you wish to override the default setting, you can select the peevish-sounding **Let Me Specify My Own Virtual Memory Settings**.

If you do decide to adjust the size of your virtual memory (swap file), I'd recommend a setting equal to approximately twice the amount of RAM you have. So if you have 64MB of RAM, 128-ish should be fine.

Before changing the size of your virtual memory, be sure to shut down all programs and run Disk Defragmenter to tidy up your hard drive so things will run more efficiently. To launch Disk Defragmenter, click **Start** ➢ **Programs** ➢ **Accessories** ➢ **System Tools** ➢ **Disk Defragmenter**.

Q. If my computer doesn't shut down properly, Windows runs ScanDisk the next time I boot up. When it finds lost file fragments, it asks if I want them saved in a file. I always say yes, but it doesn't tell me where it puts these files or what the filenames are. Any ideas?

A. These fragments are placed in files with a .CHK extension, and the filename is usually something like FILE0000.CHK, FILE0001.CHK, etc. To find these files, click **Start** ➢ **Find** ➢ **Files Or Folders**. Under the **Name & Location** tab, in the **Named** field, type *.**CHK**, and click the **Find Now** button. If you want to free up some disk space, delete any old .CHK files you may find.

Q. I recently bought a new computer. When I click the **Start** button and go to **Programs**, I see a whole bunch of computer programs. Where did these programs come from, and should I be using them?

A. Those programs arrived with your computer the day you brought it home. Some of the programs will be worthwhile, but others aren't worth their weight in modem fumes. Each computer manufacturer provides a different assortment of installed computer programs.

The best way to determine what programs you have and how useful any of them might be to you is to try each one. But don't try to learn them all at once, and don't attempt to master each one of them. Just take a quick look at one each day or one each week, as your schedule permits, and get a feel for what each program does. You'll know quickly whether it's something worth exploring in greater depth. Simply click each program to launch it and see what it does. You won't hurt anything, so have fun and explore.

Q. When I click **Start** ➤ **Programs**, the list of programs isn't entirely in alphabetical order. Some are, some aren't. How can I alphabetize the list of programs on my computer?

A. In their natural habitat, programs are listed alphabetically. Unfortunately, when Microsoft's Internet Explorer 4 browser appeared on the scene, newly installed programs started appearing at the bottom of the list. The fix is easy and only varies slightly, depending on whether you're using Internet Explorer 4.x or 5.x.

If you're using Internet Explorer 4.x, click **Start** ➤ **Programs**. Then, with the list of programs displayed, you can move a program to any location by holding down the left mouse button and dragging the program to its new location. When you arrive at its final destination, release the left mouse button.

If you have Internet Explorer 5.x, it's even easier. Click **Start** ➤ **Programs**, then right-click any program listed, and select **Sort By Name** from the menu presented.

A handy, free utility program named Q-Sort also lets you rearrange your Start menu. You can download this program from `www.hyperQ.com`.

Q. I'm using Windows 98, and I'm not sure whether I should upgrade to Windows 98 Second Edition or go with Windows 2000. Any thoughts?

A. Windows 2000 is the latest version of Windows NT (Version 5), and it really isn't intended for home users. Instead, it's designed for businesses and organizations that run large networks. I would not recommend Windows 2000 for an individual user.

Windows 98 Second Edition, as the name implies, is an "improved" version of Windows 98. It's improved because it incorporates all the bug fixes and patches that Microsoft has made available on its website since Windows 98 made its debut.

The one new feature that's worth mentioning in Windows 98 Second Edition is modem sharing. Modem sharing, technically known as ICS or Internet Connection Sharing, allows two or more computers to share a single modem and Internet connection, assuming the computers are networked. This can be a convenient feature if you have other family members online or even if you have two computers yourself and want to connect them both to the Internet. Windows 98 Second Edition also includes Internet Explorer 5 and NetMeeting 3, for Internet-based conferencing.

For more information about Windows 98 Second Edition, visit the Windows 98 Product and Technology Catalog at `www.microsoft.com/catalog/default.asp`.

So, should you move to Windows 98 Second Edition? Mr. Modem believes in keeping life simple, so my advice would be that if you're using Windows 98 and it's working well for you—and you don't have a burning need for modem sharing—leave well enough alone. The old axiom "If it ain't broke, don't fix it" is about as close to the gospel as it gets when it comes to computer software.

Mr. Modem's Related Websites

Blink   Organize and store your bookmarks online; access them from anywhere, using any web browser.

> www.blink.com/

Download.com   One of the largest directories of downloadable software on the Web. Look for software for almost any use you can imagine. Software is sorted by application category and by operating system. Also included are reviews and ratings, as well as lists of the most frequently downloaded programs.

> http://download.cnet.com/downloads/

My Updates   If you find it hard to keep current with all the updates available for your software, check out this free service. Simply register, log in, and initialize the service. It then searches the Web for available updates for the software installed on your system.

> http://updates.zdnet.com

Windows 95/98 Annoyances   Though this site's name sounds like it might be little more than a collection of rants, it actually contains lots of real tips from real users working with Windows 95 and Windows 98.

> www.annoyances.org/win95

> www.annoyances.org/win98

Windows 95, 98 and ME Home Pages   Ground zero for Windows 95/98 and Millennium Edition information.

> www.microsoft.com/windows95/default.asp

> www.microsoft.com/windows98/default.asp

> www.microsoft.com/windowsME/default.asp

Computers: Can't Live with 'Em, Can't Live without 'Em

Everywhere we turn today, we're eyeball to monitor with computers. In this chapter, I'll focus on computer-related questions in general and address questions spanning everything from buying a computer, to using a computer, to deciding what to do with an old computer.

Q. When I send a fax using a software program, is it necessary for the recipient to also have a fax modem, or can they receive it through a standard fax machine? Also, when you send a fax to a location that has its machine or computer turned off, will the fax be received automatically when it's turned back on?

A. You can use fax software to send documents to a computer with a fax modem or to a regular fax machine. However, if you're sending to a computer, the computer has to be turned on, connected to a phone line, with fax software of its own properly loaded. If the computer or fax machine at the other end is turned off, the transmission will fail. But don't take it personally. It happens to all of us at one time or another.

It's a good idea to check with the recipient to determine whether he or she needs to do anything special in order to receive a fax, such as turning on the fax machine or launching their fax software.

Q. The person who helped me set up my computer kept referring to something that sounded like ex-ee—as in "ex-ee file." I felt foolish asking because it sounded like something I should know. Are you capable of explaining what it is in terms that somebody like me can understand?

A. I certainly hope so—but you'll be the judge of that. The "ex-ee" file you referred to is actually spelled .*EXE*, which is short for *executable*. An .EXE file (a file with the .EXE extension) is a self-extracting, or self-launching file that automatically runs—meaning that it does something—when you double-click it. For example, `soli-taire.exe` is the filename of the solitaire program that is included with Windows (**Start ➢ Programs ➢ Accessories ➢ Games ➢ Solitaire**). Double-click it and you can spend hours frittering away your precious time—which, of course, is the objective of all computing.

Q. What kinds of routine maintenance should I be doing on my computer?

A. Preventative maintenance is a good idea whether it's your car, home, or computer. Here are five items that will help keep your computer in tip-top shape:

- Don't turn your computer on and off throughout the day. (See the following question and answer for additional information.)

- Use a surge protector to protect your computer from electrical spikes or brownouts.

- Use Windows ScanDisk and Disk Defragmenter at least once a month to keep your hard drive healthy. To access both utility programs, double-click **My Computer**, then right-click the C-drive icon. Select **Properties**, then the **Tools** tab. Use the **Check Now** and **Defragment Now** buttons. Always run ScanDisk first, followed by Disk Defragmenter. ScanDisk will fix any surface errors on your hard drive; Disk Defragmenter will organize the data on your hard drive so it can be accessed more efficiently.

- Always use a virus-checking software program. Any commercial program is fine as long as you keep the program updated so it can check for newly discovered viruses. My favorite virus-checking software programs are McAfee's VirusScan (www.mcafee.com) and Norton's AntiVirus (www.symantec.com).

- Clean the area around your computer regularly to eliminate the dreaded DBB (Dust Bunny Buildup) syndrome. Use compressed air to blow out dust from the cooling fan blades, but do *not* blow air on any exposed circuits or into any open ports. Instead, vacuum your ports in order to suck the disgusting filth out rather than blow it into your computer, and use a cloth to remove the lovely coating of "fur" from the fan intake cooling vents.

If you can raise your computer off the floor even a few inches, this can help decrease the amount of dust, pet fur, and small rodents that might get sucked into your computer through normal use.

Q. Should I leave my computer on all the time or turn it on and off? I keep hearing different things from different people. What's your opinion?

A. There's no hard-and-fast rule regarding when to turn off your computer. Some people leave it on all the time, especially if they use it frequently. Some people turn it on only when they need to use it and then shut it down.

If you use your desktop computer every day, I recommend leaving it on all the time, but using the Power Management features of your computer to permit your computer and monitor to gear down, or hibernate, when they're not being used. Most computer crashes and related problems occur during the boot-up, when power surges into the computer, so if you use your computer daily, consider leaving it on but in cyber-snooze mode when not in use.

To access your Power Management features, right-click any blank area of your Desktop, and select **Properties** from the menu that appears. Click the **Screen Saver** tab, then press the **Settings** button.

At the bottom of the **Power Management Properties** dialog box, you'll see **Turn Off Monitor** and **Turn Off Hard Disks**, each followed by a field. Use the little arrow to the right of this field to select the appropriate time before the desired action begins. Click **Apply**, then **OK** once you have entered your settings.

I leave my computers on all the time but, using Power Management, have my monitor set to "go dark" after one hour, and my hard drive takes a break after 30 minutes of inactivity. Go ahead and experiment with different time settings to accommodate your schedule and personal preference. Both your monitor and your hard drive will spring to life again as soon as you press any key or use your mouse.

With your Power Management features engaged, it won't hurt your computer to leave it on all the time. If you only use your computer occasionally during the week and you do elect to turn it on and off each time, just power up once a day. Don't think of your computer as you would a light switch and turn it on and off when you enter and leave the room. If you do, sooner or later, your computer will rebel, and the results won't be pretty.

CONSERVATION NOTE: If you live in an area where power shortages are an ongoing problem, follow the advice of your local power authorities. If it's recommended that computers be turned off when not in use (a computer will consume approximately $2 to $5 per month in electricity), follow that advice and do your part to conserve!

Q. I leave my computer on all the time and was wondering whether there is a program that will keep track of the amount of time my computer is running.

A. The answer is yes, but let me offer both a high-tech and a low-tech solution to this. The low-tech approach is to note the start and stop times on a piece of paper and, utilizing the miracle of tape, affix it to your monitor.

The high-tech approach uses a program that is included in Windows 98. To utilize it, follow these digital dance steps: **Start** ➢ **Programs** ➢ **Accessories** ➢ **System Tools**, and select **System Information**. In addition to lots of information about your computer system, you'll see an item labeled **Uptime**, which records the days, hours, minutes, and seconds since your last reboot of Windows.

Q. What is ScanDisk?

A. *ScanDisk* is a Windows program—it's included with Windows—that checks your hard drive for errors and corrects any errors found. ScanDisk offers two types of scans: Standard, which looks for file errors, and Thorough, which scans the surface of your hard drive looking for bad sectors. When it finds defective areas of your hard drive, it takes them out of service so data won't be written to them and possibly be lost in the process.

To run ScanDisk, click **My Computer**, right-click the icon of the drive you want to check (typically the C drive), and choose **Properties**. Select the **Tools** tab, and click **Check Now**.

When the **ScanDisk** window appears, select either **Standard** or **Thorough**, then click the **Start** button. I always run the Thorough test. It may take several hours, but it's important to check out the surface of your hard drive and correct any errors discovered, periodically—at least once a month.

Q. I'm thinking about buying a new computer, but there are so many different sizes and shapes of cases. Is there one type that's better than another?

A. There are two styles of cases: the desktop and the tower. *Desktop* cases lie flat (horizontal) on the desk, and the monitor typically is perched on top of the case—sometimes referred to as the *CPU*, or Central Processing Unit. (It's also referred to as the *box*.) *Tower* cases look like desktop cases standing on end and usually are positioned on the floor, under or next to a desk.

Tower cases come in three sizes: small (or mini), medium (or midsized), and the big boy, the full-sized tower. Tower cases are generally larger than desktop cases and allow more room for internal and external expansion by providing additional areas (called *bays*) for adding hard drives, CD-ROM drives, and other devices.

A good rule of thumb is to choose a case size that will fit in your working environment. The primary advantage of a tower case, practically speaking, is that it sits on the floor, so it doesn't tie up valuable desktop real estate.

Q. Can't I just turn my desktop case into a tower by turning it on its side and putting it on the floor?

A. Actually, you can. Years ago, there was a concern that hard drives wouldn't function properly if turned sideways, but that's not a concern with modern hard drives.

The only possible problem might be if your computer has a CD-ROM drive that needs to remain in a horizontal position to accommodate the CD. If you turn your desktop case on its side so every time you attempt to insert a CD it slips out and falls on the floor, that could get old in a big hurry.

Q. What does the *power supply* part of a computer do? If a computer uses electricity, why does it need a power supply?

A. Your computer's *power supply* is actually a power converter that transforms AC (alternating current) from your home or your office electrical outlet into the 5 and 12 volts of DC (direct current) required by your computer. In addition to this conversion process, every power supply has a cooling fan that forces air through your computer's case to keep other components within operating temperatures. (Pentium chips run particularly hot, so cooling is very important.)

When positioning your computer under a desk, for example, be sure you leave room for ventilation around the fan area. The whirring sound you hear when your computer is running is the fan. If your computer ever suddenly gets very quiet—no whirring sound to be heard—shut everything down immediately. Trying to operate a computer without a cooling fan is like trying to run a car without a cooling system: It's going to overheat very quickly and can do permanent (and expensive) damage if it's not shut down in time.

Q. What's the difference between a serial port, a parallel port, and an LPT port?

A. There are two types of *serial ports* that are easy to identify visually: 9-pin ports (with five pins on the top row and four pins on the bottom), and 25-pin ports (with 13 pins on the top row and 12 on the bottom). Serial ports are always male ports, with the pins sticking out of the actual port on the computer. Any time you see a small, 9-pin port, chances are it's a serial port. You'll rarely encounter a 25-pin serial port. So here's Mr. Modem's mnemonic device of the day: Think *s* for small and *s* for serial.

Parallel ports are 25-pin ports and are physically larger than serial ports, plus they're always female ports, meaning they have female pin slots into which a parallel cable is plugged.

An *LPT port* is the same as a parallel port. LPT stands for *line printer,* and this is typically your printer port. Usually it's specified as an LPT1 port or an LPT2 port, if your computer has more than one.

Other than the size differences between the ports, there is also a difference in the way each transmits data. A serial port transmits data one bit at a time, while parallel ports essentially transmit entire words at a time, which is why most printers use parallel ports. Serial ports are slower than parallel ports, so if you have to choose between a serial port or a parallel port for a printer or other peripheral device—assuming you have an available parallel port—opt for the parallel.

Q. What does it mean to zip a file?

A. *Zipping* refers to compressing or compacting a file. The de facto standard in the PC world for zipping is WinZip software, available at www.winzip.com.

When sending large files as attachments to e-mail, or when storing files on your own computer, zipping a file is a way to reduce the size of the file without affecting the data. Transmitting zipped files via the Internet is faster than sending uncompressed or unzipped files that, because of their size, will take longer to transmit. The recipient of a zipped file must also have the appropriate software in order to unzip, or decompress, the file.

Q. Is a Zip disk the same thing as a zipped file?

A. No, it's not. A *Zip disk* looks like a thick floppy disk. Current Zip disks can store from 100MB up to 250MB of data—more than entire hard drives could store just a few years ago. Zip disks require a special Zip drive, which can be either internal or external to your computer. For more information about Zip disks and drives, visit www.iomega.com.

A *zipped file* is a compressed or compacted file. This is accomplished using a software utility program called WinZip. For more information about WinZip, visit www.winzip.com.

Q. I downloaded a file, and now I can't find it on my computer. Help!

A. Oh, noooooo! Rule Number 1: Don't panic. The file couldn't have gone very far.

Start your search for the wayward file by using the Windows Find command to search your hard drive. Go to **Start ➢ Find ➢ Files Or Folders**.

In the **Named** box, type in the name of the file you downloaded. Let's say you downloaded a file named MrModem.txt. Type **MrModem.txt** in the **Named** box, and be sure the **Look In:** field displays your C drive or other appropriate drive. Place a check mark in the box to the left of **Include Subfolders**. Then click the **Find Now** button.

Use the **Containing Text:** field if you recall any of the contents of the file—a word or phrase, for example. Providing even a snippet of specific text can help narrow (and thus speed up) your search. Otherwise, leave this field blank.

In the bottom pane of the **Find** window, the results of your search will display where the file is located. To open the file from the **Find** window, simply double-click the name of the file, or right-click the filename, then select **Open** in the pop-up menu.

Q. My C-drive disk space is running low, but I have D, E, and F drives available. Can I transfer some of the programs from my C drive to one of the other drives? Can I program the computer to automatically install programs on the other drives from this point forward, since space is running low?

A. You can easily direct the installation of a program to a drive other than your C drive. When the **Install** Wizard shows you the directory it's going to install a new program into, it will ask you if you want to go with the default (usually the C drive) or choose a different location. At that point, simply point it to the drive you want to install to by using the **Browse** button—or there might be a little arrow that allows you to "point" to another hard drive or destination location.

As far as copying programs from your C drive to one of the other drives, that's not a good idea because there are associated files that are installed in other areas of your computer during the installation process. If you move a program after it's been installed, you're taking a chance that some of its files will not be moved with it, and that will spell trouble when it's time to run the program.

If you want to move a program from one drive to another, the best way to accomplish that is to remove the program (uninstall it) from your C drive, then reinstall it on a different drive. This is not only the recommended way to do it, but it's a lot safer than trying to copy or move programs from one drive to another.

Q. What is Linux?

A. Although it sounds like a friend of Snoopy, *Linux* is actually a computer operating system that many folks consider an alternative to Microsoft Windows, Unix, or DOS. There are many pros and cons surrounding the use of Linux. Some feel as an operating system it's much more stable and easier to use than Windows. Others feel it's so new that it lacks applications (software), and its long-term reliability isn't proven.

Linux was originally developed by a Helsinki University student named Linus Torvalds. After others began using the program, a friend of Linus dubbed his program *Linux*, short for "Linus's Unix." How's that for a piece of semi-worthless information?

For most average computer users, my recommendation is to stick with Windows. Linux has a ways to go before it's truly mainstream and a realistically viable alternative to Windows, though it is growing in popularity. You can learn more about Linux by visiting the LinuxMall at www.linuxmall.com.

Q. My computer tells me I have an error when I turn it on, and it won't start up. The error message reads "Invalid system disk. Replace the disk, and then press any key." Could the hard drive be defective?

A. Chances are, your hard drive is fine. It sounds like you have a 3.5-inch floppy diskette in the floppy drive. Take the diskette out, and then boot (start) your computer. Leaving a disk in your computer when booting up can either result in the error message you received or a "Non-system disk or disk error" message.

When your computer boots up, it looks to the floppy drive first, then it looks to your hard drive for its operating instructions. This is a good thing because if you ever do have a hard drive problem you'll be able to boot up from your emergency start-up disk, which you will insert into your 3.5-inch drive.

Q. When I start up my computer, I hear the 3.5-inch floppy drive making noises like it's trying to read a disk, but there's no disk there. Any idea what the problem is?

A. Fear not! What you are hearing is your computer going through what is known as POST, or power-on self test. (Don't you just LTA—love these acronyms?) The test is perfectly normal and is designed, among other things, to check your computer's memory, to establish contact with your hard drive and your floppy drive, and to report any start-up problems to you.

Q. What's an emergency boot disk, why do I need one, and how do I get one?

A. So many questions, so little time! An *emergency boot disk* is a "safety-net" type of back-up disk that can be used to jump-start your computer if Windows is having problems. You'll create it using Windows, and an emergency boot disk should be created on each computer for use with that specific computer.

An emergency boot disk contains the necessary files to boot up your computer in case of an emergency, as well as some diagnostic assistance to help locate and fix problems.

Create an emergency boot disk by following these steps: Click **Start** ➢ **Settings** ➢ **Control Panel**, then double-click the **Add/Remove Programs** icon. Select the **Startup Disk** tab, place a blank floppy in your disk drive, and click **Create Disk**. Disks deteriorate over time, so it's a good idea to replace your start-up disks at least once each year.

Q. I've got a 4× CD-ROM. I've been told that if I upgrade it to a 24× I'll see a big improvement in games and other multimedia programs. Is it worth the expense?

A. When it comes to games, most are going to work fine on a 4×, sometimes referred to as a *four-speed* or a *four-by* CD-ROM, because most of the game is loaded into your computer's memory. A faster CD drive could help prevent slowdowns in game action, however. When using a CD for games, the accompanying music is what's primarily running off the CD.

One big reason to upgrade to a 24× (or faster) CD-ROM drive would be to install programs and to load games faster. A 24× drive can transfer data from the CD at up to 3.6MB (megabytes) per second, compared to a relatively pokey 600KB (kilobytes) per second for a 4× CD.

A faster CD-ROM drive can also speed up the process of finding information on a CD (for example, when using a multimedia encyclopedia or one of those handy CD libraries that contain 12 billion telephone numbers). You never know when you might need to make an emergency call to Zimbabwe.

Q. I tried to play a musical CD by slipping it into my desktop computer's CD-ROM drive, but it won't play. Music from websites seem to play fine, though. Any ideas?

A. Sounds like—no pun intended—the little cable that connects your CD-ROM drive to your computer's sound card might be the culprit. It could be loose or simply not be connected. Call or e-mail your computer manufacturer's tech support folks to escort you through the repair process, if you're so inclined. As an alternative, take the computer to any reputable computer repair facility and they'll hook you up faster than your neighbors can say, "Will you turn that darned thing down?"

Q. I'm trying to create an advertising flyer but want to see what it's going to look like when it's full of text. I've seen other document samples that have dummy text or filler copy in them. How is that done?

A. Word 97 and Word 2000 provide an undocumented feature that lets you create dummy text for this purpose. To do this, type **=Rand(p,s)** on a blank line, and press **Enter**. Substitute numbers for the *p* and the *s* to indicate how many paragraphs and sentences, respectively, you want to fill. For example, *=Rand(9,6)* inserts nine paragraphs, each containing six sentences. All sentences consist of the sentence "The quick brown fox jumps over the lazy dog." (Nobody said it was going to be interesting text.)

Q. Sometimes my mouse sticks when I'm moving it. The little arrow doesn't seem to move even though I'm moving the mouse around. What's wrong with it?

A. It sounds like the little critter is just dirty or that the little ball underneath the mouse has become slick and can't get enough traction. (I hate it when that happens!) A mouse pad will help in the friction department.

To clean your mouse, first turn off your computer, then unplug the mouse, and flip it over. Unscrew the plate that holds the ball in place. Using a cloth moistened with plain water or water with a small amount of mild detergent added to it (no alcohol, please!), wipe off the ball. Then dry it completely with a clean cloth.

If you have a can of compressed air, give it a blast to blow out any dust that's taken up residence in the mouse cavity, or just blow on it yourself. Gently remove any deposits on the tiny rollers.

If the ball itself is shiny and slick from use, a few light scuffs with an emery board will put new life into it. Replace the plate, tighten the screws, and your mouse should be good as new.

Q. I've heard about USB devices that can just plug into my computer, but I understand my computer has to be "USB ready." How can I determine if it is USB ready?

A. USB stands for Universal Serial Bus, which is slightly different than the bus Ralph Kramden used to drive around the streets of Brooklyn. A USB port is a device that you plug something into, that permits you to hook up printers, scanners, digital cameras, and all kinds of digital delights to your computer.

To determine whether you have a USB port, look at the back panel of your computer. If it's USB ready, you'll see one or two rectangular USB ports tucked in there among the other strange-looking connection devices. (Don't be concerned about those other oddities; nobody really knows what they are or what they do, either.)

Windows 98 has built-in USB support, so be sure that any new hardware devices you purchase for use with a computer running Windows 98 are labeled *USB compliant.* If it is, you can plug it in and enjoy your new treat!

Q. How do I add a USB device to my computer?

A. This is where the true miracle of the USB comes into play: Just plug the device into your USB port or hub and the new device should be recognized by your computer immediately. You'll be prompted to insert the driver disk that was packaged with the device. Other than that, just follow the screen prompts—which, in most cases, involves little more than clicking the **Next** button when requested, and your new device will be installed.

 You can also unplug a USB device while your computer is turned on or can plug it back in without turning off your computer. This is referred to as being "hot pluggable."

Q. Is there any limit to the number of devices that can be hooked up to a USB port?

A. Theoretically, up to 127 devices can be connected at once through the use of daisy-chained, or linked, USB hubs. A USB hub is a device that, for example, can expand one USB into six or eight ports. String a bunch of USB hubs together and you'll have the ability to attach 127 devices. Why you would want to do this? I have no idea, but isn't it comforting to know that you can?

The concept might be easier to visualize if you think in terms of a six-outlet power strip that plugs into one electrical outlet, thereby expanding the one outlet to six.

The next time you shop for a new computer, you may see some computers that have USB ports in the back of the computer and some that have them in the front. If you have a choice, select a computer with USB ports in the front for ease of access.

This will be particularly convenient if, for example, you're planning to use a digital camera that needs to connect to a USB port in order to transmit pictures to your hard drive; it will be much easier to connect and disconnect the camera to the USB port if that port is readily accessible.

Q. One of my keyboard keys continually gets stuck and won't let me use it. Is there any way to unstick a stuck key?

A. T at appens now and t en to my " " key. Good eavens! It's appening again!

Keyboard keys are little caps pressed onto "poles" attached to switches located underneath them. All you need to do is create a small lever about the size of a Popsicle stick. With your computer turned off, run the lever under the sticking key and it will pop right up. Don't force it, though, and don't use a neighboring key as a fulcrum. (Historical Note: I've been trying to use *fulcrum* in a sentence since high school geometry class. Mrs. Guntherson would be so proud.) Once you remove the stubborn key and clean the gunk out of your keyboard as described in the next paragraph, simply reposition the key over its respective pole and press it back into position.

Board bunnies (keyboard dust bunnies) tend to collect under keys, so buy a can of compressed air at any computer or hardware store to use for springtime keyboard cleaning. Using the little plastic extension nozzle on the spray can, periodically give your keyboard a blast or two. Run the nozzle between the rows of keys, starting at the top and working your way down. You'll be amazed and disgusted by all the digital debris that has accumulated.

Q. I was shopping for a new keyboard for my computer and was amazed at the number of different models of keyboards available, some having more keys than others. Any recommendations?

A. The most common type of keyboard in use today is what's called the *enhanced keyboard,* which has 101 keys. This keyboard includes 12 function keys, a numeric keypad, separate arrow keys, and **Page Up**, **Page Down**, **Insert**, **Delete**, **Home**, and **End** keys.

Microsoft has a "Natural" keyboard that's very popular. It has three additional keys: Two **Windows Start Menu** keys and a key that works the same as pressing the right mouse button. These special keys are identified by either a Windows logo or what looks like a little mouse cursor. These keys are usually located on the bottom row of the keyboard, near the space bar.

There are also all kinds of ergonomic keyboards, and some keyboards that are referred to generically as *Internet* keyboards. The primary feature of these keyboards is the ability to program some of the keys to function as shortcut keys to specific web addresses.

There are also some very small keyboards—some of them wireless keyboards and some of them just space-saving keyboards. Be careful before purchasing one of these because they typically sacrifice some of the 101 "standard" keys in order to save space.

At a minimum, regardless what keyboard you decide on, just make sure that any new keyboard has the basic 101 keys. Beyond that, let your personal preferences dictate what keyboard is best for you. And don't forget to try out any keyboard you're contemplating purchasing to make sure the touch is comfortable for your style of typing.

Q. Can I use a regular-sized keyboard with my notebook computer?

A. Yes, you can hook up any full-sized keyboard to the PS/2 port (that's the small round one) and keep your serial port free for your mouse. Any good computer supply store will have cable or port adapters should you encounter an unusual port or keyboard configuration.

Q. I bought a USB keyboard. Do I have to use a USB mouse also?

A. Your USB (Universal Serial Bus) keyboard probably has a USB port incorporated within the keyboard that will make it very easy to use a USB mouse. That would be my first choice. However, some USB keyboards have PS/2 connectors or adapters for mice, so you can always plug your mouse into the PS/2 port located on the back or on the side of your computer.

Q. I bought a USB mouse and hooked it up, but it's not working. What's the problem?

A. I've had that happen myself. It's hard to know exactly what's causing it for sure. It could be a conflict with another device, or it could be that it hasn't been detected or identified by the Universal Serial Bus. Try unplugging the mouse, then plugging it in again. If that doesn't resolve the problem, try rebooting.

It's also possible that you need to update the relevant software included in Windows 98 that deals with USB pointing devices—the high-tech way of saying *mouse*. Software updates and drivers—even for non-Microsoft mice—can be downloaded from www.Microsoft.com/products/hardware/mouse/.

Q. What's that little wheel I see between the two buttons of a mouse?

A. That wheel, which appears on certain mouse designs, comes in very handy when scrolling through documents or web pages. If you've ever had the experience of trying to move up or down through a document using a wheel-less mouse, you know that you can zip completely through the document and whip right by the place where you want stop.

Using the mouse wheel, however, you can easily control the pace at which you scroll up or down through a document or web page, a single line at a time, if you wish.

I wouldn't necessarily recommend running out and buying a wheel mouse today, but when it comes time to replace your current mouse, be sure to take a look.

Q. What is this DVD thing I'm reading about for computers?

A. *DVD* (digital video disc, sometimes referred to as digital versatile disk) is the next-generation compact disc. It's essentially a CD with a huge storage capacity that can hold video as well as audio and computer data. A regular CD-ROM can hold 650 megabytes of data, which equates to approximately 480 floppy discs. First-generation DVD capacity is more than 5 gigabytes. This is more than enough to put a full-length movie on a single disc.

Second-generation DVD (expected about an hour and a half after the first generation makes its debut) will have a 17GB capacity, or the equivalent of almost 12,000 floppy disks. With this kind of progress, third-generation DVD may have the capacity to hold everything that ever occurred since the dawn of recorded history, with room to archive everything that occurs during the next nine billion years. Groovy!

Q. Is it true that I should use a screen saver to protect my monitor?

A. A *screen saver* is a small program that launches after your computer is idle for a specified period of time. Screen savers were originally created to prevent monitor "burn-in," a painful pixel-afflicting malady that in the olden days of computing—the 1980s—would occur if text or other images remained on screen for prolonged periods of time.

A burned-in monitor would display a shadowy image of a document or graphic appearing underneath all other screen images. Today's monitors are much more technologically sophisticated, and burn-in is just a distant, shadowy memory. If you decide to use a screen saver, use it for the fun of it, not because you have to.

Windows has within it a lovely assortment of screen savers. To review them, right-click a blank area of the Desktop, select **Properties**, then click the **Screen Saver** tab. Use the down arrow to the right of the **Screen Saver** field, and click any screen saver that you want to take a peek at. You'll see a preview displayed on the little monitor in the middle of the dialog box.

If the preview sneak-peek doesn't cut the mustard and you relish the idea of taking a look at a screen saver in full-screen view, just click on the **Preview** button. You'll get a brief full-screen look at your selected screen saver.

Q. I work with a community-based computer training facility, and we're looking for used computers capable of running Windows 95. Any idea where I can find some?

A. There are several organizations that specialize in used computers. The Used Computer Mall (www.usedcomputer.com/) is a large, used-computer marketplace, well worth visiting.

NACOMEX (www.nacomex.com/hardware.html) hosts a secondary computer marketplace where you can purchase or donate computers, and they also have a service that helps you make sure you're not purchasing stolen computers.

You might also try the American Computer Exchange (www.amcoex.com/), which will appraise your computer for $9.95. Appraisal software is also available.

Lastly, don't overlook any of the online auctions, such as eBay (www.ebay.com) or uBid (www.ubid.com). Just be sure to read the fine print regarding warranties. Some used computers are sold "as-is," while others may offer short-term (6 month) warranties.

To obtain a copy of *Mr. Modem's Top Ten Tips for Online Auction Safety*, send an e-mail addressed to auctions@MrModem.net. Leave the Subject line and body of the e-mail blank. By return e-mail you'll receive the information, courtesy of Mr. Modem. Going once…going twice…

Q. My computer is two years old, and I can't decide whether I should spend some money to upgrade it or I should just buy a new computer. What do you recommend?

A. The only upgrade recommendations I ever make apply to computers that are less than two years old. Within that context, I occasionally recommend increasing the amount of memory (RAM), but that's about it. Compatibility issues caused by introducing new components to an older computer system are a primary concern. Because these types of problems typically will not appear until the upgrade is completed, tracking down the source of a problem at that point can be challenging—which is the politically correct way of saying it can be a miserable experience. If your computer is more than two years old and you're thinking about upgrading, consider purchasing a new PC instead.

Q. I was going to buy a 17-inch monitor, but all the accompanying literature says "16.0 inches viewable" or "15.8 inches viewable." What's the scoop? Why is the viewable area so much smaller than the advertised size of the monitor?

A. As a result of a lawsuit a few years ago, monitor manufacturers agreed to list actual viewable areas alongside the physical size of a display's cathode ray tube (CRT), an inch or so of which is hidden behind the monitor's frame or bezel. Despite that agreement, most people still refer to 15-, 17-, and 19-inch monitors, though the viewing surface is always less than that. So if you want a true 17-inch viewing surface, you might want to consider purchasing a 19-inch monitor.

Q. I'm monitor shopping and must confess that I don't understand the difference between resolution and dot pitch. Can you explain what each term means and, more importantly, what you recommend for each?

A. *Resolution* refers to the number of pixels that are used to create the images displayed on your monitor. A *pixel* is the smallest individual dot you can see on your computer screen, if you put your nose right up to the glass. Every image is composed of thousands of individual pixels.

 Mr. Modem Worthless Trivia: The word *pixel* is a combination of the words *picture* and *element*.

The word *resolution*, when used in computer parlance, doesn't mean dots per square inch (dpi), as the term is used in print media. It actually refers to *relative resolution*, because all pixels aren't the same size. This might make your eyes glaze over, so get comfortable before reading further, or feel free to skip ahead; you won't hurt my feelings.

Pixel size varies depending upon the size of the monitor. A relatively low-resolution monitor setting would be 640 × 480. What that means is that the on-screen image is composed of 480 horizontal lines, with 640 pixels per line. Multiply those two numbers and you get 307,200 pixels. That's a whole lotta pixels.

If you look at that image on a small notebook computer, the picture will look pretty decent. But if you display those same 307,200 pixels on a 17-inch, 19-inch, or larger monitor, the same number of pixels are going to have to expand in size to fill the screen, so the image is going to be considerably less clear.

So, what does all this mean? It means that the term *resolution* describes how many pixels are used to create a computer display, and the numbers are always presented as *vertical × horizontal* (i.e., 640 × 480, 800 × 600, 1041× 768, etc). As far as which resolution is best, that's really up to you to decide. I prefer 800 × 600, personally, but many computer users gravitate to 1041 × 768.

Dot pitch, on the other hand, is a measurement of how closely the pixels are crammed together. The closer the pixels, the sharper the picture will be.

When monitor shopping, don't consider purchasing any monitor with a dot pitch higher than 28. A dot pitch of 26 is preferable to a dot pitch of 28. This dot pitch business can be a little confusing because the lower the number, the more closely spaced the dots are—which seems exactly opposite to how you would think things should be. But if it made perfect sense, that would be too easy.

Q. How can I change my monitor's resolution?

A. Select **Start** ➢ **Settings** ➢ **Control Panel** ➢ **Display**—or, if that's too many clicks and you *really* want to impress your friends, right-click any blank area of your Windows Desktop and select **Properties**. You'll get to the same location, your **Display Properties** dialog box. Click the **Settings** tab.

In the **Screen Area** section, you'll see a scale and a slider bar that ranges from **Less** (on the left) to **More** (on the right). Below that, you'll see the numerical resolution, 800 × 600, 1024 × 768, etc. Adjust the slider bar and you will see the screen display area change in the little preview monitor window as you change resolutions. After selecting a new resolution, click **Apply**, followed by **OK.** You'll have to restart your computer for the new resolution to take effect.

Mr. Modem Bonus Tip: Here's a very handy, though little-known feature that for some strange reason is generally disabled by default. To have the ability to change your monitor's resolution *without* having to restart your computer, follow these steps:

1. Right-click any blank area of your Windows Desktop, select **Properties**, then the **Settings** tab, and press the **Advanced** button.

2. Place a check mark in the box that says **Show Settings Icon On Taskbar**. Click **Apply**, then **OK** to exit **Display Properties**.

Now that you have the ability to change resolutions without restarting your computer, here's how you do it:

1. Right-click the monitor icon located in the System Tray (to the left of the time display at the bottom of your screen). This will bring up a list of available monitor resolutions.

2. Select a new resolution from the displayed menu by clicking it. If this is the first time you're changing resolutions, a message may appear asking if you want to change the resolution without restarting your computer. Select the option to hide that dialog box in the future, and click **OK**.

Presto! Your monitor resolution will be changed without the need to reboot. Try different resolutions and see what works best for your monitor and your eyes.

Q. How can I tell which COM port my modem is using?

A. If you're using an external modem, just check which serial port it's plugged into on the back of your computer. Usually the small serial port is designated as COM1 and the larger serial port, if you even have one, is designated as COM2. If you only have one serial port, dollars to donuts it's COM1.

Another way to check is to click **Start** ➤ **Settings** ➤ **Control Panel**, and click the **General** tab. Click your modem on the list displayed, and choose **Properties**. It will display which port your modem is using.

Instead of selecting the **General** tab, you can also select the **Diagnostics** tab, which will display a list showing what devices are using which COM ports.

Q. I'm continually getting knocked offline when a call-waiting call comes in. Is there anything I can do about that, short of getting another phone line?

A. All you need to do is disable call-waiting while you're online. (As soon as you terminate your online session, call-waiting will automatically return to action.) In most areas of the U.S., the code to disable call-waiting is *70, but better check with your phone company to be sure.

If your disable code is *70, you'll want to insert *70, (star, seven, zero, comma) before the Internet service provider's dial-up phone number. For example, if the number your modem usually dials in order to connect to the Internet is 555-1212, you would enter ***70,555-1212**. (The comma forces the modem to pause for one second after dialing the **70* to allow time for the call-waiting to be disabled and for the new dial tone to begin.)

 If you're trying to connect to the Internet from a hotel room or other facility where you need to dial a 9 first to obtain an outside line, do the same thing: In the field where you provide the number for your modem to dial, insert *9,* (9 comma), then the number. That will allow time for your modem to secure the outside line dial tone and then to continue with the dialing sequence.

If you're using the Windows Dialer, to insert **70,* in the dialing field, click **My Computer ➢ DialUp Networking**. Right-click the name of your Internet Service Provider or your Internet account, and select **Properties**. Click the **General** tab. In the **Telephone Number** field, enter ***70,** followed by the number your modem would usually dial to establish your connection to the Internet. Click **OK**, and back your way out to your Desktop.

That's all there is to it. Next time you log on to the Internet, call-waiting will be disabled while you're online, so you won't be unceremoniously dumped offline again—at least not by incoming calls.

Q. Somebody e-mailed me a document file that I printed, but when we compared documents, it didn't look like the original that the person who sent it to me printed. Why is that?

A. It's probably due to a difference in the fonts available to you on your computer. Many times, documents and graphics files that you receive from other people have been created using fonts that you may not have on your computer, or formats (such as HTML) that your e-mail program may not be equipped or enabled to handle.

If you try to print something created with a font that you don't have, your software will substitute a similar font. Unfortunately, that substituted font may result in a document that looks substantially different from the original created by the sender.

You could ask the sender to also e-mail you the font or fonts used to create the document you're attempting to print and then copy or drag them into your Fonts folder, usually located in your `C:\Windows` folder. Just be aware that it could be a violation of the font software company's copyright for you to install somebody else's fonts on your computer. The font police do not look kindly upon such violations.

Another option would be to purchase and install a font-set software package that includes the font used by the creator of the document, or you could ask the person to reformat their document using any of the default fonts that are included with Windows.

Q. Several times in the past week my monitor went black for no apparent reason— once when I was typing and another time when a screen saver was running. Should I open up the monitor and check for loose wires?

A. Only if you have a death wish. There are parts inside your monitor that retain electricity even when the monitor is unplugged, so do not open your monitor for any reason.

The next time your monitor goes dark, try moving your mouse and see if that breathes any life into it. If so, your computer's power management features are probably causing the blackouts. And when it comes to blackouts, better your monitor than you.

You can turn Power Management off or increase the amount of time before the monitor turns off by right-clicking on your Desktop and selecting **Properties**. Select the **Screen Saver** tab and you should see the energy-saving features toward the bottom of your screen.

If moving your mouse doesn't bring your monitor back to life, my best recommendation is to get thee to a repair facility and ask them to check it out.

 Monitors don't last forever and, unless they're new, are rarely worth repairing. Be sure to evaluate the estimated cost of a monitor repair versus the cost of replacing the monitor with a new one.

Q. How can I install a new printer so my computer will recognize it and know it's available?

A. Through the miracle of Windows, installing a new printer has never been easier. With your computer and printer turned off, hook the printer cable up to your computer. Boot up your computer and you may receive the always-welcome "New Hardware Found" message. Click **Next** to continue, but be sure to follow any special instructions that may appear. Double-click **My Computer**, navigate to **Printers**, and then **Add Printer**.

If you receive a message that says that the appropriate driver cannot be located, don't panic! A driver is a small program that transmits instructions between a device, such as a printer, and the software applications that use that printer. Simply insert the floppy disk or CD-ROM that came with your printer.

Follow the on-screen instructions that will ask you to identify or to confirm the specific model printer you're installing. It will then ask you if you want to install the drivers, or it may just do it for you without asking. Once the setup is complete, right-click the printer icon, and make sure that there's a check mark next to **Set As Default**.

Q. I'm using a contact manager program as my computerized address book. I notice that searching for names is getting slower and slower. Anything I can do to speed things up?

A. Sometimes sluggish address-book searches can be eliminated by changing the way you enter data. One of the most common mistakes is entering the word *the* first (for example, "The Save-the-Kumquat Foundation" or "The Adopt-An-Aardvark Association"). Always put the *the* after the name of the entity, such as "Save-the-Kumquat Foundation, The." While this may sound like a terribly simplistic piece of advice—and would you expect anything less from Mr. Modem?—it really works.

Q. Sometimes my computer doesn't seem to perform a function when I've clicked on something, so I'll click on it again and again. The more I do that, it seems like the command isn't "getting through" to the computer and I'll have to reboot. What's the problem?

A. I operate on the theory that if one click is good, 17 clicks is even better, but that's not the case when it comes to computers. If your computer doesn't perform an action when you click something or press **Enter**, repeating the action numerous times won't help. It's like yelling at your car when it won't start. You can yell all you want, but it's not going to make a whole lot of difference.

When it comes to computers, repeatedly entering the command is likely to freeze up your computer, necessitating a reboot more than anything else. So just have patience.

Sometimes the big freeze is caused by one program being uncooperative, so shutting down that one program alone may get you back in action. If you're stuck in a program, press **Ctrl + Alt + Del**, which will display the **Close Program** dialog box. Select the program that's frozen or not cooperating from the list of programs displayed, and click the **End Task** button. Sometimes it takes a few clicks of the **End Task** button to force the program to shut down. Once the program shuts down, try relaunching the program. If you can relaunch the program, chances are everything will be fine.

However, if things are frozen more solidly than a birdbath in Buffalo in February and you're sure nothing is going to happen—by waiting 20 to 30 seconds—save yourself the frustration and just reboot. Rebooting will force your hardware to reset and your software to reload, presenting you with a clean slate from which to operate. Your computer will thank you.

Q. Viruses terrify me, and I'm afraid I'm going to get a virus from something somebody sends me online. What can I do?

A. Many people have a self-imposed (and very smart) rule of never opening file attachments that accompany incoming e-mail received from people they don't know. With today's increasingly sophisticated viruses, even before opening an attachment you receive from somebody you *do* know, you should e-mail the sender and ask if he or she intended to send the attachment. If so, ask for a description—what is it you're sending me? You may decide it's something you're not interested in under any circumstances and can save yourself some time by simply deleting it.

Intelligent viruses today can attach themselves to e-mail address books, making it possible that the sender won't even know they're sending virus-laden attachments with their outgoing e-mail. That's why it's important to ask the sender if they intended to send a particular attachment.

In addition, be sure to use a virus-checking software program. My personal favorites are McAfee's VirusScan, available at www.mcafee.com, and Norton's AntiVirus, at www.symantec.com. Both programs will scan e-mail attachments for any lurking critters that could cause your computer harm.

Mr. Modem's Recommended Websites

Gator   A free program that serves as a savvy online companion by filling forms and remembering all your passwords. Gator is secure, with your information being stored only on your own computer.

www.gator.com

File Converter   This handy resource can convert files in the most popular graphic, document, and sound formats.

http://wheel.compose.cs.cmu.edu:8001/cgi-bin/browse/objweb

Used Laptops   Used notebooks and laptops, sold with a 30-day warranty and starting as low as $295. All top-quality, brand-name computers, including IBM, Dell, Compaq, Toshiba, and Uncle Beauford's JiffyPute. Well, maybe not *all* top brands.

www.usedlaptops.com

File Extensions, Part I   I never met a file extension I didn't like, but if you have encountered some that you didn't recognize, this is a site to behold. Enter the three mystery letters and find out what program created the file. You'll find everything from .TXT files to things that go .BMP in the night. Currently more than 1,500 file extensions are catalogued in this database.

http://extsearch.com/

Internet Software   Excellent resource for downloadable, Internet-related software.

http://cws.internet.com/

How to Build Your Own Computer   A wonderful tutorial, complete with photos. If you have ever been interested in building your own computer (something that falls just below hot-coal walking and blindfolded sky-diving on Mr. Modem's list of priorities), check this website out.

http://freepctech.com/index.php

Computing in the Palm of Your Hand

Palm-based computers (computers using the Palm Operating System) are forgiving, friendly, and fun. Whether you've never had the pleasure of using one or you've been using one for years, you'll find answers to frequently asked questions in this chapter that will help you get the most out of Palm's basic programs and features (including the Date Book, Address Book, To Do List, and Memo Pad) and your Palm Desktop software.

Conventions and Definitions

If you are just now familiarizing yourself with palm-computing, you'll find the terminology and functionality to be different than what you're accustomed to for your gargantuan desktop computer. So please read the following for some handy (har-har) background and fundamental information.

The **Applications** screen is accessed by tapping (with your stylus) the Applications icon (sometimes referred to as the **Applications** button), which is represented by a picture of a house, located in the upper-left corner of the Graffiti area (where you enter data via handwriting). Tapping the Applications icon from any location within the Palm device takes you back to the main screen of a given category of applications. Repeatedly tapping the Applications icon will cycle through all top-level applications categories.

An instruction to tap **System** ➤, followed by additional taps as designated, refers to tapping the Category arrow located in the upper right-hand corner of any main or top-level Applications screen. A drop-down menu of categories will appear. One of the categories displayed will be **System**.

A sequence of instructions such as tap **System** ➤ **Preferences** ➤ **General** means to navigate to (and then select) the **System** category as explained in the previous paragraph; at the **System** screen, tap **Prefs** (which I'll refer to as **Preferences** from this point on), and look in the upper right-hand corner of the **Preferences** screen. If **General** is not displayed, tap the arrow to reveal the drop-down menu of additional **Preferences** categories; locate **General** and tap it to select it.

An instruction to tap **Menu** ➤, followed by additional taps as designated, refers to tapping the Menu icon located in the lower-left corner of the Graffiti area.

Palm Desktop refers to the Palm software loaded on your desktop computer.

Address Book refers to the application itself. When you tap **Address**, your contacts are displayed in alphabetical order in a view called the *Address List*.

Q. I was planning to buy a Palm computer but became thoroughly confused by the number of models and products available. I thought it was a matter of going into a store and purchasing a Palm. Not so. Can you help me sort through this?

A. The whole Palm arena can be a bit overwhelming at first, but it might be helpful to think of it in terms of the operating system (OS) rather than the actual hardware device—the little computer you can hold in your hand.

By definition, when we talk about the Palm OS, we're talking about a software product that has been licensed to, and incorporated within, a large number of hardware devices. The Palm computer—of which there are a number of models—is one such example.

Devices that use the Palm operating system include all the current Palm computer models: The Palm IIIxe, IIIc, Vx, VIIx, M100, M105, M500, M505, as well as all previous Palm devices. For the latest information about current Palm models visit www.palm.com. Handspring (www.handspring.com), founded by one of the individuals who created the Palm but then went on to develop the Visor line of handheld devices, which also use the Palm OS, includes the Visor, Visor Deluxe, Visor Platinum, Edge, and Prism. For more information about the current line of Visor products, please visit the Handspring website at www.handspring.com.

In addition, there are handheld devices using the Palm operating system available from IBM (www.ibm.com), Franklin Covey (www.franklincovey.com), Kyocera (www.kyocera.com), Nokia (www.nokia.com), Samsung (www.Samsung.com), Sony (www.sony.com), Symbol (www.symbol.com), and TRG (www.trgpro.com/).

The bottom line is this: Palm OS handheld computers are one of the fastest-growing sectors of today's emerging technologies. Because this technology is developing so rapidly, the best place to obtain current information about these cutting-edge devices is on each product's website, as referenced here.

Q. Where can I find the best prices on a Palm device?

A. I recommend any of the following price-comparison websites. At any of these sites, enter the product, model number, and whatever other information you have, and let your browser do the walking!

Website	URL
Internet Mall	www.shopnow.com
mySimon	www.mysimon.com
PriceSearch	www.price-search.net
PriceComparison	www.pricecomparison.net
Street Prices	www.streetprices.com

If you're an auction enthusiast, you might consider some of the more popular online auction sites, such as eBay (www.ebay.com), uBid (www.ubid.com), or Yahoo! Auctions (http://auctions.yahoo.com).

Q. Can my Palm safely go through the X-ray machine at airport security? Will it lose any data?

A. Yes, it can, and no, it won't. Yes, it can safely ride the conveyor belt through airport security checks without losing any data.

Speaking of traveling with your Palm: On an airplane, the Palm is considered to be a "portable electronic device," so do not use it at the beginning or end of a flight when the flight attendants give their instructions about using such devices.

It's also a good idea not to enable any alarms in your Palm when flying so your device doesn't start beeping during a period when all portable electronic devices should be turned off and secured.

Q. I've loaded a lot of programs on my Palm, and I'm not sure how much room I have left to add additional programs. How can I check?

A. Tap the **Applications** icon ➤ **Menu** ➤ **Delete**. At the top of the **Delete** screen, you'll see how much free memory you have remaining and what your maximum memory is.

Q. I'm trying to find a note I entered somewhere—it might be part of an address entry or a memo—but I can't remember where I put it. Is there any way to locate it?

A. The Find feature is a fine feature and perfect for this situation. Tap the **Find** icon—it looks like a little magnifying glass and is located in the lower right-hand corner of the Graffiti screen. That will bring up the **Find** screen, where you can enter a word or the first few letters of a word or name—anything that you can remember that might be part of the record you're trying to find. Capitalization doesn't matter, but bear in mind that **Find** only searches the beginnings of words, so it's the first few characters that matter.

If you think the record is in your Address List or another application, open the appropriate application *before* launching Find. Find will search the current or open application first, before moving on to the others.

Once you enter your search word or characters, tap **OK**, and any search results will be displayed. Tap the **Find More** button to see additional search results.

Q. When I'm not entering data into my Palm or otherwise using it, it shuts off very quickly. I know that's to save battery life, but it's a little too quick. Is there some way I can slow it down so it gives me a bit more time before shutting off?

A. You bet. Select **General** from the drop-down menu in the **Preferences** screen. The third item on the list is **Auto-off After**; tap the little arrow and you'll have your choice of setting the unit to wait one, two, or three minutes before shutting off.

Q. I've had my Palm device for a while, and it's worked great, but lately when I tap something, nothing happens. It's like I'm tapping in the wrong place, but I'm not. What's going on, and is there anything I can do about it?

A. You're experiencing what's known as dreaded Digital Drift. But don't worry, your secret is safe with me. What's happening is this: Over time, the point of your stylus isn't quite registering precisely where you're tapping. The good news is that it's very easy to fix if you get thee to the Digitizer.

Tap **System** ➤ **Preferences**, then, using the Category arrow in the upper-right corner, select **Digitizer** from the drop-down menu.

A small target will appear on screen with the instruction to tap the center of the target. Go ahead and tap it. The target will then move to two other locations on your screen, and you'll be asked to tap the center of the target again in each instance. That's all there is to it. As soon as you make the third tap, the target will disappear and you'll be back to the **Preferences** screen with the peace of mind of knowing that your stylus will hit the mark from that point forward.

Q. How can I change the font that appears throughout the Palm? It's so small that I can hardly read it.

A. You can change the font in each of the four included programs (Address Book, Date Book, To Do List, or Memo Pad), as well as most programs that accommodate font changes, by launching the program and then tapping **Menu** ➤ **Options** ➤ **Font**.

This will display the **Select Font** dialog box with several font options. Just tap the appropriate font to make your selection, then tap **OK**.

 You must change the font in each program. You cannot change the font in the Address Book, for example, and have it automatically change in the Date Book as well.

Q. Whenever I open my Palm Desktop program, it always opens to the Date Book. I hardly ever use the Date Book. Can I change something so it always opens to the Address Book instead?

A. You bet! Go ahead and launch your Palm Desktop, then click **Tools** ➢ **Options**, and select the **General** tab. The first item you'll see is **Startup Application**, with a little arrow to the right of that field. Click the arrow to display choices of **Date Book**, **Address Book**, **To Do List**, and **Memo Pad**. Use your cursor to make your selection, then click **OK**.

Next time you launch your Palm Desktop, it will open with your preferred application.

Q. When I first got my Palm, I recall going through a Graffiti tutorial—it was a place to practice writing. Now I can't find it. I'm sure it's here someplace. Can you help?

A. If people new to the wild and wacky world of Palm computing are challenged by anything, it's Graffiti. Graffiti is the Palm's handwriting-recognition software and the method of entering data into your Palm by writing special characters on screen using your stylus. The tutorial can be found by tapping the Applications icon, using the Categories arrow located in the top right-hand corner of the screen, and then selecting the **All** category to display all applications. From the applications displayed, tap **Graffiti**. It's worth spending a little time practicing Graffiti. It won't take long until you'll be Palm-writing like a pro!

Q. Graffiti is driving me crazy. I've been practicing it, but sometimes I forget how to write a character. I saw a quick reference guide somewhere, but I can't remember where I saw it or how to make it appear for a fast brush-up on my Graffiti skills.

A. The Graffiti Reference Guide is always just a quick stylus stroke away. Place the point of your stylus at the bottom of the Graffiti area and draw a vertical line all the way up to the top of the Palm screen. That will bring up the Graffiti Reference Guide, and you can use your scroll buttons (located between the four program buttons) to review the different Graffiti characters and how to write them. Tap **Done** when you're through reviewing and you'll be returned to the place where you detoured into the Guide, so you won't miss a beat.

Q. How do I create categories for the different programs I'm loading onto my Palm?

A. I'm glad to hear you're interested in using categories. Many people don't invest the few minutes required to learn how to create categories and, as a result, wind up with lots of clutter—too many icons, not enough room to display them all on the small Palm screen. Creating categories of programs makes it easy to keep things organized and, even more importantly, gives you the ability to quickly find what you're looking for!

To create a category, follow this sequence: Tap the small arrow in the upper-right corner of the **Applications** screen to display a drop-down list of existing categories. Tap the last option, **Edit Categories.** This will display a screen where you can add, rename, and delete categories.

To create a new category, tap the **New** button, then enter the name of your new category. Click **OK** when you're finished.

Q. I have a number of categories created. How do I assign programs to those categories?

A. Now the fun begins! You've created your categories, so it's time to start filling them up. On the **Applications** screen, tap the **Menu** button, then select **Category.**

A listing of all the programs on your Palm device will appear. To the right of each program name is the category to which the program is currently assigned, or it may say **Unfiled** if the program is not currently assigned to any category.

Tap the little arrow to the right of a program. This will display a list of available categories. Select the appropriate category by tapping it. When you're finished assigning programs to categories, tap **Done**.

Once you have assigned programs to categories, you can either use the Category arrow in the top-right corner to display categories or, if you continue to tap the **Applications** button, you can cycle through each of your categories, displaying the contents of each category. Try it! It's much faster than using the Category arrow and the drop-down menu.

Q. How can I delete a category?

A. To delete a category, tap the Category arrow, which is the small arrow in the upper-right corner of the **Applications** screen, to display a drop-down list of existing categories. Tap the last option, **Edit Categories**. This will display a screen where you can, among other things, delete categories.

Tap the category you would like to remove, then tap **Delete**.

Q. Can I print directly from my Palm device?

A. If you have an IR (infrared)-capable printer and a software program like PalmPrint, you can. All you have to do is point your Palm at the printer, beam the record, and print. More information about PalmPrint software and the large number of supported printers is available at `www.stevenscreek.com`.

Q. When I enter data, I use a lot of the same phrases. How do I create shortcuts or shorthand strokes so I can enter phrases with a minimum amount of text entry?

A. Shortcuts can really speed up the process of data entry. As an example, let's say you're an attorney and *contributory negligence* is a phrase you use frequently when using your Memo Pad or another feature of your Palm device. Wouldn't it be convenient if you could just enter the letters *c n* instead and have the phrase *contributory negligence* appear on screen? You bet it would! Therein lies the magic of shortcuts.

To create the shortcut used in our example, select **System ➤ Preferences**, select **Shortcuts** from the dropdown menu in the upper right-hand corner, and then tap the **New** button.

In the **ShortCut Name:** field, enter the shortcut you want to use. (In our example, we would enter the letters *c n*.)

Next, tap the first line in the **ShortCut Text:** field, which will move your cursor to that position. Here's where you enter the word or phrase you're creating a shortcut for. (So, in our example, we would enter the words *contributory negligence*.) Tap **OK** when you're done.

To use this or any other shortcut, you first have to enter the magical *shortcut stroke* in the Graffiti area of your screen; this is a signal to your device that what follows are letters that comprise a shortcut. The shortcut stroke looks like a handwritten, or cursive, lowercase *l* (that's the letter *L*).

 To see the actual stylus stroke required, use the Graffiti Reference Guide, which is a quick stylus stroke away. Just place the point of your stylus at the bottom of the Graffiti area and draw a vertical line all the way up to the top of the Palm screen. That will bring up the Graffiti Reference Guide. Use your scroll buttons (located between the four program buttons) to locate the shortcut stroke and observe how to enter it. Tap **Done** when you're through reviewing the Guide and you'll be returned to the place where you detoured into it.

Once you enter the shortcut stroke, which will appear on your screen, then enter your shortcut letters (the *c n* in our example) and the words *contributory negligence* will appear.

 When you first visit **Shortcuts** from the drop-down menu in the **General Preferences** screen, you'll see a number of shortcuts created for you. Practice using these included shortcuts to get the hang of this very handy feature.

You'll find the following shortcuts included with your Palm:

Enter This	This Text Will Appear
Bk	*breakfast*
Cc	*conference call*
Din	*dinner*
Ds	[date stamp]
Dts	[date and time stamp]
Lu	*Lunch*
Me	*meeting*
Ts	[time stamp]

Be creative! Use shortcuts for people's names, word prefixes and suffixes (*pre-, inter-,* and *-tion, -ing,* etc.).

Q. Is there a shortcut stroke or other way to add a reminder to call somebody other than manually entering a To Do List item?

A. It's not a shortcut stroke, but there is a way to quickly add a person or a company, with the telephone number, to the To Do List—assuming the person or company is already entered in your Address Book. The Palm has lots of capabilities, but it can't read your mind—at least not yet. Give it another year.

Open your **To Do List** and tap **New**. Then tap **Menu** ➣ **Options** ➣ **Phone Lookup**. Tap the name of the person or company in the **Phone Number Lookup** dialog box, then tap **Add**. The name of the person or company, with the accompanying telephone number, will pop right into your To Do List.

> Because the To Do List can be difficult to read if you try to cram too much information into an item, try limiting the To Do List item itself to two or three descriptive words. Then add any additional information as a note by tapping the **Details** button, then selecting **Note**. Here, you can wax expansive without cluttering up the To Do List itself. Tap **Done** when you've finished entering your note. Your To Do List item will appear with a little "page" icon next to it reminding you that there is a note attached.

Q. Can I convert a To Do List item into an appointment in the Date Book, similar to the Phone Lookup feature that will bring an Address Book entry into the To Do List?

A. If I understand your question correctly, the answer is yes—but only using the Palm Desktop. You can't perform this function within the Palm device itself. Of course, once you have changed the data in your Palm Desktop, a quick HotSync will ensure that the same information exists in your Palm handheld device.

To have a To Do List item appear in the Date Book, follow these steps:

First, open your Palm Desktop and click the **Date Book** button, (labeled **Date**). Select the **Day** tab, and go to the specific date to add your new appointment. In the lower-right corner pane on your computer screen will appear your To Do List. If your Address List appears in that pane instead, click **To Do**, which appears above the pane. You can toggle this pane to display your Address List (names and telephone numbers) or your To Do List.

With the To Do List displayed, select the desired item, then drag and drop it into the appropriate time slot in your Date Book. Presto! What once was a To Do List item is now a scheduled meeting or appointment. (Your original To Do List item remains on the To Do List.)

This process only works in one direction: You cannot drag and drop a Date Book appointment to the To Do List.

Q. When I complete an item from my To Do List, I want it to disappear from the list, like a paper list where I would cross out an item. How do I do this?

A. Display your To Do List, then tap the **Show** button. That will display the **To Do Preferences** screen. Remove the check mark from **Show Completed Items**, and tap **OK**. From this point forward, any time you place a check mark by a To Do List item to indicate the task has been completed, the item will disappear from your To Do List.

Completed items are not deleted, however; they are simply hidden from view. Return to the **To Do Preferences** screen at any time and replace the check mark next to **Show Completed Items** to bask in the glow of your completed tasks list.

 As long as you're fiddling with your To Do Preferences, one very useful item is the **Record Completion Date** option. Place a check mark by this item, and each time you complete a task, the date of completion will automatically be added.

Q. How do I delete completed To Do List items that are hidden from view?

A. Display your To Do List, then tap the **Show** button. That will display the **To Do Preferences** screen. Place a check mark next to **Show Completed Items**, and tap **OK**.

With your completed To Do List items displayed, tap an item to select it, then tap **Details** ➢ **Delete**. You will be prompted to confirm your request to delete this item, so just tap **OK** and it will disappear before your eyes.

Q. Can you explain the synchronizing process? I know I can enter information on my Palm and it will get loaded into my Desktop. Does it work the other way around, too?

A. That's exactly right: The process of synchronization (it's referred to as a *HotSync* in Palm parlance) accomplishes three things:

- Data entered into your Palm device is added to your Palm Desktop.

- Data entered into your Palm Desktop is added to your Palm device.

- Any data changed in your Palm Desktop or your Palm device will be changed in the other location.

If you regularly enter data into either your Palm Desktop or your Palm device, it's important to HotSync frequently so your data is kept current on both.

Q. I bought a Palm device and the HotSync cradle that came with it can be plugged into either a serial port or USB port. Does it matter which one I use?

A. The HotSync cradle is the holder your Palm device slips into so you can HotSync with your Palm Desktop. If you have a choice between connecting with the USB port or serial port, and you have a USB port available, definitely go with the USB port because it's much faster than a serial-port connection.

Q. I travel a lot and always enter data into my Palm device, not through my desktop computer. When I was away on a trip, somebody in my office entered some incorrect data into my Palm Desktop software. When I did a HotSync after I returned, the "bad data" was copied into my Palm device. Can I change settings in some way so that only data from my Palm device is copied to my desktop computer? In other words, I don't want any data from my Palm Desktop software copied to my Palm device; I just want the data to flow in the other direction, from my Palm device going to my desktop computer. Does that make sense?

A. I understand what you're asking. It's a little unusual, but the answer is yes, it can be done. I would just encourage other readers *not* to do this unless there's a very specific reason, similar to yours. For most users, performing a HotSync that updates both the Palm device and the Desktop is the best method of keeping your data current.

Having said all that, in order to accomplish what you have requested, just click the **HotSync Manager** icon located in the System Tray of your desktop computer, and select **Custom** from the pop-up menu that will appear.

In the **Custom** dialog box, you'll see a listing of your Palm programs, such as Date Book, Address Book, To Do List, etc. To the right of each application appears the action to be performed during each HotSync; most will probably say **Synchronize The Files**.

Select the application or applications (with your cursor) and the action you would like to change, then click the **Change** button.

In the **Change HotSync Action** dialog box, select **Handheld Overwrites Desktop**, then click **OK**. Place a check mark in the box to the left of **Set As Default** to make this new action the default to be used in all future HotSyncs.

Each time you perform a HotSync, your Palm device will update the data in your Palm Desktop software, but your Palm Desktop will *not* update any data in your Palm device.

Q. I enter most data into my Palm from my desktop computer. Is there a faster way to get into the program than through the Windows **Start** button, going to **Programs**, clicking **Palm Desktop**, then **Palm Desktop** again from the submenu? That seems like an awful lot of steps.

A. Many Palm enthusiasts, myself included, prefer to use the Palm Desktop for data entry. The easiest way to gain speedy access to your Palm Desktop program is through a Windows shortcut to the program from your Desktop.

There are several ways to create Windows shortcuts, but here's a really easy way to create this one: Click **Start** ➢ **Find** ➢ **Files or Folders**. In the **Named:** field, type **palm.exe**.

 Make sure the **Look in:** field shows your C drive—or whatever the appropriate drive is if you installed your Palm software into a drive other than the C drive.

Click the **Find Now** button. When the search of your hard drive is completed, you'll see the file `palm.exe` shown in the lower window. Right-click the file, and select **Create Shortcut**. You'll be cautioned that Windows cannot create a shortcut in that location, but one can be placed on the Windows Desktop. Click the **Yes** button to create this shortcut.

An icon labeled **Shortcut To Palm.exe** will appear on your Desktop. Right-click the name of the shortcut, and select **Rename** from the menu that will appear. Rename the shortcut *Palm* or *Palm Desktop*—whatever name you would like to use.

With your new shortcut created, any time you want to enter data into your Palm Desktop or to use your Address Book, Date Book, To Do List, or Memo Pad, just double-click the shortcut to launch the program.

Q. I usually work in Microsoft's Word on my desktop computer. How can I reformat those documents so I can work with them on my Palm?

A. Try a very useful product called Documents To Go (`www.dataviz.com/products/documentstogo/`), which was voted "Best Handheld Software Product of 1999" by *Mobile Computing and Communication* magazine. With this program, there's no need to specially format files created on your desktop computer because Documents To Go does it for you. The cost of the program is approximately $30.

Just drag your files into the Desktop's Documents To Go program and, the next time you HotSync, those files will be moved to your handheld and reformatted for Palm-size viewing.

Q. I've used Outlook as my contact manager for years and I'd like to continue using it. Do I have to use the Palm's Address Book instead?

A. No, you don't. When you install your Palm Desktop software from the CD-ROM that comes with your Palm device, the software will detect whether you have Microsoft Outlook on your desktop computer. If you do, a message will appear on your desktop computer's screen during the installation process advising that Outlook was found on your computer.

It will also ask whether you would you like to link your handheld data to Microsoft Outlook or to the Palm Desktop Application. Just click to place a dot next to your program of choice.

Q. I've installed my Palm Desktop software, and I've used the HotSync a few times. I was just getting ready to HotSync again, but the HotSync Manager icon is gone from the System Tray. How do I get it back?

A. Once you install the Palm Desktop software, the HotSync Manager icon (it looks like a little circle with two arrows, one red and one blue) appears in your Windows System Tray—the area to the left of the time display at the bottom of your screen.

If the HotSync Manager icon disappears, that just means that the program was shut down and that it simply needs to be started again like any other software program. To do that, from your Windows Desktop, click **Start ➢ Programs ➢ Palm Desktop ➢ HotSync Manager**.

Q. I'd like to organize my Palm memos in a certain order other than the default alphabetical sort order. How can I do that?

A. While viewing your Memo Pad, tap **Menu ➢ Options ➢ Preferences**.

In **Preferences**, you'll have your choice of sorting memos manually or alphabetically; select **Manually**. Then, using your stylus, tap the memo you would like to move and drag it to its new location.

Q. I never use the Memo Pad, so I never use the Memo Pad button. Can I change that button so it brings up a program that I use more frequently?

A. The four program buttons located on the lower portion of your Palm case, below the Graffiti area, provide a fast way to launch four of the most popular Palm programs: the Address Book, Date Book, To Do List, and Memo Pad. But if you don't use one or more of these basic applications, you can easily assign another program to any of the buttons.

First, tap **System ➢ Preferences ➢ Buttons**. That will bring up a screen displaying **Select An Application To Customize Each Button** followed by five icons, one each for the Date Book, Memo Pad, Address Book, calculator, and To Do List.

Each icon has a little arrow to the left of the name associated with that icon. Tap the arrow to view a list of all applications on your device. Tap (to select) the application you would like to associate with a particular button. When you have reassigned the button, tap any of the program buttons to save the change and to exit.

Button Pushing 101

Located at the bottom of the **Button Preferences** screen, you'll see three options labeled **Default**, **Pen**, and **HotSync**. Think of the **Default** button as a safety net, and select this option to restore the program button assignments to their original settings—the way things were before you started getting creative.

The other two options, **Pen** and **HotSync**, are rarely used, but for the sake of completeness and in the interests of excruciating detail, here's what they do:

Tapping **Pen** allows you to elect what happens when you drag the tip of your stylus from the Graffiti area to the top of the screen in one fell stroke. You can decide if you would like that stylus action to launch Graffiti help (the default action), activate the on-screen keyboard, turn on backlighting, turn off and lock your device, or beam data.

Tapping **HotSync** is asking for trouble, so my best advice is to not even go there. What this option does is permit you to reprogram the **HotSync** button on your device docking cradle—something you really don't want to do. So just pretend it doesn't exist. Life will be simpler that way.

Q. How do I remove software from my Palm? I like to try new software but don't always want to keep some of the programs after trying them out.

A. Deleting programs is fast and easy. Tap the **Applications** icon ➤ **Menu** ➤ **Delete**. A list of all the applications on your Palm will be displayed. Just tap (to select) the program you would like to delete, then tap the **Delete** button. A confirmation screen will appear that displays the name of the program you have selected to delete. If you wish to proceed and delete the program, tap **Yes**.

 When you delete a program, you also delete all the data contained within that program that you may have entered or added.

Q. Is there a faster way to enter people's names into the Date Book when scheduling appointments other than by manually entering their name?

A. There is, but only if the name you wish to enter is already in your Address Book. The lesson to be learned here is to be *sure* to enter into your Address Book anybody with whom you schedule an appointment. If you do that consistently and build your Address Book database, adding appointments or meetings with specific individuals will be a much faster process in the future.

Assuming the person you're meeting with is already in your Address Book, tap the **Date Book** button, and select the **Day** view (displaying a single day's entries) as you would to enter a meeting or other appointment.

Tap the blank line associated with the desired time of your appointment. Then tap **Menu ➤ Options ➤ Phone Lookup**. This will display all the names in your Address Book. Simply tap the name of the person you're planning to meet with to select it, then tap **Add**. The person's name and telephone number will pop right into the time slot selected for your meeting.

Q. How can I hide data on my Palm? Sometimes I'll enter personal events like doctor's appointments, etc. that I don't want anybody else to see.

A. Before you can make any data private, you'll need to activate or enable the Private Records feature. To do this, the first thing you'll need to do is select a password that must be entered in order to view a record designated as private. Be sure to select a password that you can remember. If you ever forget your password, you're out of luck. Oh, sure, there's a way out for the *truly* desperate, but it's not pretty. I'll mention that in a minute, but first select a password.

Tap the small arrow in the upper-right corner of the **Applications** screen to display a drop-down list of all categories, then select **System ➤ Security**.

Tap the **Password: Unassigned** box, and enter the word or whatever you would like to use for your password. Try to keep your password fairly short so it won't be a hassle to enter it each time, but it should also be something unique to you—like the zip code of the town in which you were born or the date of a significant event in your life written without punctuation (such as *0704* for the Fourth of July). Be creative, but not so creative that you won't remember your password.

After entering your password, this warning will appear: **If You Assign A Password, You Must Enter It To Show Private Records.** Makes sense to me. This will only go into effect once you designate a record as private. It won't affect existing records.

Tap **OK** and you'll be asked to confirm your new password by entering it again, followed by the same warning again. If once was good, twice is better, I assume.

Tap **OK** once more and the word **Unassigned** will change to **Assigned**. You can return to this location at any time to change your password, but you will have to provide your existing password before you can change it. You can also elect not to use a password.

Next, at the top of the **Security** screen, right above where you assigned your new password, is the **Private Records** option, and your choices are **Show** or **Hide**. Tap **Hide** to enable this feature, and confirm the confirmation that will appear by pressing **Hide** a second time.

You can designate as private any record entered into your Address Book, Date Book, Memo Pad, or To Do List. To designate a record as private, select the record you wish to make private by tapping it.

Next, tap the **Details** button. (For some strange reason, in the Address Book only, you first have to tap **Edit**, which will take you to the screen that has the **Details** button. Don't ask me why.) A box that contains one or more options for the selected record will be displayed, along with a box labeled **Private**. Tap **Private** to place a check mark in the box, then tap **OK**.

As long as the **Private Records** option is set to **Hide**, any record designated as private will not be visible.

To view a private record and all private records, return to the **Security** screen and tap **Show**. You will be prompted to enter your password first, of course.

When you HotSync, any records designated as Private on your Palm device will also be hidden on your Desktop, and vice versa. To make private records visible on your Palm Desktop, click **View** from the menu bar, and select **Show Private Records**. You will be asked for your trusty password.

Break Glass in Case of Emergency (or Forgotten Password)

I mentioned previously that I would share with you what to do if you absolutely, positively cannot remember your password. This is a drastic step and is intended for the truly frenzied: Return to the **Security** screen where you first selected your password. Under **Password Features**, you'll see a box labeled **Forgotten Password**. (Can't you just feel the tension?)

When you tap the **Forgotten Password** button, your password will be vaporized—deleted forever, *along with all your private records*. That's right, all your private records will be deleted. That's the bad news. The good news is that those deleted private records will be restored to your Palm device the next time you HotSync—assuming, of course, that you've been regularly performing HotSyncs so your Palm Desktop and Palm device contain the same data. Your restored private records will still be private, but without a password.

Q. How do I password protect the Palm Desktop?

A. The same password you select for your Palm device is automatically used to protect your Palm Desktop.

To activate password protection for your Palm Desktop, click **Tools** ➢ **Options** ➢ **Security**, and place a check mark next to **Require Password To Access The Palm Desktop Data**.

Once the check mark is in place, any time the Palm Desktop is started, the correct password will be required to access the program.

Q. I'd like to change the way names are displayed in my Address Book. Is there a way to do that?

A. You can display Address Book entries in alphabetical order by Last Name, First Name—which is the default Address List View—or in Company, Last Name order.

To change between the two, tap the **Address Book** button, then tap the **Menu** icon, followed by **Options** ➢ **Preferences**. Make your selection by tapping **Last Name, First Name** or **Company, Last Name**. Then click **OK**.

If you select the **Company, Last Name** view and there is no company name associated with an entry, the individual's last name will be displayed.

Q. I'm a Service Rep and visit a lot of clients during the day. I keep my contact info in my Palm Address Book, but in addition to the address, phone, fax, e-mail, etc. fields, I'd like to add a field for account numbers and also a credit status line for information provided by my home office. Can I add these additional fields to the form that pops up when I tap New to add a new Address List item?

A. You sure can. You can add up to four additional, custom fields. To add new fields, press the **Address List** button, and tap **Menu** ➢ **Options** ➢ **Rename Custom Fields**.

Under **Create Your Own Field Names By Editing The Text On The Lines Below**, you'll see **Custom 1**, **Custom 2**, **Custom 3**, and **Custom 4**. Select the text that says **Custom 1**, and enter the name you would like to use for that field. Go ahead and name as many of the others as you wish. Tap **OK** when you're done.

Your new fields will be located at the bottom of each Address Book data entry form, including records you have already created.

Q. How can I add a note to an Address Book entry? Sometimes I like to include additional information that won't fit on the form itself. There must be a way to attach a note to an entry, isn't there?

A. Absolutely! If you're in the process of creating a new Address Book entry, just tap the **Note** button after you've entered your information on the Address Book form itself. Tap **Done** when you're finished.

If you would like to add a note to an existing Address Book entry, just display the entry, then tap the **Edit** button. On the **Address Edit** screen, tap the **Note** button that appears at the bottom, and add your note. Tap **Done** when you're finished.

It's not *really* necessary to tap the **Edit** button to edit a record. All you have to do is display the address record you would like to edit (called the *Address view*) and tap it. The **Address** view will immediately change to the **Address Edit** view, and you can make any changes you wish.

So why is there an **Edit** button? Mr. Modem is clueless. If you're a button kind of person, go ahead and use the **Edit** button; otherwise just tap the address record and start editing.

Q. Can I print my To Do List?

A. Using your Palm Desktop program, you can print any record, category of record, or the entire contents of an application (Address Book, To Do List, etc.). After launching your Palm Desktop program, click the **To Do List** button, then, from the menu bar, select **File ➤ Print**. You can also press **CTRL + P** on the keyboard.

Be sure to take a look at the **Print Options** section of the **Print** dialog box to determine which printing options are available to you for your specific printing task.

Q. I've been using an old DOS address book program for many years and have hundreds of entries in it. Can I import that data into my Palm Address Book?

A. As long as your old program is capable of saving its data in either a comma-separated or a tab-separated (sometimes called *tab-delimited*) format, you can.

To do this, in your old program, locate the menu option used to export the data in either of the two formats I just mentioned. When prompted, you'll want to save that data to a file on your hard drive. Be sure to pay attention to where you save the file. I always recommend saving files to the Windows Desktop so you can find them easily and not forget about them.

Next, launch your Palm Desktop program and select **File ➤ Import**, which will bring up the **Import** dialog box. Locate the file you just created with your old program, and highlight it with your cursor to select it.

From the **Type Of File** field, you may have to choose the type of file by using the drop-down list in order for it to appear. Its file extension could be something like .CSV (comma-separated view). It shouldn't be difficult to find, though. Once you select the file, click the **Open** button.

That will bring up the **Specify Import Fields** dialog box. Because the data in your old program won't be arranged in the same way as the Palm's data fields are arranged (first name, last name, company, etc.), this is your chance to give your Palm a helping hand.

On the left side of the screen you'll see the Palm's data fields, such as **First Name**, **Last Name**, etc. On the right side of the screen, you'll see **Data In** *Old Filename*. (Instead of *Old Filename*, you will see the name of the data file saved from the old program.)

All you have to do is drag each field on the left (the Palm fields) until it lines up with the appropriate data on the right (your old program fields). Line up **First Name** with **First Name**, **Address** with **Address**, etc. If there is any data you do not want to import into your Palm, just remove the check mark that appears to the left of the Palm fields' name.

Once you finish lining up the fields, click **OK**. With any luck at all, you'll see all those old contacts appear highlighted in your Palm Desktop Address List. You can then go through the entries and delete any duplications.

Q. Can I import a file from my PC into the Palm Memo Pad?

A. You can if it's in ASCII or in plain text (.TXT) format. You'll import the file using your Palm Desktop program on your PC, then HotSync the information into your Palm device.

Launch your Palm Desktop program, and select **File** ➢ **Import**, which will bring up the **Import** dialog box. In the **Files Of Type** field, select **Text (*.txt)** from the drop-down menu.

Next, use the **Import** dialog box to navigate to the file you would like to import, located on your hard drive. Select it and click the **Open** button.

In the left frame of the **Specify Import Fields** window, you'll see your Palm fields. Be sure **Memo** has a check mark by it and that the Memo field is lined up with the top of your file text appearing in the right frame. If it isn't lined up, just drag the Memo field, appearing in the left frame, to the point that it does line up with the start of the text appearing in the right frame.

Click **OK** when you're finished.

If your text file is a whopper (larger than 4,097 characters) and thus too large to fit into a single memo, your Palm Desktop program will slice and dice it into several memos—however many are needed—and will report **2 Record(s) Imported** (or however many were created).

Q. Can I add to the different types of expenses included with the Palm's Expense program? Sometimes I have expenses that don't fit into any of the types provided.

A. No, you can't. The list of expense types, which range from **Airfare** to **Train** and include such items as **Incidentals**, **Laundry**, and **Subway**, is fixed and cannot be edited. If you have an expense to enter and feel that none of the 28 expense types provided will work for you, my best suggestion is to select **Other** and use it as a catch-all category.

Q. I frequently travel to Europe, so my expenses often involve using foreign currencies. Do I have to convert to U.S. dollars, or can I enter the local currency into my Palm?

A. The Palm Expense program includes dollars, Euro dollars, and Deutsche marks, but you can easily add four additional countries by using the **Custom Currencies** screen.

To add additional countries, launch the Expense program, then tap **Menu** ➢ **Options** ➢ **Custom Currencies**. Tap **Country 1**, **Country 2**, **Country 3**, or **Country 4**, then enter the name of the country and its monetary symbol. (Hint: Monetary symbols appear on the Graffiti numeric keyboard and the Graffiti Reference Guide.) Tap **OK** to return to the **Custom Currencies** screen.

To access the Graffiti Reference Guide, which is always just a quick stylus stroke away, place the point of your stylus at the bottom of the Graffiti area and draw a vertical line all the way up to the top of the Palm screen. This will bring up the Graffiti Reference Guide. Use your scroll buttons (located between the four program buttons) to find the dollar sign ($) and other currency symbols available. Tap **Done** when you're through reviewing the Guide and you'll be returned to the place where you detoured into it in the first place.

Q. Can you explain really briefly how to create categories for expenses? I want to set up an expense category for several different clients and projects. A real "cut-to-the-chase" answer would be appreciated.

A. Sure—oops. Is that too chatty? Okay, okay, here's the no-frills answer:

1. Launch your Expense program. Tap the arrow in the upper right-hand corner to display existing categories.
2. Tap the last item, **Edit Categories**.

3. Tap **New**, enter a new category name, then tap **OK**.

To add additional categories, tap **New** again, and repeat this process as many times as necessary to add new categories.

4. When you're finished adding categories, tap **Done**.

The next time you need to enter an expense, your new categories will be available to you from the drop-down list of categories.

Q. How do I delete expenses after a business trip or after they have been submitted?

A. Launch your Expense program, then tap **Menu ➢ Record**, and select either **Delete Item** (to remove one specific expense item) or **Purge** (to delete an entire category of expense). If you tap **Purge**, a list of existing categories will be presented; tap the category you want to purge, and tap the **Purge** button.

 As soon as you tap **Purge** to delete a category, it's gone. You won't receive a courtesy confirmation. Instead, the category just vaporizes, so be sure you want to delete the entire category before tapping **Purge**.

Q. I'd like to put my memos into categories. How do I create categories for the Memo Pad?

A. Press the **Memo Pad** button on your Palm to launch the Memo Pad.

Tap **New** to create a new memo, or start to write anywhere on the Memo Pad screen and you'll automatically be at the data entry screen, as if you had tapped the **New** button. Cool, huh? (So do you need to tap the **New** button to add a new memo? No, you sure don't.)

Tap **Details**, which will bring up the **Memo Details** dialog box. Tap the arrow that appears to the right of the word **Category** to display a list of existing categories. Tap the last item on the list, **Edit Categories**.

Tap **New**, and enter the name of a new category. Tap **OK** when you're done.

The next time you write a Memo, tap **Details ➢ Category**, and assign your memo to an appropriate category.

Q. I just did a HotSync to copy the expense information I entered into my Palm to my desktop computer. How do I access that information in the Palm Desktop?

A. I hate to be the bearer of bad news, but you can't—without some outside assistance in the form of Microsoft Excel. However, the other Palm programs, like the Date Book, Address Book, Memo Pad, etc., can be accessed from your Palm Desktop program. In fact, that's an easy and convenient way to get data into your Palm handheld—by entering the data into your Palm Desktop and then doing a HotSync to get it into your Palm device.

But the Palm Expense program doesn't work the same way, even though the **Expense** button does appear on the Palm Desktop Toolbar along with the Date Book, Address Book, and other programs.

The expense data from your Palm is copied to your Palm Desktop program during a HotSync, but you'll need Microsoft Excel installed on your desktop computer to view it, to print a report, or to otherwise work with the data. That may sound troublesome, but it's really not—well, unless you're not an Excel user.

Working in this way, your expense data is placed directly into an Excel spreadsheet, which you can access simply by clicking the **Expense** button in your Palm Desktop program. That will launch Excel (assuming you have it installed on your desktop computer) and open a file named `expense.db`. This file is physically located on your hard drive at `C:\Palm\YourUsername\Expense`—just in case you're curious.

 When you launch Excel, you may receive a warning from Mr. Gates & Company about using macros and how they may be infected with creepy-crawly viruses. Because the `expense.db` file was created within your Palm device—which is a "sealed" or closed environment—the file in all probability isn't going to be infected with any viruses, so it's okay to elect to enable macros. In fact, if you don't elect to enable macros, you won't be able to access your Expense data. How's that for irony?

Q. How do I create a business card so that I can beam my information to other Palm users?

A. *Beaming* (transmitting) information between devices is one of the many ultra-cool things Palm users can do. It feels very space-age and high tech, for sure. Every Palm device since the Palm III has an IR (infrared) port that looks like a small, dark-red window.

A *business card* in this context is really any record in your Address List that you designate as a business card for beaming purposes. You can easily change the designation at any time. For example, if you're at a computer show, going from booth to booth, many vendors will welcome beamed information instead of a hard-copy business card to send follow-up materials. In this situation, you may wish to designate your business address, work telephone number, and e-mail address as your beamable business card and exclude any personal information. In other situations, you may wish to designate a record that contains your home address and home phone number.

To designate information in your Address List as your business card, open the address record, then select **Menu ➢ Record ➢ Select Business Card**.

The **Select Business Card** dialog box will appear and ask whether you would like to make the selected name (the record you selected) your business card. If so, tap **Yes ➢ Done**.

A small Rolodex card icon will appear at the top of this record indicating it has been designated as your beamable business card.

Q. How can I beam a business card to another Palm device?

A. Assuming the other Palm also has an IR (infrared) port, hold down the Address Book button (it looks like a little telephone handset) for about two seconds.

 Before you tap **Beam**, line up the two Palm devices so their IR ports face each other and are between six inches and three feet apart. Once the beaming begins, a dialog box will appear to let you know that the beaming is in progress. The first thing you'll see is a message that says your Palm is searching for the other Palm. Once the two devices "handshake" and establish their connection, the data is transmitted.

Q. When beaming information to another unit, how far apart can the units be positioned? Is there a maximum distance?

A. Most infrared devices have a range of approximately five feet.

Q. I tried to beam data, but nothing happened. I think I'm doing everything right, but nothing gets beamed. Any thoughts?

A. Sounds like your **Beam Receive** option is toggled off. (Sounds very Star Trekish, doesn't it?) You need to turn on the ability to beam data before you can actually beam it.

Tap **System** ➤ **Preferences** ➤ **General**. The last item on the list of **General Preferences** is **Beam Receive**. Tap the arrow next to the word **Off** and select **On.** Now try beaming again.

Q. How do I select an Address Book item or Memo Pad entry for beaming?

A. Though the specifics vary depending on what you want to beam, the general procedure is the same: If it's a single item—a single Address Book entry or a single Memo Pad entry—display the entry you would like to beam, tap the **Menu** icon (in the lower-left corner of the Graffiti area), then, from the drop-down **Record** menu, select the appropriate item: In the Address Book, you'll have a choice of **Beam Address** (to beam a single record); in the Memo Pad, **Beam Memo**; in the To Do List, **Beam Item**.

If you would like to beam an entire category of items—every address in your Address Book or every entry in your Date Book—open the Address Book (or other application) and select a category by tapping the little arrow in the top-right corner of your screen to display the categories. Tap a category to select it, then tap the **Menu** icon. From the drop-down **Record** menu, select **Beam Category**.

 Before you beam an entire category, be sure it's something you *really* want to do. Not only can it require a lot of time if you have hundreds of entries, but it can also consume a lot of your Palm's memory.

Q. How can I beam one of my Palm programs to another Palm user? Is it legal to do that?

A. I'm glad you asked about the legality of beaming applications. Stealing or pirating software is illegal, and it's not very nice, either. Programs that aren't free should never be shared. Instead, provide the web address of the program so your friend or colleague can download and register (and pay for) his or her own program. The good folks who write this fabulous software for us deserve to earn a few dollars for their efforts. Most of this software is very inexpensive, so let's help the folks who are helping us and be sure to pay for the software we use.

As you'll soon discover, if you do try to beam programs, not all programs are beamable. (And, yes, *beamable* is Mr. Modem's new word of the day.) The basic programs that come with the Palm device (Address Book, Date Book, To Do List, Memo Pad) are not capable of being beamed, for example. Other commercial programs are locked to prevent beaming. Some programs require the use of an accompanying database, and those programs can't be beamed either.

However, if you do discover a really neat, free game, utility, or other program and you're just dying to share it with a friend, here's how you do it. (It's very similar to beaming data from your Address Book or Memo Pad, for that matter.)

First, tap the **Applications** icon to bring up your **Applications** screen. Next, tap the **Menu** icon and select **Beam** from the drop-down menu that will appear.

It may take a few seconds, but in short order you'll be presented with the **Beam** dialog box that lists all the applications on your Palm device. (The apps—that's the groovy-cool way of saying *applications*—that cannot be beamed will appear with a little padlock. Get the picture?) Tap an application to select it, then tap **Beam**.

As the sender (or beamer), when the beaming has finished you won't receive a message saying **Congratulations!** or even any acknowledgment that you've successfully completed your beaming. The receiver (the beamee) is presented with a dialog box that asks whether he or she wants to accept the data that was beamed. A tap on the **Yes** button means the data is received, accepted, and integrated into the receiver's Palm.

A program received is placed into the Unfiled category, where it will remain until the Palm user decides to place it in another category.

You can't receive duplicate applications, but you can receive duplicate data, so if somebody beams you a copy of information you already have in your Address Book or Memo Pad you'll end up with two of the same records. You can delete one of the records at some point in the future when you encounter a duplicate.

Mr. Modem's Recommended Websites

DDH Software   www.ddhsoftware.com

Handango   www.handango.com

Hands High Software   www.handshigh.com

Handspring   www.handspring.com

LandWare   www.landware.com

MemoWare   www.memoware.com

Palm   www.palm.com

Palm Boulevard   www.palmblvd.com

Palm Gear HQ   www.palmgear.com

PalmPower Magazine   www.palmpower.com

Peanutpress   www.peanutpress.com

Quartus   www.quartus.net/products

Tucows   www.tucows.com

Must-Surf TV!
(WebTV, that is)

Hundreds of thousands of people surf the Internet, exchange e-mail, chat, and participate in newsgroups every day—without a computer, thanks to WebTV. Despite being easy to use and a breeze to configure, a few questions always remain. In this chapter, we hear from some WebTV enthusiasts and some folks thinking about making the switch to WebTV.

Q. What is WebTV?

A. In its simplest form, WebTV is a device that permits you to access the Internet but uses your television, instead of a traditional computer and monitor, to display web pages. Even if you know absolutely nothing about the Internet and even less about computers, you can be accessing the Internet and receiving junk e-mail and get-rich-quick schemes within minutes of using WebTV. Sounds like a dream come true, doesn't it?

WebTV is an excellent choice if you're not particularly interested in learning about computers. You'll need three items to use WebTV: the WebTV terminal (and remote), a keyboard, and the cables to connect your terminal to the phone lines and TV. Monthly service costs $9.95 to $24.95 (depending upon the level of service you select), and you can save $10 if you use your own ISP. Add to this the cost of the equipment, which is typically less than $200. Of course, if you're a bells-and-whistles kind of person—my kind of person—you can always add a few goodies.

WebTV is available at finer consumer electronics stores everywhere. For readers with Internet access, additional information is available at `www.webtv.net`.

Q. What is WebTV Classic?

A. The WebTV Classic Internet is the basic WebTV service and includes the ability to search or find a variety of topics on the Web, to save your favorite websites in folders, and to find out what's going on in your area. It also includes e-mail and chat.

Q. What's WebTV Plus?

A. WebTV Plus Interactive includes all the features of WebTV Classic Internet service plus a few extra goodies: a "home base" for television viewing with a show-in-progress program description, an electronic program guide, and a picture-in-picture feature that allows you to watch television while surfing the Internet.

You must have a WebTV Plus receiver to gain access to the WebTV Plus Interactive Network. WebTV Plus works with all major cable systems and supports closed captioning. There is an additional monthly charge for WebTV Plus Interactive service.

Q. I can't remember what name I used when I first registered with WebTV. Is there some way I can find that out?

A. There sure is. From your WebTV Home screen, select **Switch User**. The username shown at the top of the list on the **Choose Your Name** screen is the name you selected when you registered. It's also referred to as your **Primary Account**.

Q. Can I remove my real name from the primary user's e-mail address?

A. You sure can. From **Mail**, select **Settings**, then **Mail Name**. Delete the names in the boxes, or change them as you wish. Select **Done** when you're finished.

Q. How can I add additional users? I'd like to set up an account for my wife and two children. How do I do that, and do I have to pay extra for those accounts?

A. You can add up to five additional user accounts at no additional charge, so you're in good shape! Each user will get a different e-mail address, their own list of favorites, plus an optional password.

To add additional users, you'll need to be connected to the WebTV network using your primary user account. From your WebTV Home screen, follow these on-screen steps:

1. Choose **Settings** ➤ **Extra Users** ➤ **Add User**. Enter a first name and/or last name. (You don't have to enter a first *and* last name unless you want to.) Select **Continue** when you're ready to proceed.

2. Enter the name you want to use as part of a new e-mail address. `@webtv.net` will be added to the name you provide. Once you've entered the name, choose **Continue**. (If somebody else—another WebTV subscriber—is using the name you selected, you'll be invited to enter another name. Go ahead and try another name, then choose **Continue**.)

3. The next step invites you to add a password. You don't have to do this. If you would like to use a password, type your password in the **Password** box, then type it again to confirm it. Your password will appear as dots rather than English letters as you type them in. Choose **Continue** when you're ready.

4. You'll then have an opportunity to prevent this account from accessing X-rated or adult-oriented websites. If you want to impose this restriction, choose **Kid-Friendly** or **SurfWatch**. A red dot will appear in front of the restriction you elect. If you don't want to impose any restrictions, leave the red dot in front of **Unrestricted Access**. Press **Continue** when you've made your selection.

SurfWatch doesn't promise absolutely, positively that your kids won't be able to get into any adult-oriented sites. SurfWatch blocks sites according to a "no access" list that it maintains and presumably updates regularly. But if a website isn't on the SurfWatch list, your kids will be able to access the site. But if your kiddos do try to access a blocked site, a message will appear on screen telling the user that access to that site is blocked, courtesy of SurfWatch. For more information about SurfWatch or related products, visit `www.surfcontrol.com/`.

Kid-Friendly takes a reverse approach. Rather than attempting to block access to adult-oriented sites, Kid-Friendly *only* permits access to approved sites. In other words, everything is off limits other than sites that are approved by Kid-Friendly. There are still no guarantees that your young 'uns won't wind up at the International Naked Jello-Wrestling Championship website, but odds are very heavily stacked against it happening.

5. Next, you'll have the ability to impose even more restrictions by preventing the user from using e-mail, chat rooms, or the Web Page Builder feature. Just make your selection regarding what, if any, of these limitations you would like to impose. If you don't make any changes on this screen, the user will be able to send and receive e-mail, access chat rooms and newsgroups, and use the Page Builder to construct web pages. Press **Continue** when you're ready to move to the last step.

6. As a last step, review the information you provided for this new account, and make any changes by choosing the blue text. Select **Done** when you're finished.

Q. I bought WebTV, but connecting requires a long-distance telephone call. Is there any way to avoid that?

A. If a long-distance call is required to connect to the WebTV network, you should look into signing up with a local Internet Service Provider (ISP) for your access to the Internet. Ask some friends and neighbors whether they have Internet access and, if so, who is providing that access.

Once you obtain the name of one or two local ISPs, call them and ask whether their service works with WebTV. It probably will, but it's always worth asking.

The cost for unlimited access (an unlimited number of hours connected) to the Internet should be approximately $20 per month. There are also free Internet access providers, though not all will accommodate WebTV. Be safe, and ask first to be sure.

Once you sign up with a local ISP, you'll be asked to create a username for your account and a password, and you'll be provided with the local telephone number that WebTV is going to dial to connect to the Internet. With this information in hand, follow these steps to provide this information to WebTV so you can connect to the WebTV network and get rid of those long-distance charges you've been paying—well, after this last time.

First, connect to the WebTV network using your primary user account. I know this is a long-distance call for you, but it's the last long-distance call you'll have to make to log on!

From your Home screen, select **Settings** ➤ **Dialing** ➤ **Dialing Options** ➤ **Use An ISP**.

From the **Billing** screen, select **Signing Up To Use An ISP**. Then, from the **Using An ISP** screen, press the **Sign Up Now** button.

Here, you'll be asked to enter the name of your ISP, your username (this is your username with your ISP, not your WebTV account) your ISP password, and the local telephone number provided to you when you signed up with your ISP.

After providing this information, press the **Use Your ISP** button.

At this point you should receive a message telling you that your WebTV unit needs to reconnect in order for the changes you just made to take effect. Select **Continue**, and WebTV will reconnect.

After the connection is established, you'll see a confirmation screen. Select the **Use Your ISP** button, and your WebTV unit will connect to the WebTV network using the local telephone number you just provided.

Adios, long-distance telephone calls!

Q. I have a Windows 98 computer. Can I set things up to watch TV on my PC?

A. Sure, but first you'll need a TV tuner card, which costs anywhere from $70 to $140. That's what enables you to actually plug your cable, satellite, or broadcast TV signal into your computer.

You'll need to install and set up the WebTV application that is part of Windows 98. To do this, click the **My Computer** icon from your Windows Desktop, then **Control Panel**. Click **Add/Remove Programs**, select **Windows Setup**, and check the **WebTV** box—it's located at the bottom of the **Components** list.

Finally, consult the instructions that came with your tuner card to set up the TV display on your PC. You'll be running *Bewitched* reruns in no time.

If you subscribe to WebTV Plus Interactive service, press your keyboard's **Options** key while you're surfing, then select **TV Window**. You can also open the TV Window by pressing **Command** + **W**. If you would like to bounce the TV Window from side to side on your screen—even if it's just for the fun of it—just press **Command** + **M** or, even easier, just press **Enter** on your remote and follow the bouncing window.

Q. I have WebTV Plus, and I've tried changing channels by using the Up and Down buttons on my remote, but nothing happens. Any idea what the problem is?

A. Sounds like you need to hit the **WebTV Mode** button on the remote to toggle it into channel-changing mode. That should take care of it.

When using the keyboard to change channels, you'll need to check and be sure that the **TV/WebTV** switch is on the **WebTV** side.

Lots of WebTV users prefer the keyboard for changing channels, even if that does sound a bit strange. But it's actually very convenient if you're surfing the Web and keeping an eye on the TV at the same time.

To further enhance your channel-switching pleasure—something that annoys the heck out of Mrs. Modem, I might add—you can program your WebTV unit so that it switches between a limited number of specific stations when you're channel surfing. To do this, follow these steps:

1. Select **TV Home** ➢ **Settings** ➢ **Channels**.

2. Designate the channels you want to include in your channel surfing expeditions by placing a check mark by the channel(s) to be included.

3. When you're finished, select Done.

If you select the **Auto Select** mode, your WebTV unit will select channels that have programs currently being broadcast and ignore any "blank" channels. Maybe some day we'll have an Infomercial Repellent Option so we can program WebTV to skip over any channels showing infomercials. I'd pay big bucks for that myself.

Bonus Tip: WebTV can surf up to six channels at a time! To activate this feature, press the **Recent** button on your keyboard or remote unit, then move the yellow selection box to any of the small TV windows to update that window. Pressing the **Recent** button a second time will update all six windows at once. Happy days are here again!

Q. How do I know when I can interact with a TV program I'm watching? Isn't that one of the features of WebTV Plus?

A. It sure is! You can interact with a television broadcast whenever you see the I-link logo. (It's the interactive-setting logo that looks like a lowercase *i* inside a little square.) The I-link logo will only appear in the upper right-hand corner of the screen, and only when you're watching in full-screen mode.

As soon as you see the I-link logo, that's your invitation to join in by pressing the **Go/OK** button on your remote unit. You can also press **Return** on your keyboard. Then select **Go Interactive**.

Every interactive show will present something special for WebTV viewers that will allow you to participate in some manner.

To obtain a list of Interactive links, press **TV Home**, and select **TV Sites**.

Q. Can I capture a picture from a TV broadcast and send it to a friend by e-mail?

A. Yes, but only if you have the WebTV Plus service, not WebTV Classic.

From the WebTV Home screen, select **Mail**, or you can press the **Mail** button on your keyboard. Either one will work fine. However you get to Mail, once you're there, select **Write**.

Type in your message as you would for any e-mail message, by filling in the **To:** and **Subject** lines, along with the body of the e-mail.

Next, select **Photo** from the sidebar and the **TV/Video** switch. As soon as you select it, it will change to the **TV** position from its default **Video** position.

This next step is designed to bring out the artiste in you: As soon as the image in the video window is perfecto—just the way you want it to be—hit the **Freeze** button. If you fumble it or you manage to capture a picture of somebody while they're blinking their eyes, just hit **Freeze** again. This will cause the image to begin moving, and you can make as many attempts as you wish to capture the perfect image.

Once you have achieved success—or lowered your expectations, whichever comes first—press the **Add To Message** button. Your captured image will appear at the bottom of your e-mail message.

Hit the **Send** button to send your e-mail with the attached image, or if you want to take one more stab at capturing another image, just scroll down to the bottom and press the **Detach** button to jettison that image and try it again.

Q. How do I delete a message in WebTV e-mail?

A. To discard a message, first select the message you want from the list of mail in your mailbox. Go to your mailbox and, with the arrow keys, move down the list until the message you want is selected, or highlighted, with the yellow box around it.

Then, hit the **Return** key to open the message as if you were going to read it. While you're looking at the message, you'll see a menu on the left of the screen. On that menu is the option **Discard**. With your arrow keys, move to the menu on the left of the screen and down the menu until the word **Discard** is highlighted. Then hit **Return**. A box will pop up asking if you want to discard. Select the button at the bottom to confirm that you want to discard the message, and press **Return**.

Q. How can I get back to watching the TV from my WebTV mailbox?

A. Use the **View** button on the remote control to toggle between **TV** view and **Web** view.

Q. I know I can program my WebTV remote control unit, but I haven't done it yet. It's like programming the VCR to me: I've tried it, but it's a bit over my head. Can you explain how to do it—and keep it simple?

A. I think the word *programming* is what sounds intimidating, so let's just substitute the word *enjoying* instead. The process is really simple, straightforward, and well worth doing so you can use your WebTV remote to control your TV. (Mrs. Modem swears I enjoy remote control units more than any person ought to enjoy remote control units. I think it's a "guy" thing.)

If you have WebTV Classic Internet, you can use your WebTV remote to control your TV's volume and to mute the TV, if your television has that feature. Just follow these easy steps for WebTV Classic Internet:

1. From your **WebTV Home** screen, choose **Settings** ➤ **Television** ➤ **Remote Control**. At this point, just follow whatever instructions appear on your screen.

 WebTV Plus Interactive users can use their remote control units in a similar manner by following these slightly different steps: From your **WebTV Home** screen, select **Help** ➤ **Tips And Tricks** ➤ **Remote Control Setup**. Then just follow the instructions that will appear on your screen and proceed to the next step.

2. You'll soon need the 3- or 4-digit code that controls your TV, but that will be displayed on screen as you move through the instructions, so don't be concerned if you don't have those numbers at hand.

If you have a cool wireless keyboard, you can use your keyboard to control your TV by pressing **Help** from your Home screen, then select **Keyboard Setup**.

Q. Do I need to disable call-waiting with WebTV?

A. Unlike people connecting to the Internet via a personal computer with a dial-up account, WebTV works very well with call-waiting, though you do have the ability to disable call-waiting, as well.

If you prefer to let WebTV work with your call-waiting service, all you need to do is configure WebTV to receive calls while you're connected to the WebTV network. Then, when an incoming call arrives, you'll be automatically disconnected from WebTV, your telephone will ring, and you can take the call—or let your answering machine pick up. When you're finished with the call or a message has been left on your machine, press the **Return** key on the keyboard or the **Go/OK** button on your remote to reestablish your connection to the WebTV network. Once you're connected again, you'll be right back to the screen you were viewing before you disconnected.

To configure your WebTV to interact with call-waiting as I describe here, you have to be connected to the WebTV network and using your primary WebTV account. Follow these steps from your **WebTV Home** screen: **Settings** ➢ **Dialing** ➢ **Call Waiting**. Select **Accept Calls (Disconnect If a Call Comes In)**, then select **Done**.

Q. I'd like to disable call-waiting so I'm not interrupted while I'm online. Is that possible?

A. Sure! If you prefer, you can elect not to be interrupted while using WebTV. To disable call-waiting during your online sessions, follow these steps: **Web Home** ➢ **Settings** ➢ **Dialing** ➢ **Call Waiting** ➢ **Block Calls**. Here, you'll need to enter the prefix used to temporarily disable call-waiting. The prefix is *70 (star symbol, 7, 0) in most areas of the U.S., but check with your telephone company to be sure. After you terminate your WebTV session, call waiting will be automatically enabled (activated) again.

When you're done, choose **Done**.

Q. I keep getting disconnected while I'm online and it's really annoying. Any suggestions?

A. WebTV will disconnect you automatically after 10 minutes of inactivity on any one screen. That means if you're reading a rambling e-mail or a particularly lengthy web page, you need to create the appearance that you haven't fallen asleep at the keyboard or walked away. Any keyboard or remote control action that results in screen activity will keep your connection alive, so just scroll around the screen, press a key on your keyboard or remote—anything to provide a little interaction will do it.

Q. I think the credit card that's charged for my WebTV account each month is about to expire. How can I update that information?

A. First, establish your connection to the WebTV network with your primary user account. Then, from **Web Home**, select **Account ➤ How You Pay**.

Next, select the payment method you would like to change or modify—in this case, **Credit Card**. The **Payment Method** screen will show how you're currently paying for the WebTV network.

When your credit card information is displayed, make the appropriate changes, and select **Done**. That's all there is to it.

Q. How can I review my entire billing history online?

A. You can't review your entire billing history online—well, unless your entire billing history consists of the last three months. You can review your last three months' billing history, however—nothing beyond that.

You must be logged on to the WebTV network using your main user account—the account you created when you first registered with WebTV.

Then, from your WebTV Home screen, choose **Account ➤ Billing Statement**. After you review your statement, select **Done**.

Q. What is the WebTV Today feature?

A. WebTV Today provides the latest information on WebTV, as well as summaries of news, money, weather, and sports. WebTV-specific information resources include the Club WebTV Newsletter as well as WebTV Tips.

Q. Where can I find the Club WebTV Newsletter?

A. Club WebTV is located in the WebTV Today section of your Home screen. To find the Club WebTV Newsletter, select **WebTV Today** from your WebTV Home screen, then choose **Club WebTV**, located in the upper right-hand corner of the page.

Q. What does the time stamp on my WebTV e-mail indicate?

A. The time reflected in time stamps on e-mail or other postings shows the local time where the message was sent from. Time is usually either shown with an offset from your local time zone (*EST-3*, for instance, means eastern standard time, less three hours) or shown as Universal time, which is Greenwich mean time (GMT) that nobody really understands.

Bear in mind that time stamps are only as accurate as the mail server that sends out the message, and sometimes those clocks are off. Also, some online services use mail servers located in other time zones, so it can really be tricky relying on time stamps. I use time stamps to provide a rough idea when a message was sent, nothing more specific than that.

Q. I'd like to have WebTV check e-mail automatically the first thing every morning, so it's waiting for me when I log on. How can I do that?

A. Under normal circumstances, WebTV will check for e-mail once a day at a randomly selected time, but you can change that time so your e-mail can be waiting for you first thing in the morning, or you can disable this feature (explanation follows) so WebTV never checks for e-mail on its own.

To set up a specific mail-check time, first be sure you're connected to the WebTV network and that you logged on using your primary user account. Then, with your connection established, go to **Mail List** and select **Settings**.

Choose **Message Light**, then press the **Time** button. A list of time selections will be presented to you.

Choose the time you would like WebTV to check for any new e-mail. You can use the down arrow on your keyboard to move through the list of times. Once you make your selection, select **Done**.

To disable automatic e-mail checking, go to **Mail List** and select **Settings**, followed by **Message Light** ➢ **Time**. (Once again, you must have your connection to the WebTV network established and be logged on with your primary user account.)

When the list of times is presented, use the up arrow on your keyboard, and go to the top of the list, then select **Don't Check**—which will instruct your WebTV unit not to check for e-mail automatically. When you're finished, select **Done**.

Q. I've used a computer for years but just purchased WebTV. I'd like to create some folders to hold e-mail that I've sent and also for incoming e-mail that I might want to save. How do I create folders with WebTV?

A. What are known in the personal computer world as *folders* are accommodated by the use of a *storage area* in the world of WebTV. Your WebTV account includes 2 megabytes of storage. Each user account has its own e-mail account so you can create a storage area for each of these accounts.

When you read an e-mail message without discarding it, that e-mail will continue to appear in your Mail List until you toss it or move it to your Saved folder. Your Saved folder will be created automatically when you create a storage area.

Depending on the size of your e-mail messages and whether they contain graphics or sound files, you should be able to store between 100 and 150 e-mail messages.

To create your storage area, follow this sequence: **Mail List** ➢ **Settings** ➢ **Extras**. Place a check by the box to indicate that you want to **Create A Storage Area For Your Saved, Sent, And Discarded Messages**. Then select **Done**.

Once your storage area is created, you'll see a little sidebar area in your Mail List that will have a **Storage** menu item. Select that to access your storage area.

To place an e-mail into your Saved folder, select the e-mail you want to save from your Mail List, and press **Save**.

 WebTV automatically saves (in the Sent folder) your outgoing messages for one week. If you want to *permanently* save them, you'll need to move them to the Saved folder as described here.

Q. I accidentally deleted an e-mail. Can I get it back, or is it gone forever?

A. WebTV provides a lot of flexibility for saving and disposing of messages. As you already discovered, to delete (discard) an e-mail message, you select **Clean Up** from the Mail List. You'll be presented with a list of all your saved e-mail. Just place a check mark next to those you would like to discard, then press **Discard**. Poof! Faster than you can say "Oh, no! I didn't want to discard that message," it's gone.

Knowing that we all make mistakes, the good folks at WebTV thoughtfully provided a way for us to have a second chance by allowing us to retrieve a discarded message. Thank you, WebTV!

To fish your discarded e-mail out of the trash, choose **Storage** from the Mail List. Select the **Discarded** folder and you'll see a list of the message you've tossed out for the past week (longer than a week and you're out of luck).

Select the message or messages you want to retrieve. Unpoof! The body of the message is displayed.

Select **Save** to move the retrieved message into your Saved folder.

Q. I like to save some of the e-mail that I send to other people, but not every one of them. Is there a way to do that?

A. Yes, you can be selective about which of your own sent e-mail messages you save. It's a good idea to be selective, particularly if you send a lot of e-mail. Many times, an e-mail will be little more than a casual note of little importance, so it's not worth the storage space to retain it.

Follow these steps to save an e-mail you sent to others:

1. Select **Mail List** ➢ **Storage** ➢ **Sent** (folder).

2. Select the e-mail you would like to save, and press **Save** from the sidebar.

To review an e-mail you saved in the Save folder, select **Storage** from your Mail List. Select the Saved folder, and then the e-mail message you would like to read.

Q. If I send an e-mail to somebody and they respond, my original message appears along with their response. When somebody writes to me and I respond to them, their original doesn't appear with my response. What am I doing wrong?

A. For context purposes, most e-mail software programs automatically include the e-mail to which you are replying. This is called a *quote back*.

WebTV does not include the original (or *parent*) message in your reply by default, but you can quickly adjust your mail settings so you will have that ability in the future. Just follow these steps:

1. Select **Mail List** ➢ **Settings** ➢ **Extras**.

2. You will see a box labeled **Add An Option To Include The Original Message When You Reply**. Place a check mark by this box, and select **Done**.

Your response should appear *before* the quote back, not after. Responding before the quoted material is an on-line courtesy (called *netiquette*) and will prevent the recipient of your response from having to scroll through his or her own e-mail to get to your response.

Once you have changed your settings and have the ability to include the original message with your reply, follow the following steps to actually include the original. (Even though you changed your settings, it will not be included automatically with every reply)

1. Select the e-mail message to which you want to reply, and select **Reply** from the sidebar.

2. In the area under the **Subject** line, enter the text of your reply.

3. Press the **Attach Original Message** button, then press **Send**.

Q. When I receive an e-mail along with several other recipients, how can I send a copy of my reply to everybody who received the original e-mail?

A. This is called *replying to all,* and the ability to reply to all needs to be activated by turning on the cleverly named Reply All feature. Here's how:

1. Select **Mail List ➢ Settings ➢ Extras**.

2. Place a check mark next to the box that invites you to **Add A Cc: Line For Carbon-Copy Recipients On Outgoing Messages**, and press the **Reply All** button. Then, press **Done**.

 Since there are no carbon copies today—when was the last time you saw a piece of carbon paper?—the cc: field is frequently referred to as the *cyber copy* or the *courtesy copy* field.

When you would like to reply to a message sent to two or more individuals and have all recipients receive a copy of your response, select **Reply All** from the sidebar (instead of **Reply**) to copy the sender and all other recipients of the original message.

Warning: When you include one or more e-mail addresses in the cc: field, those addresses *will* be visible to every recipient of your e-mail. Please keep in mind that most of the people you include in your cc: field probably didn't give you permission to publish their e-mail addresses, but that's the effect of using the cc: field. Be sensitive to the fact that you are distributing other individuals' e-mail addresses if you include them in your cc: field.

Unfortunately, WebTV at this time does not support a bcc: (blind carbon copy) field, which would permit you to hide other individuals' addresses. Hopefully, that feature will be forthcoming soon. WebTV, are you listening?

Q. If I want to send an e-mail to several family members and friends, do I just type in each e-mail address in the To: field?

A. As long as you separate each e-mail address with a comma, that's exactly right.

However, if you frequently send e-mail to the same group of individuals, create a mailing list instead of typing in each individual address on every e-mail you send to the group. You can create as many mailing lists as you wish.

To create a mailing list, select **Mail List ➢ Addresses ➢ Add.** In the **Name:** field, give your mailing list a name such as *Family, Office,* or some other name that describes the individuals who will be included in the list.

In the **E-mail:** field, enter as many e-mail addresses as you wish, each one separated by a comma. Select **Add** when you're done.

Q. How do I set up a printer to work with WebTV?

A. Essentially, it's just a matter of plugging everything together and hoping for the best—just like with computers. It's a good idea to unplug the terminal before attaching any devices (such as a printer) to the terminal. With WebTV Classic Internet, you need to plug the adapter into the terminal. If you're thinking that you need a tool to remove the side plate, you're right, and that tool comes with the adapter.

Before plugging in the adapter, remove the washers from the mounting screws, which will permit a snugger connection. (I've been trying for years to work *snugger* into a grammatically incorrect sentence. Finally!) If the connection is a good one, a little green light will appear at the side of the adapter. At this point, just follow the instructions that came with your specific printer to complete its setup.

Connect the printer cable from the printer to the terminal on the back of the WebTV Plus Interactive or to the adapter on the WebTV Classic Internet. The terminal should automatically recognize the model of printer you're hooking up. If it doesn't, disconnect the device, then reconnect it, and try it again, making sure that all connections are firmly in place.

Instruct the printer to print a sheet for you if it doesn't happen automatically. Press the **Options** key, and look for **Printing Options**. For most printing, you'll only need to have the **Print Text In Black** box checked. (The **Black Cartridge Installed** option is for single-cartridge printers only.) If you feel like exploring, try it with each box checked just to see what it does, for future reference.

Q. If I want to print just one page out of many pages, how do I do that?

A. If what you want to print is only enough to fit on one screen, use the **Print Screen** button. If it's more than a screen's worth, then you can use **Cut**, **Copy**, and **Paste** to copy the text to a word processor, an e-mail message, or to another destination location.

Q. How long can I leave the printer turned on with WebTV?

A. Many people leave their printer on all the time, so there really isn't any limit on how long you can leave the printer on.

Q. How do I cancel the service for WebTV?

A. To cancel your WebTV network service, please give a call to 800-GO-WEBTV (800-469-3288). You can also visit the WebTV website at www.webtv.net/.

Q. Can I hook up two WebTV terminals to the same telephone line?

A. Yes, you can connect two boxes to a single phone line, but you can only be online with one of them at a time. You'll also have to pay for two subscriptions for service.

Q. How do I use the shortcut keys on my wireless keyboard?

A. The *shortcut keys,* labeled **F1** through **F7** on the top row of your keyboard, enable you to press a single key to go directly to a preassigned Favorite website. To create a shortcut, follow these steps:

1. Select **WebTV Home** screen ➤ **Favorites**, then select the folder that contains the Favorite you would like to create a shortcut to.

2. Select **Organize** ➤ **Shortcut**, and press the button to the right of the Favorite to assign a shortcut to a specific key, **F1** through **F7**.

3. Once you have made your selection, press **Done** to record the change.

Q. Sometimes I get stuck at the WebTV logo when I try to log on. How do I break free from it?

A. The *logon logo* can drive you loco! When that happens, try pressing a few keys on your keyboard (or on your remote), which may get the yellow connection light flickering again. If you get stuck on the logo every single time, it may be the result of some other device on your phone line, so try disconnecting any answering machine, fax machine, or cordless phone that may be connected to the same line.

A sure-fire test to see whether the line is available is to pick up the phone and listen to the dial tone. If you hear a nice, strong dial tone with no static, that's a good sign. Static is not a good sign and could be the cause of your problems.

If you do hear line noise or static, contact your telephone service provider and ask them to check your phone line. Explain that you're having difficulty sending and receiving faxes. It's been my experience that telephone companies may be more responsive to line problems relating to faxing than to data transmission or connecting to the Internet. It's worth a try, anyway.

Last, set the terminal's dialing in **Setup** to **Audible**. The next time you connect, note the local access number being used. Then call WebTV Networks at 800-469-3288 and ask whether there's a problem with that specific number.

Q. How do I change the size of the text when using the **Print Screen** key?

A. Go to the WebTV Home screen, and select **Using WebTV**. Go to **Text Settings**, and change them to either **Small**, **Medium**, or **Large**. This will also affect the size of the text you see on your screen in your e-mail, on web pages, while chatting, and in newsgroups.

Q. What is the red dot that appears at the bottom of my screen on occasion?

A. The red dot indicates that you have activated **Caps Lock**. Pressing the **Caps Lock** key causes everything you type to appear in ALL CAPITAL LETTERS. Typing in ALL CAPS is considered to be shouting online and is best avoided. To type in lowercase, press the **Caps Lock** key again to toggle it off.

Q. What does the **Options** button do?

A. Press the **Options** button on your remote while watching a TV program. You can then save the channel as a Favorite to your TV Listings, delete a Favorite channel, or view program information.

Q. Is there a way to clear out my terminal's RAM memory cache?

A. You can clear out your terminal's RAM memory cache by turning the unit off and then back on again. You can also clear the memory cache by switching users.

Q. I saw two people talking about WebTV in a chat room, and they both said their WebTV played music in the background. Is that true? How can I do that?

A. While the "Sound of Silence" was a big hit for Simon & Garfunkel, there's no reason for you to be surfing in silence, and WebTV will be happy to provide a little background music. Just follow these steps and you'll be tapping your toes, as well as your keyboard or remote, in short order:

1. From your WebTV Home screen, select **Settings** ➤ **Music**. Place a check mark in the box by the **Background Music** option.

2. Next, press the **Choose Music Styles** button, and select the type or types of music you would like to listen to. When you select a style of music, you'll see the songs included in that style. You can even select a song title to hear what the little ditty sounds like.

3. When you've made your selections, select **Done**, which will return you to the **Music** screen, then press **Done** again—and you're done!

Q. I have WebTV Classic Internet, and my neighbor has WebTV Plus Interactive. Can I use my WebTV Classic keyboard with his WebTV Plus outfit?

A. A qualified yes. The WebTV Classic Internet keyboard will work with the WebTV Plus receiver, but it will not be able to perform all the Plus keyboard's functions. Features such as volume controls, channel switches, and the **View** key are available on the Plus keyboard only.

Q. Is it true that I can use WebTV to automatically record a program on my VCR?

A. It is true if you're a subscriber to WebTV Plus Interactive. If you know the name of the show—which I assume you do, otherwise why would you be recording it—from

TV Home, select **TV Listings**. You can then choose **By Program Title Or Category**. Enter the name of the show, and hit **Return** or select **Search**.

Then enjoy a leisurely scroll through the names of all the shows presented until you find the show you would like to record. Select it with your cursor and press **Record**.

If you want to record this show every week, select **Record Regularly**, and then how often you want to record that time slot. If this is a one-time taping, just ignore this step.

 WebTV Plus Interactive has a handy feature to remind you when a show is about to be recorded. The reminder comes in the form of a message that scrolls across the top of your screen. If you don't want to see the reminder message, uncheck the **Remind Before Program Begins** box by selecting the box and toggling the check mark on or off, as appropriate.

When you've completed the above steps, select **Done**.

Q. Sometimes when I type, the wrong letters appear. Why is that?

A. If the characters you type do not match the text on the screen, or if you get no response from the keyboard at all, check to see whether your keyboard batteries are low. Weak batteries can cause the keyboard to send mixed signals and may cause the power to cut off erratically.

If you continue to experience problems after replacing the batteries, your keyboard may not be functioning properly. In this case, you'll need to contact the manufacturer for further assistance at one of the following numbers:

- Mitsubishi: 800-332-2119
- Philips/Magnavox: 888-813-7069
- Samsung: 800-726-7864
- Sony: 888-772-7669

Q. How can I send an interesting web page that I stumble upon to somebody else?

A. When you're viewing the web page that you want to send, just press the **Send** key, enter the intended recipient's e-mail address (or select **To:** if they're already in your address book), and select **Send Page**. This will result in an e-mail being sent that contains a "live," or "hot," link at the bottom of your message.

All the recipient has to do is click the link to be transported to the page you would like to share with them. If you want to include a message with the link, just select **Edit Message** before sending the page. When you're done writing the message, select **Send**, and off it will go.

Q. I'd like to try a chat room. How do I find one, and what do I do when I get there?

A. WebTV's chat affiliate is one of the largest providers of chat rooms on the Internet: Talk City. To find a Talk City chat room, and to participate in one, follow these steps:

1. Select **WebTV Home** screen ➤ **Community** ➤ **Chat**. If you click the **Talk City** link at this point, you'll see a list of available chat rooms, listed by general topic.

2. At the **Welcome To Talk City** screen, select a topic of interest, and enter the chat room.

   Since this is your first time chatting, look for the New2WebTV chat room. It's a great place to start. You can practice, get help from others, and there's a very nice feeling of camaraderie associated with it.

 Once you enter a chat room, it's a good idea to *lurk* (read what others are saying) before jumping in so you can get a feel for what's going on. When you enter a chat room, however, other participants will know you arrived, so don't be surprised if one or more people say hello.

3. To respond or participate in a chat room, type your words in the box located to the left of the **Send** button. Keep your messages fairly short and don't type in ALL CAPS because that's considered shouting online—definitely something to be avoided.

4. After you compose your message, select **Send** to pop it into the chat room so all other participants can read it.

Q. Why do pictures only print on half a page?

A. A picture that fills one screen will only print on a half sheet of paper. The farther you have to scroll down to see the picture, the more it will print on the page. It takes just over two screens to print out on a full sheet of paper.

Q. What does the Cmd key do?

A. The **Cmd**, or **Command**, key is used in conjunction with other keys on the keyboard for shortcuts. Pressing **Cmd** and another key at the same time will perform many different functions. Note the following key combinations and the functions they activate.

Cmd + left arrow	Moves the cursor to the beginning of a line of text
Cmd + right arrow	Moves the cursor to the end of a line of text
Cmd + **Delete**	Deletes an entire line of text
Cmd + **F**	Finds specified text within the page you're viewing
Cmd + **G**	Finds the next occurrence of the text you're searching for
Cmd + **R**	Reloads the page you're currently viewing
Cmd + **P**	Opens the print window
Cmd + scroll down	Moves to the bottom of the page
Cmd + scroll up	Moves to the top of the page
Cmd + **Ctrl**	Displays the URL of a link when the link is highlighted

Q. My e-mail signature seems to be growing; it's longer than it's ever been. Is there a way to shorten it?

A. Sometimes lots of extra returns (*carriage returns* in the old days) take up residence above your intended signature line or lines. To remove the extra lines, from the main Mail page select **Setup** ➤ **Signature**. Move the cursor into the text input field. And then, while holding down the **Cmd** key, press the letter **A**, and press Delete.

Press **Done** ➤ **Write**, and press **Cmd** + **R**. That should result in a slimmer, trimmer signature.

Q. What do the special keys—not the letters of the alphabet—do on my wireless keyboard?

A. Each *special key*, not surprisingly, has a special function. Following is an overview list of the function each key performs.

Alt	In conjunction with another key, types a special character, such as a fraction or a symbol from a character set.
Back	Moves you back one page.
Cmd (or **Command**)	Creates and executes, in conjunction with other keys, shortcuts.
Edit	Allows you to move the cursor within a text entry field.
F1 through **F7**	Takes you to your first seven Favorites.
Go To	Goes directly to a page, if you type in the URL.
Home	Returns you to the Home screen.
Info	Displays the web address (URL) of the website you are currently viewing. It also displays the date and time the site was last updated (very useful information).
Mail	Takes you to the e-mail features.
Options	Displays the **Options** panel, which includes **Find**, **Info**, **Go To**, **Save**, **Hang-Up**, and **Reload** if the Advanced options are activated.
Recent	Displays a list of the last 12 websites you visited.
Save	Saves a website to your Favorites list.
Scroll Up/Down	Moves the cursor up and down through a page.
Search	Takes you to the Search page.
Send	Sends a website to a specific e-mail address.

Mr. Modem's Recommended Websites

Andresen Family WebTV Home Page   Includes the WebTV Special Interest Group, an online discussion group focusing on WebTV and related topics.

www.webtvsig.com/splash2.htm

Bill's Games   Free WebTV-compatible games for the whole family—card games, word games, puzzles, board games, mazes, and more.

www.billsgames.com

Help for WebTV Users   Having problems viewing pages, sending cards, and working with graphics and sound files? Whatever your difficulty, you'll probably find the answer here.

http://rats2u.com/clipart/vault/clipart_webtv.htm

WebTV's Addict Test   Take this simple (and fun!) test to determine if you're addicted to WebTV.

www.geocities.com/SiliconValley/Pines/6810/test.html

WebTV   Ground-zero for WebTV product and service information.

http://Webtv.net

Glossary:

Mr. Modem's Internet Terms of Endearment

As you immerse yourself in the Internet culture, you will encounter certain cryptic terms often referred to as *geek-speak*. The following glossary is not intended to be all encompassing, but rather an attempt to present some of the terminology you are most likely to encounter along the Information Super—well, you know.

A

account   An arrangement for access to the Internet through an Internet service provider. Uses a designated username and password for each individual subscriber.

active window   The window you are currently using; the window that contains your cursor.

ActiveX   A Microsoft application that allows a program to run within a Web page.

address   The unique location of a Web page on the Internet.

address book   A feature of e-mail programs that catalogs and retains e-mail addresses.

ADSL (Asynchronous Digital Subscriber Line) A high-speed connection to the Internet using copper wire connections. Speeds range from 6Mbps downloading (from the Internet to your computer) to 640Kbps uploading (from your computer to the Internet).

alias   An abbreviation, alternative, or shortened form of an e-mail address Sometimes called a nickname, a user can enter an alias into an e-mail's address field instead of remembering an entire e-mail address. For example, MrM might be an alias for MrModem@home.com.

Alt key   Alt stands for *alternate*. This key is used in conjunction with other keys to perform certain functions. Within instructions or keystroke sequences, Alt + F means to press the Alt and the F keys simultaneously.

angel   Business angels are wealthy private investors who help launch Internet start-up companies. A very rare species today. (*See* **IPO meltdown**).

anonymous FTP   Accessing an FTP (File Transfer Protocol) site without the necessity of entering a username. Enter **anonymous** as the username and your e-mail address as your password.

Any key   A cyberspace version of an urban legend: The novice computer user who observes the instruction on screen to "Press any key," and cannot locate the *Any* key. Bulletin to all readers: There is no Any key; the instruction simply means to press any key on your keyboard. However, if you insist there is an Any key and this is simply a vast computer conspiracy, may I suggest you also consider obtaining the Sky Hook module to enhance your Internet experience.

AOL   America Online.

applet   A small application or software program that can be embedded in a Web page. Applets make Web pages more enjoyable or useful by providing animation, calculations, and generally permitting interaction between you and a Web page.

application   A high-tech sounding term that means *program*. Apparently too many people became comfortable referring to software programs, so it must have been time to change the terminology. If you see *application*, think *program*. Technically, an application is a collection of commands and protocols that permits or commands a computer to perform certain tasks or functions. But who cares about technical definitions? Surely, not Mr. Modem.

Apply button   A button you click when changing computer settings to implement and save changes without having to close the dialog box. You may have to restart (reboot) your computer for the changes to take effect and will be notified on-screen if this additional step is required.

Article   A message posted to a newsgroup.

ASCII   Rhymes with *PASS-key* and should never be pronounced *ASK-2*. If you do pronounce it ASK-2 and we ever meet, let's pretend we don't know each other. ASCII stands for American Standard Code for Information Interchange. ASCII is the worldwide standard for the code numbers used by computers to represent all the upper and lower case Latin numbers, punctuation, etc. There are 128 standard ASCII codes, each of which can be represented by a seven-digit number, 0000000 through 1111111. (Insert yawn here.)

associate   No, not the newest member of a law firm, but rather it means to connect or relate files having a particular extension to a specific program. When you double-click on a file with a certain *extension*, the associated program is launched (started) and the file clicked on is opened. When you download (receive) files from the Internet and attempt to open them (after checking them for viruses, of course), the correct association of the downloaded file is necessary in order for the file to open. Associated files are often referred to as *registered* files.

attachment   A file or other document that is sent with an e-mail message. This file is said to be "attached" to the e-mail message.

autocomplete   The feature that kicks in when you type part of a Web address in a browser's location or address bar; the browser tries to make things easier for you by guessing the rest of the address based on sites you have previously visited.

autoresponder   A computer program that automatically replies to anyone who sends an e-mail to a particular e-mail address. For a demonstration, send an e-mail addressed to `index@MrModem.net`. Leave the Subject line and body of the e-mail blank. By return e-mail you will receive a listing of free Mr. Modem articles available via autoresponder.

B

B2B   Business to business. Any Internet business that sells goods or services to other businesses.

B2C   Business to consumer. Any Internet business that sells goods or services to consumers.

backward compatible   Referring to a software program that will work with earlier versions of the same program. Example: software written for Windows 98 that will run under Windows 95.

bandwidth   The amount of data you can send through an Internet connection. Usually measured in bits per second. The greater the bandwidth of a connection, the greater your connection speed, assuming you're accessing via that connection.

baud   Often confused with how many bits per second a modem can transmit data. Technically, baud is the number of times per second that the carrier signal shifts value—whatever that means. For example, a 1200 bit-per-second modem actually runs at 300 baud, but it moves four bits per baud—and that ain't good. (4 × 300 = 1200 bits per second.)

BBS (Bulletin Board System)   A computer network to which members can connect via modem to read and post messages.

Bcc   What was known as a blind carbon copy in the era of typewriters is also an available feature of e-mail. Other recipients of an e-mail will not see the name or names of individuals receiving Bcc copies. Referred to in Internet parlance as a blind cyber copy or blind courtesy copy.

beltwear   The name given to the many devices geeks and bearded authors wear affixed to their belts. Devices include Palm computers or other PDAs, cell phone, pagers, security cards, etc.

binary file   A non-ASCII file that contains special codes that can be destroyed or corrupted when traversing the Internet. For example, word-processing files, sound files, graphics, etc. *See also* **UUEncode**.

BIOS (Basic Input/Output System)   An information area inside your computer where software programs look in order to determine how your computer is configured, so they can run properly.

bit   Short for Binary digIT, a bit is the smallest unit of data that a computer recognizes. There are eight bits in one byte and one byte equals one character, such as the letter *A* or a numeral. Bits are usually depicted with a lower case *b*: 40Mb, meaning 40 megabits.

bitmap   A graphical image composed of thousands of dots, which are saved as bitmap files. Bitmap files carry the extension .bmp. Graphical images that make noises during the evening hours are referred to as "things that go .bmp in the night."

Bluetooth   A technical industry standard that allows wireless connections between portable devices. With a special transceiver chip, PDAs (personal digital assistants), notebook PCs, and cell phones can connect with other devices, such as desktop computers, within a limited range.

bookmarks   A Netscape file used to store Web site addresses. Also called a Hotlist or Favorite Places list. *See* **Favorites**.

Boolean logic   A method that provides specific instructions to a search engine yielding more precise search results.

Boolean operators   Sometimes called Boolean expressions, these are specific terms that provide instructions to a search engine. Used with keywords they broaden or narrow a search. Major Boolean operators include **AND**, **OR**, **NOT**. Example: Searching for *tuna* **AND** *Charlie* narrows or refines a search. Searching for *tuna* **NOT** *Charlie* broadens the search.

boot up   To start a computer. Also referred to as "power up."

'bot   A robotic program on the Internet that performs a function such as cataloging Web sites for search engines.

bounced mail   E-mail that has been returned to sender. This could be due to an erroneous e-mail address, technical problems at the receiving end, or an attached file that's too large for the recipient's mailbox.

bozo filter   An e-mail function that monitors e-mail received from certain less-than-welcome individuals and routes the e-mail to trash or deletes it upon receipt. *See also* **filter**.

bps   Bits per second. The quantification of speed at which data is transmitted between modems. Analogous to miles-per-hour (mph) in an automobile.

brick and mortar   Pertains to the physical office or store location of a retailer, as opposed to its online presence.

broken link   A clickable link that's not working properly. Broken image links appear as a broken icon in Netscape Navigator and as a box with a red cross in Microsoft's Internet Explorer.

browse   1) To peruse information on the Internet. Often referred to as *surfing* 2) To search through existing drives, directories, and files on your own computer.

browser   A software program used to view documents on the World Wide Web. The two most popular browsers are Microsoft's Internet Explorer and Netscape.

BUI (Bonus Useless Information)   A full page of English text is approximately 16,000 bits.

bus   The path or pipe through which data is transmitted between a computer's memory (RAM) and its microprocessing chip.

byte   A set of bits that represents a single character such as the letters *a* or *b*. Bytes are usually depicted with an upper case *B*: 40MB, meaning 40 mega-bytes. A kilobyte is one thousand bytes; a megabyte is one million bytes; a giga-byte is one billion bytes; an overbite is reason to see your orthodontist.

C

cable modem   A device used to access the Internet via high-speed cable, the same type cable that carries television into millions of homes. Telephone access to the Internet requires a dial-up modem as opposed to a cable modem.

cache   Temporary storage space on a hard drive. Web browsers store copies of Web pages in cache for faster viewing on subsequent visits. Pronounced *cash*, not *ca-shay*.

cartridge   A plastic container in an ink-jet printer that holds black or col-ored ink.

case sensitive   Meaning that you must pay attention to upper- and lowercase letters. Online passwords are frequently case sensitive For example, if I designate `MrModemIsGroovy` as my password for any case-sensitive, password-protected Web site, when I return to that site in the future, I won't be able to type `mrmodemisgroovy`. Case sensitivity requires the use of upper- and lowercase letters as originally provided.

cave dwellers   Technical Support people who work in confined office spaces or work areas.

Cc   Once referred to as a "carbon copy," in today's parlance, it's a courtesy or cyber copy. Used to send a copy of an e-mail to one or more other recipients.

C2C   Consumer to consumer. Describes networks such as Gnutella (`www.gnutella.com`) or FreeNet (`www.freenet.com`) where consumers do online business directly with other consumers.

CD-ROM   Compact Disk–Read Only Memory. A multimedia device that installs software and plays music. Recordable disks are designated as CD-R disks, and rewritable disks are CD-RW.

CGI (Common Gateway Interface)   A set of rules that describes how a Web server computer communicates with another piece of software on the same computer and how the other piece of software (the CGI program) talks to the Web server computer. Usually, a CGI program is a small program or script that takes data from a Web server and does some-thing with it, like putting the contents of a form into an e-mail message.

channel   A Web site designed to deliver content from the Internet to your com-puter; an area on Internet Relay Chat (IRC) where users gather to discuss a topic of common interest. There are thousands of different channels in exis-tence at any given time.

chat Live, online conversation between two or more people. Typed comments appear instantly on each participant's computer screen.

click To quickly press and release a mouse button to select something, such as a menu item.

click and drag Besides being a great name for a law firm specializing in computer and software related matters, it also means to point to an object, press and hold down a mouse button, and move the object (said to be *clicked*) to a new location.

client A computer that's part of a network that requests files or information from another computer called a server or host computer. Your home computer is a client in relationship to the Internet. A software program located on your computer within this context is referred to as client software.

click and mortar An online retailer or merchant that also has an offline, physical presence in the marketplace.

clipboard A temporary storage area for data that's been cut or copied before the information is pasted to a new location. Frequently used on the Internet to accurately preserve convoluted, case-sensitive Web site addresses and other information gleaned from Web pages for personal use.

Close button An X in the upper right-hand corner of a Web page viewed within Windows. When you click the Close button, the window or Web page closes.

.com An Internet domain extension that stands for *commercial*.

COM port Communications port. A place typically on the back or side of a computer where you can plug in a modem or other peripheral device. Also called a serial port.

compress The process of compacting a file to make it smaller so it will transmit faster over the Internet.

connect speed The rate at which your modem receives data from another server's modem. When you type in a URL and press Enter, the connect speed regulates how fast the site can transmit its information back to your modem. V.34, V.42, and V.90 are terms used to describe modems capable of a particular connect speed. V.34 modems can download up to 33.6K; V.90 describes 56K-capable modems.

cookie A very small piece of information sent by a Web server to a Web browser (software program) that the browser saves and then sends back to the server whenever the browser makes additional requests from the server. Most frequently used to customize or personalize and thus enhance a user's visit to a Web site. Note: Cookies do not read your hard drive or send your life story to the CIA.

cornea gumbo A visually busy Web page that incorporates too many colors, graphics, fonts, advertisements, and other visual distractions.

CPU (Central Processing Unit) Specifically, the microchip "brains" of a computer. Generically, CPU is used to refer to a computer "box" or tower case. Also refers to the intake facility for inmates at federal and state prisons. When it comes to worthless information, think "Mr. Modem."

cracker Criminal hacker; an individual who breaks into computers with the intent of doing damage or stealing data or other information. *See* **hacker**.

crash When a computer or software program bytes the dust. Could be a temporary meltdown or the destruction of a hard drive, in which case all data will be lost. Truism: If you use a computer, at some point you will experience a crash.

cross-post Posting the same article (message) to multiple newsgroups. Don't do it.

Ctrl key The Control key, which is used in conjunction with other keys to perform certain functions. Within instructions or keystroke sequences, Ctrl + C means to press the Ctrl and the C keys simultaneously.

cursor The little blinking line on your computer screen that you can move with your mouse or directional keys. It indicates where information you type on your keyboard will appear on screen.

cyberspace A term originated by author William Gibson in his 1982 novel *Neuromancer*. The word *cyberspace* is currently used to describe all the informational resources available through computer networks.

cybersquatters Individuals who register domain names of companies or celebrities with the intention of selling the domain name to the company or individual for a very high price.

cybrarian A person who makes a living conducting Internet-based research.

D

daemon Originating with the Unix operating system, a program that is continually operational and awaiting input to which one or more predetermined responses will be made.

data sponge Slang for a handheld scanner.

default The *normal* setting; a configuration created and installed by a computer manufacturer or software publisher.

defrag Short for defragment. The process of organizing file fragments on your hard drive to improve access speed. Windows 98 has a built-in disk defragmenter. Click Start ➤ Programs ➤ Accessories ➤ System Tools ➤ Disk Defragmenter.

Desktop   The main screen of Windows that contains icons representing shortcuts to files located on your hard drive. When downloading files from the Internet, I recommend downloading to the Desktop.

dialog box   A window that appears presenting questions that force you to make crucial-yet-uninformed decisions at inopportune moments, thus elevating your anxiety. Dialog boxes were designed to keep us all humble in the face of continually updated technology that nobody really understands. When installing programs downloaded from the Internet, dialog boxes will frequently appear requesting additional information or personal preferences, which can usually be changed at a later time.

dial-up connection   The way most of us connect to the Internet using a modem and a telephone line. Internet service providers (ISPs) offer dial-up service. *See also* **direct connection**.

digest   A grouping of mailing list postings distributed via e-mail as a single message. Rather than subscribing to a mailing list and receiving multiple e-mail messages, some individuals prefer to subscribe to mailing list digests.

digital signature   Encrypted data attached to a message or e-mail used to identify the sender.

digirati   The digital version of *literati*. A reference to a nonspecific group of people believed to be knowledgeable or otherwise in-the-know in regard to the digital revolution at hand. *syn*: *technorati*

direct connection   A full-time, high-speed connection to the Internet such as that provided by cable access. Direct connections are generally more expensive than dial-up connections, but they're also a lot more fun.

DLL (Dynamic Link Library)   Usually seen as a filename extension, .dll files contain information needed by specific software programs. Unless you've got a yearning for computer problems, don't delete .dll files. You life will never be the same if you do.

domain extension   The three characters appearing to the right of the final dot in a Web address. These three characters, sometimes referred to as Moe, Larry, and Curly, display the type of organization that owns a particular domain name. For example, the extension .com denotes a commercial organization, .edu, an educational institution, .org, a nonprofit organization, .gov, a branch of the government, .mil, a part of the military.

domain name   The unique name that identifies an Internet Web site. Domain names have two or more parts—the host name and name extension—separated by periods, or "dots." In the Web site address for this book, www.mrmodem .net, the domain name is *mrmodem.net*.

DNS (Domain Name Server or Domain Name System) Computers that translate Internet Protocol (IP) addresses into user-friendly domain names for ease of reference. For example, without a domain name, instead of typing in *website.com*, we would have to type in the numerical IP address, which would be something like 123.456.78.9.

DOS (Disk Operating System) An older operating system for running software programs. I just included it in this glossary for old time's sake. Gone, but not forgotten.

dot-com An Internet company. It derives from articulating the company's Web address that typically ends with the words "dot-com" as in MrModem.com.

double-click Pressing and releasing the left mouse button twice in rapid succession. Generally, you will double-click to launch or open a program, by clicking on a small, graphical image or *icon*.

download To retrieve data (files) from the Internet to your computer.

drownload To download multiple files from the Internet simultaneously and accidentally crash or freeze up your computer in the process.

dpi Dots per inch. A unit of measurement that represents the sharpness or clarity (resolution) of printed materials or the image on a computer monitor.

drag Make up your own jokes if you must, but within the context of computers, it's a mouse movement that transports an object (such as a file or icon) to a new location. This is accomplished by holding down a mouse button while simultaneously moving the selected object.

driver A small program that serves as a translator of commands or instructions between a piece of hardware (such as a printer) and the software that uses that printer. A small driver is sometimes referred to as a Minnie Driver. Sometimes not.

drop The last step in the dragging sequence. An object is dropped when the mouse button is released.

DVD No, not a brand of underwear, but rather Digital Versatile Disc or Digital Video Disc, depending whom you talk to. Think of DVD disks as very high-capacity CD-ROMs. A CD-ROM has a capacity of approximately 650MB (megabytes or million bytes). A DVD disk has the capacity to hold 4.7GB to 17GB (gigabytes or billion bytes) of data. One DVD disk can hold nine hours of studio-quality video or 30 hours of CD-quality audio, or 47 years of scratchy, static-laden radio.

E

e-book An "electronic book" that's been published on the Internet and can be read by downloading and installing on an e-reader or Palm-type device.

.edu An Internet domain extension that stands for educational, as in educational institution.

EFF (Electronic Frontier Foundation) A lobbying group with a focus of protecting and preserving freedom in cyberspace.

egoboo Short for ego boost, it refers to the joy of seeing your own name online or in print.

ego surfing Using a search engine to search for your own name on the Web. *See* **googling.**

e-mail Electronic mail; private communication between the sender and recipient. (Is this easy or what?)

e-mail address A unique Internet address to which your e-mail is sent. Always appears in the format *username@host.domain*. Example: MrModem@home.com.

e-mail filters Rules that you define for your e-mail program to forward, redirect, or block incoming messages. Your e-mail program will "look" at a sender's e-mail address, the subject line or any other data contained in an incoming e-mail and perform a particular action.

e-mailingering A tongue-in-cheek reference to individuals who do little work but instead do a great deal of Web surfing and sending e-mail in order to create the illusion of being busy and productive.

emoticon The use of punctuation marks and other symbols or characters to convey moods in online communication. Turn your head sideways to view. An example is a wink ;).

encode To convert by any method a document or data file into a format in order to attach it to an e-mail message.

encrypt To jumble the contents of an e-mail message or file so that it cannot be read by individuals who do not have the appropriate encryption code or key.

Ethernet A very common method of networking computers in a local area network (LAN). Ethernet can transmit approximately 10 million bits per second and can be used with almost any kind of computer.

Eudora A very popular e-mail software program.

executable file A file that automatically runs when you click it. It usually has an .exe extension.

extension The three digits that appear after the period or *dot* in a filename; for example, the last three digits of Windows.exe or Readme.txt. Extensions tell us mortals what kind of file we're looking at. Extensions also permit computers to recognize files as particular types so they can *associate*. For more information about file extensions, send a blank e-mail to **filetypes@MrModem.net**.

You'll receive information by return e-mail.

e-zine   A Web-based magazine.

F

FAQ (Frequently Asked Questions)
Documents located on most Web sites that list and answer the most common questions about a particular subject relating to the site.

Favorites   An Internet Explorer file used to store Web site addresses. Also called a Hotlist or Favorite Places list. *See* **bookmarks**.

56K line   A digital phone line connection (sometimes also called a leased line), capable of carrying 56,000 bits per second. At this speed, it would take about three minutes to download a one-megabyte file.

file   Anything stored in electronic format on a computer. Examples: software, graphics, spreadsheets, documents.

filter   A personal mail sorter that monitors incoming e-mail and performs certain designated functions such as moving e-mail received from a particular sender into a designated e-mail box, opening it, playing a sound, or in the case of a bozo filter, routing it directly to the trash. Also used with newsgroups to avoid viewing articles posted by certain individuals.

firewall   For security purposes, a combination of hardware and software that protects computer networks against unauthorized entry by Internet users.

flame   A hostile or negative response to an e-mail message or newsgroup posting. Most flames are intended to be provocative and cause the recipient(s) to respond. Don't take the bait. The person sending such a message is referred to as a *flamer*. A series of flames and counter-flames is referred to as a *flame war*.

folder   A means of organizing files. Folders are what we used to know as *directories*, but since many of us knew, understood, and felt comfortable with the term *directory*, it was obviously time to change the terminology.

follow-up   A reply to a newsgroup message.

forward   To send an e-mail on to another Internet user.

FQA   Frequently Questioned Acronyms.

frames   A way of dividing Web pages into separate areas or compartments that can be scrolled individually.

free-mail   A Web-based e-mail service that allows you to send and receive e-mail from a Web page rather than an e-mail software program. Free e-mail services typically contain one or more advertising messages that appear with each e-mail transmitted.

freenet   Free public access to the Internet, typically sponsored by a municipality.

freeware   Free software available for downloading from the Internet. *See* **shareware**.

FTP (File Transfer Protocol)   A common method of moving files between two computers. The same as uploading and downloading. Visit www.mrmodem.net for more information about FTP.

FUQ   Frequently Unanswered Questions.

G

garbage   Computeresque characters that telephone line noise or static may cause on computer screens.

Gates, Bill   Is it possible that anybody doesn't know who Mr. Gates is? On a personal note, Mr. Gates and I enjoy a wonderfully harmonious professional relationship: He doesn't know I exist; I refer to him as Mr. Gates. It works like a charm.

gateway   A threshold to the Internet. For example, America Online and Compu-Serve both serve as a gateway to the Internet for their respective members.

geekosphere   The area in and around a computer user's desk and workspace.

generation lap   The phenomenon of seniors becoming *more* technologically savvy than their children and *as* technologically savvy as their grandchildren.

GIF   Stands for Graphic Image File or Graphics Interchange Format, depending on whom you're talking to. Regardless, it's a format used frequently on the Internet. Files in this format have a .gif extension. Pronounced "gif," as in Gifford, not "jiff," as in jiffy.

gigabyte   1,000 megabytes. Abbreviated GB. If you're trying to sound ultra cool and computer savvy, you might refer to it as a "gig." But hopefully, not often.

googling   Looking up one's potential romantic interest on the Internet, specifically by putting their name into the Google search engine. *See* **ego surfing**.

.gov   An Internet domain extension used by any nonmilitary branch of the government.

GUI (Graphic User Interface)   A method of utilizing software through the use of windows, pictures, icons, avatars, buttons, etc. Pronounced "GOO-ey."

guru   Highly regarded spiritual advisor or computer nerd. Mr. Modem is often referred to as a guru, though guru of what has yet to be determined.

H

hacker   Cyberspace scoundrels who break into computers and computer networks, often just for the fun of it. *See* **cracker**.

history file   A record kept by your Web browser of all the sites you have visited within a certain period.

hit As used in reference to the World Wide Web, a hit means a single request from a Web browser for a single item from a Web server or Web site. In order for the Web browser to display a page that contains three graphics, four hits would occur on the server: one for the HTML page and one for each of the three graphics.

home page The first screen of a Web site that contains pointers (links) to resources located within the Web site.

host A computer that provides services or information to other computers connected to it or having access to it. May also be called a *server*. Connected computers are called *clients*.

Hotlist A bookmark or favorite places list of Web site addresses. *See* **Bookmarks** or **Favorites**.

HTML (Hypertext Markup Language) The coding language used to create Web pages.

HTTP (Hypertext Transfer Protocol) The protocol for transmitting hypertext files across the Internet.

hyperlink No, not an over-stimulated link, but rather a navigational element within hypertext that allows users to navigate the World Wide Web. A hyperlink can be text, a graphic, or multiple links within a single graphic.

hypermedia A combination of hypertext and multimedia. Of course, it could have been called textmedia, but that wouldn't be nearly as impressive.

hypertext Any text that contains links to other documents. Words or phrases in a document can be selected by mouse-click, which causes another document to be retrieved and displayed.

I

IAD Internet Addiction Disorder. A questionable phenomenon and not a recognized disorder by the American Psychiatric Association. Some individuals suggest that certain people become addicted to the Internet; others contend the Internet is just another form of escapism, such as television.

icon A technologically motivating chant or mantra recommended by Mr. Modem. When confronted with computer or Internet difficulties, keep repeating, "Icon if I think icon." An icon is a little picture that represents an object, program, file, or command.

.ini Short for initialization and pronounced "inny." An .ini file extension appears on files that contain special programs or system settings. Despite rumors to the contrary, there is no .outi extension.

ink-jet A type of printer that employs small nozzles to spray ink onto paper. Ink-jets can print in black or color and are usually less expensive than laser printers.

instant messages Private exchanges or communications between two individuals online at the same time. The communication takes place in real time, like chat, though not within a chat room.

internesia The experience of finding a Web site or other online item that you want to show someone but then forget where on the Internet you saw it. Checking your browser's history file (Ctrl + H) can sometimes cure internesia.

Internet The vast collection of interconnected networks that all use the TCP/IP protocols that evolved from the ARPANet of the late 1960s and early 1970s.

internet Any time you connect two or more networks together, you have an internet. The *inter* prefix has the same meaning as in international or interstate.

Internet Explorer Microsoft's Web browser software. Biggest rival: Netscape.

Internet incubator A company that offers a vast range of services, including financing, to young online companies (start-ups) in order to help get them launched. Incubators will often take a 30 percent to 70 percent stake in the new company in lieu of hard-dollar compensation.

Internet Phone A protocol that permits individuals with a microphone, sound card, and speakers to speak with other similarly equipped individuals via their computer. Sure, it's easier to pick up the phone, but that's not the right attitude.

InterNIC Internet Network Information Center. The organization responsible for registering Web site domain names. Go to www.networksolutions.com.

interstitial advertising Annoying pop-up advertising that appears when you're visiting Web pages.

intranet A private network inside a firm or company that uses the same types of software that you would find on the public Internet. However, an intranet is for internal use only.

IP (Internet Protocol) The basis for the Internet, defines how packets of data are transmitted from point of origin to destination.

IP address The numerical address (Internet Protocol address) assigned to computers on the Internet. In the Address field of any Web browser, you can type in a domain name or numerical IP address and navigate to the same location. *See also* **domain name**.

IPO Initial Public Offering. When a privately held company's stock becomes publicly traded.

IPO meltdown When a new dot-com or other company drops dramatically in value on the stock market the first day it's offered to the public or shortly thereafter.

IRC (Internet Relay Chat) An Internet protocol or system through which you can talk in real time with other chat participants utilizing the same system.

ISDN (Integrated Services Digital Network) A standard for digital communications using telephone lines. Data is transmitted at 64 or 128Kbps.

ISP (Internet service provider) An organization or business that provides access to the Internet, typically for profit.

issue A euphemism for a bug or problem. Some companies will alert users to "issues" with their software. Mr. Modem's interpretation: "Run for your life!"

J

Java A programming language invented by Sun Microsystems that is designed for writing programs that can be safely downloaded to your computer through the Internet and run immediately, without fear of viruses.

JavaScript A scripting language developed by Netscape that is embedded into the HTML code of a Web page. JavaScripting, confusingly enough, has nothing to do with the Java programming language.

JPEG A preferred graphic file format popular on the Internet, as opposed to GIF. A file in this format will have a .jpg extension. Pronounced "JAY-peg."

K

Kbps Kilobits per second. The speed at which data is transmitted online. Newer modems transfer data at 56Kbps. Not to be confused with kilobyte. Bits, bytes, it's enough to drive anybody crazy.

key In encryption, the code that permits you to unscramble a message or document.

keyword The word, words, or phrase you enter into a search engine to try to find a Web site of interest.

kill file A newsgroup newsreader software file that acts as a filter. Enter keywords and e-mail addresses to prevent receiving articles with those words or from those individuals.

kilobyte A thousand bytes. Technically, it's 1,024 bytes, but what's a few bytes between friends? Abbreviated K or KB.

L

laganoia The fear of being ignored in a chat room or other online community. Brought about by a delay or lag between the time you post a message and the time you receive a response.

LAN (Local Area Network) Two or more computers connected together within a relatively small area such as a home or office setting. *See also* **WAN**.

landscape A printer setting in which words and graphics are printed sideways along the 11″ length of an 8.5″ × 11″ sheet of paper. See also portrait.

lapjack The practice of stealing unattended computers, usually in airports.

LCD (Liquid Crystal Display) The type of screen found in most notebook computers.

link In a Web page, a link is a connection to another Web page. When you click a link, that document will be displayed through your Web browser software.

Linux A freeware operating system that is thought by many to be an up-and-coming challenger to Windows. Created in 1991 by Linus Torvalds. Pronounced "LYNN-ex."

Listserv A type of mailing list.

lockware Software programs that you can download but not use until you purchase a password or key that will allow you to unlock and run the program.

login (noun) The account name or username used to gain access to a computer system. Not private, such as a password. *See also* **username.**

log in (verb) The act of entering into a computer system: e.g., to log in to CompuServe or America Online or the Internet.

log out *or* log off To terminate an Internet session; go offline.

Love Bug The fastest-spreading computer virus to date. The Love Bug appeared in the Spring of 2000 and infected millions of computers around the world, in part because of the "ILOVEYOU" subject line and attachment in many messages.

lurking Nonactive participation on the part of an individual in a newsgroup or other online discussion group. To be a *lurker* means that you're generally just reading what others are saying without participating yourself. Lurking is acceptable and recommended when you first join any online community in order to get a feel for it; however, the success of any discussion group depends on everybody's participation.

M

Mac An abbreviation for Apple Macintosh; a popular type of computer, often used by Web designers and other artistic types.

mail server The hardware and software used by an Internet Service Provider to send, receive, and store e-mail.

mailing list An automated system that allows people to send e-mail to one address, whereupon their message is copied and sent to all of the other subscribers to the list. Sometimes referred to as a *mail list*.

Majordomo A type of mailing list software.

MAPI (Messaging Application Programming Interface) An e-mail standard that allows different kinds of Windows-based e-mail programs to exchange e-mail messages with each other.

megabyte One million bytes or one thousand kilobytes. Technically, it's 1,024 kilobytes, but who's counting? Abbreviated MB.

memory "Light the corners of my mind, misty watercolor memory…" An area computers use to store frequently accessed data.

Metoobies Chat participants who contribute little more than "Me, too!" or "Ditto" sentiments.

MHz Megahertz. A measure of the speed of your computer's processor, referred to as clock speed. Example: 400 or 450MHz.

microprocessor Often referred to as a computer's brain, it's really a small silicon chip located inside your computer that determines, among other things, how fast your computer can process information.

MIDI (Musical Instrument Digital Interface) A standard adopted by the electronic music industry governing sound cards and synthesizers.

.mil An Internet domain extension used by branches of the military.

MIME (Multipurpose Internet Mail Extensions) The standard for attaching nontext files to standard Internet e-mail messages. Nontext files include graphics, spreadsheets, formatted word-processor documents, sound files, etc.

mirror Generally speaking, to maintain an exact copy of something. The most common use of the term on the Internet refers to *mirror sites*, which are Web sites or FTP sites that maintain exact copies of material available at other locations. FTP sites, for example, that receive a great number of visitors are typically *mirrored* to provide additional download locations in order to minimize accessing delays. If hamburger stands were FTP sites, McDonald's would represent the McMirrored site model.

modem 1) An acronym for MOdulate/DEModulate. A device connected to a computer and phone line that allows your computer to talk to other computers through the telephone system. 2) Adopted surname of a beloved bearded author.

moderated Messages submitted for posting to moderated mailing lists and newsgroups are first screened for acceptability by a moderator, usually a volunteer.

Mosaic The first Web browser developed by NCSA, the National Center for Supercomputing Applications.

motherboard   The main circuit board inside your computer on which chips, dips, and other gizmos are attached.

mouse   A hand-held pointing device used to select and move objects displayed on a computer monitor.

moved to Atlanta   A humorous reference to Web pages that cannot be accessed, resulting in 404 File Not Found error messages in their place. 404 is an Atlanta area code.

MP3   A file format that stores compressed audio files, but without distorting the sound. MP3 files have an .mp3 file extension. A player is required to listen to MP3 files. For more information visit www.mp3.com.

MPEG   A compressed video file format. Files in this format are named filename.mpg.

MSN   Microsoft Network.

MUD   MultiUser Domain, sometimes referred to as a dungeon. A fantasy, role-playing arena.

Multimedia   A combination of graphics, text, video, sound, animation, and photographs integrated within a software program, Web page, CD-ROM, or other device.

N

nag screens   Messages incorporated within shareware programs that remind you that you need to register the software. In 30-day trial periods, every time you launch a program it will count down, "25 days remaining, register now! 24 days remaining, register now!" Nag, nag, nag.

Net, the   Shorthand for the Internet. Used by those who want to sound like they're cool, groovy, and in the know. Also used in Sandra Bullock movies.

Netiquette   Etiquette for using the Internet. For example, rules of courtesy regarding use of e-mail, posting forum messages, etc.

netizen   Derived from the term *citizen*. Referring to a citizen of the Internet. The term connotes civic responsibility and participation.

netopath   An Internet sicko; people who are online stalkers and hackers who do millions of dollars damage. Chronic spammers can be classified as netopaths.

Netscape   Netscape Communication's Web browser software. Biggest rival: Microsoft's Internet Explorer.

network   A group of computers connected together that share information, hardware, software, etc.

newbie   A newcomer to the Internet; recent arrival. Not a disparaging term.

newsgroups   Also called Usenet; ongoing public discussion groups devoted to particular topics of interest.

newsreader   A program used to read Usenet newsgroup messages.

NNTP (Network News Transfer Protocol) The standard for sending and receiving Usenet newsgroup articles across the Internet.

O

OCR (Optical Character Recognition)   Refers to converting data from a scanned image into text.

offline   Not connected to the Internet.

offline mail reader   An e-mail program that connects to the Internet, retrieves e-mail, then disconnects. You can then read and compose replies to e-mail offline, before going back online and sending or uploading responses.

offline news reader   Similar to an offline mail reader except it connects to Usenet newsgroups, retrieves unread articles, then disconnects. Articles can then be read and responses or replies composed offline.

online   Connected to the Internet.

online trading   The ability to buy and sell stocks via the Internet.

.org   An Internet domain extension for nonprofit organizations.

OS   Operating System. The software that allows your computer to run. Examples: DOS, Linux, Unix, Windows.

P

packet   A standard unit of data sent across the Internet. Packets usually contain identification and address information regarding the destination location.

packet loss   Speaking for myself, not nearly as troubling as hair loss, but rather the failure of data to transfer successfully between two or more points on the Internet.

packet switching   The protocol used to transmit data over the Internet. It's the Popeil DataMatic approach to data transmission. Data is sliced and diced into small units, called packets. Each packet is assigned an address. The data is then routed through the Internet, taking the most expeditious route possible, and using the assigned addresses, reassembled at its final destination.

parallel port   The larger connection thingy (term of art) on the back of your computer, usually used to attach a printer.

parental filters   Browser and other software settings that can be configured by parents to restrict access to certain Web sites and Web activities inappropriate for children.

password   A textual key, usually a word or a combination of words and numbers, without which access to a specific area, program, or feature is prohibited.

patch　A temporary fix to resolve a software problem.

PC　Personal computer. Usually refers specifically to what we used to call "IBM clones" as opposed to Macintosh computers.

Pentium 4　Intel's latest microprocessor chip that will offer processing speeds above 1GHz (gigahertz).

peripheral device　A geekspeak way of saying "piece of hardware." Modems, printers, and monitors are all peripheral devices.

phreaker　A person who hacks or breaks into telephone systems.

Ping　Not referring to golf clubs, but rather an Internet-based program that sends a signal to a host computer to see if it's available or functioning. Derived from a sonar *ping* sound.

pixel　One of hundreds of thousands of tiny dots or points of light that compose any image you see displayed on your computer monitor. If you put your nose right up against your monitor, you can see the pixels.

platform　A computer operating system like Windows 98, or more generically, any computer-based environment such as a chat platform, newsgroup platform, etc.

Plug and Play　A technological miracle for all novice computer users. Technology that identifies the existence of a new device—such as a printer—once it's been attached to the computer, and then configures the computer accordingly.

plug-in　A small piece of software that adds features to a larger piece of software. Common examples of plug-ins are used for the Netscape and Internet Explorer browsers or some chat software. Plug-ins are sometimes referred to as *helper applications*. See "Plugging Along with Plug-Ins" in Chapter 8.

POP　Two commonly used meanings: Point of Presence and Post Office Protocol. A Point of Presence usually means a city or location where a user can connect to a network. Post Office Protocol refers to the way e-mail software, such as Eudora, retrieves mail from a mail server computer.

port　A connector, usually located on the back or side of your computer, into which you plug a printer, modem, scanner, etc.

portal　A point of entry to the Web that offers a wide selection of services such as access to search engines, free e-mail, and access to other sites.

portfolio tracking　The ability to monitor the performance of your financial portfolio via Web page. A free service offered by many financial Web sites.

portrait　The usual way a page of text is printed, with lines of text running across the 8.5" width of an 8.5" × 11" sheet of paper. *See also* **landscape**.

port speed   The rate at which data is transferred between your modem and your hard drive. Speed is measured in kilobits per second or Kbps. Typical port speeds are 33,600, 57,600, 115,200.

post   A message contributed (by uploading) into an online discussion group is said to be *posted* by the writer of the message.

PostScript   A computer language that controls the positioning of text and graphics on a page. More popular with graphics professionals, print shops, and Macintosh users than with personal computer users.

ppm   Pages per minute. Refers to the output speed of a printer.

PPP (Point-to-Point Protocol)   The most popular protocol that allows a computer to use a regular telephone line and modem to make an Internet connection.

propagation   The process of distributing and disseminating information throughout the Internet, as it passes from computer to computer.

protocol   An agreed-upon method or standard by which computers "talk" to each other and transmit data, files, graphics, etc.

proxy server   A computer located between a client, such as your Web browser software, and the host server. Generally used to improve performance by delivering frequently requested Web pages. Rather than a request going out from your browser to the Internet and retrieving a popular Web page, the request will only need to go as far as the proxy server, which will then return the requested page to you faster. At least that's the theory.

push technology   Technology that delivers customized news and information to your computer as contrasted with the "get" model of information retrieval that requires you to go to an Internet source for information.

Q

query   A search request, typically a keyword, submitted to a search engine database.

queue   Pronounced "Q"; refers to the printing order of documents.

QuickTime   A free plug-in player that enables short audio-visual movies, but not full-screen motion pictures, to be played over the Web. For more information or to download the latest version, visit www.apple.com/quicktime.

R

RAM   An acronym for Random Access Memory. RAM is the area of memory accessed by your computer to perform the tasks you see taking place on your computer screen.

RealAudio   A standard for transmitting or *streaming* compressed audio over the Internet. Supported by Web browsers

Internet Explorer and Netscape. A player device is required that can be downloaded for free from www.real.com.

real time   Without any delay. For example, when talking in a chat room, participants communicate in real time; one person types words and all other participants see those words on their computers. Contrasted with a newsgroup posting where the words are posted and a response may appear sometime later.

refresh   A command issued to update the information displayed on the computer screen. Sometimes referred to as Reload in the case of retrieving a current and up-to-date copy of a specific Web page or Web site.

register   *See* **associate**.

Registry   The command center for Windows that houses system and program configuration settings.

removable storage   Floppy disks, backup tapes, Zip disks, portable hard drives.

resolution   The number of horizontal and vertical rows of pixels that compose an image displayed on a computer monitor. 800 × 600 is a frequently used resolution. *See also* **pixel**.

right-click   Clicking and releasing the right mouse button to display a shortcut menu of commands related to the object you clicked.

robot   A program that automatically performs certain functions on the Internet. One example is a program that prowls the Internet cataloging newly arrived Web sites. Sometimes referred to as a *'bot*, for short.

S

scanner   A hardware device that plugs into your computer and converts documents and photographs into electronic format or files. This data can then be imported into documents, attached to e-mail messages, or saved. The objective is to save as many things as you can until you reach the point where you can't remember what you've previously saved, so you can start saving things again.

search engine   A program that will allow you to enter keywords and launch a search for Internet resources containing those keywords. Yahoo! and WebCrawler are two examples of Web search engines. See Chapter 10, "Internet Search Engines."

secure server   A computer that handles encrypted data for secure (usually financial) transactions.

serial port   A place typically on the back or side of a computer where you can plug in a modem or other peripheral device. Also called a COM or communications port.

server A computer that provides or serves data and information upon request to software residing on other computers called *clients*.

shareware Downloadable software that you can try before you buy. If you use shareware software, you are on your honor to register it if you decide to keep it. The good folks who write this software depend on our honesty, so please register any shareware you intend to use.

shelfware Software programs that are purchased but never used. The ultimate objective of computing is to see how much shelfware one can collect.

Shockwave A plug-in that enables interactive multimedia to display over the Web. Download the latest version at www.macromedia.com/shockwave.

signature An ASCII text file that can be automatically attached to the bottom of e-mail that identifies the sender.

SLIP (Serial Line Internet Protocol) A standard for using a regular telephone line (a serial line) and a modem to connect a computer to the Internet. SLIP is being replaced by PPP.

SMTP (Simple Mail Transfer Protocol) A popular protocol for transmitting outgoing e-mail. SMTP stores e-mail messages on your computer, not on a remote server.

space hogs A term of endearment that refers to extremely large software programs, graphics files, sound files, and video sequence files. Making snorting sounds can often alleviate the anxiety one feels when installing programs that are known to be space hogs.

spam An inappropriate attempt to use a mailing list, newsgroup, or other networked communications capability as a broadcast medium—which it is not—by sending the same message to a large number of people who didn't ask for it. The term is believed to have originated from a Monty Python skit that featured the word *spam* being repeated over and over. Another school of thought believes that the term may have originated from someone's low opinion of the food product, which is perceived by some to be a generic, content-free waste of resources. (Spam is a registered trademark of the Hormel Corporation.) In its simplest form, spam is junk e-mail.

spampoena A subpoena distributed to multiple recipients via e-mail. During litigation in March 2000 in Massachusetts, a U.S. District Court judge approved the prosecution's request to serve subpoenas to certain Web sites in this manner. The ACLU (American Civil Liberties Union) objected on the grounds that e-mail service of subpoenas violated the rights of third parties receiving subpoenas as well as the spirit of laws governing service.

spamouflage   Bulk e-mail messages delivered from generic e-mail addresses with innocuous subject headers in order to confound filtering programs and spam-intolerant readers.

SSL (Secure Socket Layer)   A means of providing a secure environment for transmitting data (such as credit card information) via the Internet.

start page   The first Web page that appears on your monitor when you launch your browser. This can be any Web page you want it to be or the default page, typically the Netscape or Internet Explorer home page.

stopword   A word that a search engine ignores when doing a search. These words occur so commonly in language that they do nothing to narrow a search. An example would be the word *the*.

streaming   Around the holidays, Internet users are usually streaming of a white Christmas. Sorry. Streaming refers to the process of retrieving data (audio or video) in realtime as opposed to downloading and then executing or launching a program. A good example of streaming is RealAudio, which permits audio to begin playing via your computer's speakers without having to wait to download large audio files. *See also* **RealAudio**.

Stuffit   You should pardon the expression. Nothing personal intended, I assure you. Stuffit is a Macintosh file compression program and Stuffit

Expander is the Windows version. Stuffed files display a `.sit` file extension. For additional information visit `www.aladdinsys.com/products/index.html`.

subdomain   A portion of an Internet domain, typically a network host such as an Internet service provider. In my e-mail address `MrModem@home.com`, *home* is the subdomain, also referred to as the host.

subscribe   To join a mailing list or begin to receive posts or participate in a newsgroup. There is typically no charge for subscribing. *See also* **unsubscribe**.

surf   Arguably the most overused term associated with the Internet, though *Information Superhighway* can't be far behind. Surfing refers to moving from Web site to Web site following hyperlinks.

SVGA (Super Video Graphics Array)   A video standard that provides more colors and higher clarity than its predecessor, VGA standard.

T

T1   A leased-line connection to the Internet capable of carrying data at a blistering 1.54 million bits-per-second rate.

T3   A very expensive leased-line connection to the Internet capable of carrying data at 45 million bits-per-second. Not practical for home or office access.

tabs A dialog box feature in many Windows-based programs that permits a single dialog box to contain several layers. You can navigate among the layers by clicking on what appear as file folder tabs to reveal a different set of formatting or setup configuration options.

TCP/IP (Transmission Control Protocol/ Internet Protocol) A collection of rules that defines how data is transmitted on the Internet.

telephony Never talk to phonies, so I wouldn't recommend telling them anything. Nobody likes a groaner, so let's move on. *Telephony* refers to the technology that lets us use our personal computers to make and receive telephone calls without incurring long-distance charges. Ma Bell has her cables in a knot over this issue.

Telnet Also called *remote login*. Telnetting to a site is very similar to logging onto America Online or CompuServe. Using your modem, you connect to a host computer, where you are then presented with a menu. You can use this menu to navigate the Internet, explore remote computer sites, and execute programs as well as rodents or other annoying household pests.

temporary Internet files Internet Explorer's version of a *cache*, where the data from previous Internet sessions is stored.

terabyte One thousand gigabytes.

terminal A device that allows you to send commands to a computer located elsewhere—said to be in a *remote* location.

thread An online conversation consisting of messages and responses.

time out To fail to connect to a Web site, usually because the remote host— the computer you're attempting to connect with—fails to respond in a timely manner. When this happens, just try again later. It's often the online equivalent of getting a busy signal on the telephone.

TLA Three-letter acronym.

toolbar One or more rows of icons and buttons used as shortcuts for a program's frequently used commands.

tooltips Short, descriptive words and phrases that appear when you place your mouse cursor on a toolbar or other navigational button.

Trojan horse A type of computer virus that masquerades as normal software, but instead contains harmful or destructive programming code. *See also* **virus**.

Trumpet Winsock A Windows-based program that provides dial-up SLIP or PPP access to the Internet. The predecessor to Windows 95/98 Dial-Up Networking.

U

Unix   An operating system upon which the Internet was constructed. Used mostly by Internet service providers. Avoided like the plague by most Internet users.

unsubscribe   To remove yourself from a mailing list or newsgroup. *See also* **subscribe**.

upload   The opposite of download. Duh! To send data (files) from your computer to the Internet.

URL (Uniform Resource Locator)   A Web page address, typically beginning with `http://www`.

USB (Universal Serial Bus)   A standard that has been touted as the successor to the serial, parallel, mouse, and keyboard connectors. A one-size-fits-all port into which you can plug a printer, monitor, scanner, digital camera, Zip and Jaz drive, and other devices. *See also* **bus**.

Usenet   Users Network. Topical discussion groups referred to as newsgroups. *See also* **newsgroups**.

username   The name you log in or connect to the Internet or a Web site with. Typically used in conjunction with a password. It's also the part to the left of the @ sign in your e-mail address. For example, in my e-mail address `MrModem@ home.com`, *MrModem* is my username.

utilities   Software tools that perform specific functions, typically maintenance related.

UUEncode (Unix-to-Unix Encoding)   A popular method of converting files from binary to ASCII format so they can be transmitted on the Internet. *See also* **binary file**.

V

vaporware   Nonexistent software. Vaporware often makes a nonappearance when a company announces a new product that never materializes.

viewers   Software that permits you to view certain types of files on your computer screen.

virtual   Used to describe computer simulations. For example, virtual tours, virtual buildings, virtual cities. In the world of computer simulation, it can be virtually anything.

virus   A program created by cyberhooligans and often spread through attachments to e-mail, which intentionally causes harm to infected computers.

voice recognition   The ability to enter computer commands or text in word-processing software by speaking as opposed to using a keyboard or mouse.

W

WAN (Wide Area Network)   Unlike a LAN (Local Area Network), a WAN spans large distances and usually connects LANs in multiple locations. *See also* **LAN**.

WAP (Wireless Application Protocol)   A standard for Internet content that is delivered to handheld wireless devices, such as mobile phones, pagers, two-way radios, and other similar devices.

Web authoring   Creating Web pages using HTML.

Webmaster   The person responsible for keeping a Web site up, running, and available to the public by maintaining the Web server that hosts the Web site.

Web page   A document written in HTML that you can view using your Web browser software. Every Web page has its own unique URL or Web page address.

Web ring   A collection of Web pages, typically individual home pages, all linked together, all with the same theme or special interest.

Web site   A collection of Web pages usually sharing a common focus. A Web site is typically owned or managed by a single entity, company, organization, corporation, association, club, or individual. *See also* **home page**.

Windows ME   Windows Millennium Edition. The name of Windows newest operating system designed specifically for home users. Soon to be supplanted by the even more recent Windows XP.

WinZip   A compression program for Windows. *See also* **Zip**.

World Wide Web (WWW)   The fastest-growing portion of the Internet in which Web pages containing text, graphics, audio, and video are linked together and easily searchable with browser software.

worm   Not technically a virus, but close enough. A worm is a bit of computer nastiness that replicates itself and can gobble its way through a computer network.

WYSIWYG   What You See Is What You Get. What you type on your keyboard and what appears on your monitor is the way it will appear in printed or other format. Pronounced "Wizzy-Wig."

Z

Zip   A file compression format for personal computers using PKZip or WinZip software. Zipped files display a .zip file extension. It's the approximate equivalent of Stuffit or Zipit for Macintosh users. For more information visit www.winzip.com.

Index

Note to the Reader: Page numbers in **bold** indicate the principle discussion of a topic or the definition of a term. Page numbers in *italic* indicate illustrations.